THE CONCERTGOER'S COMPANION

Also by Antony Hopkins

Beating Time (*autobiography*)
The Nine Symphonies of Beethoven
Pathway to Music
Sounds of Music
Talking About Music
Understanding Music

THE
CONCERTGOER'S
COMPANION

VOLUME 1
BACH TO HAYDN

ANTONY HOPKINS

J.M. Dent & Sons Ltd
London & Melbourne

This book is set in 10pt Bembo
Typeset by Inforum Ltd, Portsmouth
Made and printed in Great Britain by
Biddles Ltd, Guildford, for
J.M. Dent & Sons Ltd
Aldine House   33 Welbeck Street   London W1M 8LX

Dedicated to the Malcolm who asked for it
but doesn't need it and to the Malcolm
who didn't ask for it but does.

CONTENTS

FOREWORD

Analytical notes in programmes can often cause more confusion than illu-
mination since of necessity they are so concentrated that two or three
sentences may have to cover music taking a substantial time to perform. All
the same, major symphonic works are not always easy to understand fully
unless the listener has an educated ear. This book is an attempt to offer
guidance to the musically uninitiated by the use of descriptive analysis which
is (so far as possible) free from technical jargon. Such musical examples as
there are are virtually all confined to a single line, omitting the additional
complexity of supporting harmony which the average reader finds difficult
to imagine in terms of sound; any musical terms that may be unfamiliar are
explained at the time. Ideally the book should be read while listening to the
chosen work on tape or disc since all the significant events are described in the
manner of a running commentary.

The many omissions need more justification than the inclusions – for
instance, why no Bruckner? It seemed to me impossible to give an adequate
description of a symphony on Bruckner's scale without a very considerable
number of music examples. Furthermore to have included him with Bach,
Bartók, Beethoven, Berg, Berlioz, Brahms and Britten would have sufficed
to fill an entire book without ever escaping from the Bs. The original
intention was to produce a single volume, an A – Z of orchestral music; the
scheme was quickly abandoned when I realised that if I reduced the list of
composers drastically to twenty and allowed each one twenty-five pages I
would still end up with a book of five hundred pages. The solution was to
expand to two volumes, the second of which will follow in due course. In the
first, 'Bach to Haydn' (there are no As worthy of such distinguished company,
but no matter . . .), I have tried to include a representative collection of the
standard works in the orchestral repertoire. Composers as prolific as Haydn
presented the biggest problem since I could hardly allow him space for 104
symphonies; I have therefore chosen a small selection of what are generally
considered to be his finest.

   The brief biographical essays are intended to make the composers themselves seem less remote, for I feel that the ability to identify oneself with the
composer is often the way to enhance one's appreciation of his music. To take
an obvious example, which of us can listen to late Beethoven without being
affected by a knowledge of his deafness? While it is not always true that 'to
know is to love', the prime purpose of this book is not to add to the sum of
knowledge but rather to enhance affection and understanding. If it succeeds
in doing that, I shall feel that my function of 'guide' will have been adequately
fulfilled.

   May 1984   A.H.

INTRODUCTION
The Need for Form

Music is not like a picture. We cannot look at it in a single glance and then take in all the detail at our leisure. It exists in motion; it passes by, affecting us in one way or another, thrilling us with its climaxes, soothing us with its soft passages, puzzling us with its complexities, sometimes boring us or even rousing our antagonism. Within the span of a large-scale movement many events will happen, events that may be closely related or deliberately contrasted. If we are to understand music rather than merely to feel its emotional stimulus, we need to be aware of such relationships, to appreciate the contrasts, to understand the way a movement is planned. To do this we need to know the *form* of a piece, for listening to a Nocturne is a different experience from listening to a Fugue; listening to a Prelude by Bach is not the same as listening to a Prelude by Chopin or Debussy.

Most of the works described in this volume are symphonies or concertos. Many readers may already have a fairly clear idea of the ground-plan of such works; all the same it may be worth while to give a brief description of basic forms so as to avoid having to make the same points over and over again. At once we are confronted with a paradox; not one work in this book is called a sonata and yet nearly every work has at least one movement (usually the first) in 'Sonata form'. The word Sonata literally means a 'sounding' piece as opposed to Cantata, a 'singing' piece. Symphonies are really large-scale Sonatas for orchestra; Concertos are Sonatas for soloist and orchestra. Therefore although we are not concerned with Sonatas as a *genre*, we certainly need to have some understanding of the conventions of Sonata form, even if only to appreciate the way in which composers use form to create a sense of expectation and then to deny it. Surprise is the frustration of expectation; you cannot have a surprise unless you are expecting something to behave in a normal or orthodox manner and it then deviates from normality. Composers take much delight in this since to surprise us is to keep our interest alive. The reason why we need an understanding of form, then, is not so that we can apply the chilling hand of analysis but rather so that we can better appreciate inspired *departures* from it. It is these that help to give a work its vitality and originality.

Science fiction has given us an instinctive dread of clones; we value what is individual to each of us though we share a common mould of physical similarity. Sonata-form movements are not clones and it is a fundamental mistake to expect them all to conform to a pattern; but just as most people have the same number of eyes, arms, legs and ears and yet are all different, we can expect sonata-form movements to have some common factors. What they are I shall endeavour to explain.

The simplest analogy is to think of a play in three scenes. In Scene I we meet the characters; naturally there will be a contrast between them – masculine/feminine, aggressive/soothing, cheerful/sad – as the playwright chooses. Some link needs to be established between them to justify their being in the same scene.

In musical terms Scene I is the Exposition in which we meet two contrasting groups of ideas, the First Subject (seldom a single theme) and the Second Subject, usually more lyrical in character. The link that joins them is called a Bridge Passage. It has another function, though, and that is to 'modulate', to shift the music into a different key, or 'family' of notes. The 'home' key is called the Tonic and the Bridge Passage will most probably modulate to its nearest relative, the Dominant, the key whose 'home' is a fifth higher. If a symphony or sonata is 'in' C, the First Subject will be in that key; the Bridge Passage will modulate to G, a fifth higher, and the Exposition (Scene I) will end in that key.

In Scene II of our play we learn a lot we didn't know before about the characters; their relationships towards each other change; the aggressive man may show unsuspected tenderness, the unhappy girl may become more cheerful.

This in music is the Development in which the composer manipulates the material, effecting such changes as he wishes and even introducing new ideas if it suits his purpose. (This is especially likely to happen in a concerto where the soloist is liable to be permitted to roam free.) The music will probably modulate to more 'distant' keys – ones whose notes differ markedly from those of the 'home' key – while themes may change in mood or be disguised in numerous ways.

Scene III of our play appears to start exactly as Scene I did; the same characters appear in the same surroundings, but we now know much more about them and view them in a different light. To conclude there must be a denouement, a summing-up.

Musically this third section is known as the Recapitulation. It usually begins with a reprise of the First Subject followed by a modified Bridge Passage that does *not* modulate, allowing the Second Subject to appear in the 'home' key for the first time. To round the movement off we have a Coda, usually brief but sometimes very substantial.

This, with many subtle variations, is the basic form of the first movements of most symphonies, concertos, quartets and sonatas written between approximately 1750 and 1880. Many such movements have an Introduction, but it is by no means essential. Sonata form may also be used in finales or even, more rarely, in slow movements. What I have omitted to mention, because it departs from my theatrical analogy, is that the Exposition was normally repeated. This was to enable the listener to absorb the material and in particular to take in the relative proportions of the various ideas so that the changes carried out in the Development could be better appreciated. In this respect Concertos have an advantage over Symphonies since the first Exposition was usually given to the orchestra alone while the repeat featured the soloist.

The four-movement Symphony derives partly from the orchestral Suite of dances from an earlier period, partly from a type of Overture that was divided into contrasting sections. Essentially it was designed to satisfy the need for contrast but also to show that the composer could write music to appeal to the intellect (first movements), the sentiments (slow movements), wit (minuets or scherzos) and aspirations to glory (finales). But many finales are pure entertainment, in which case a likely form is the Rondo. As its name suggests a Rondo is a circular form in which one theme returns a number of times with intervening and contrasting episodes.

Slow movements are often in the form of Theme and Variations, a self-explanatory title, while the Minuet and Trio – later to become Scherzo and Trio – falls into several sections. The traditional Minuet form begins with two matching sections, each of which is repeated. There follows a central section called a Trio which is also usually in two parts, both repeated. The players then return to the beginning of the movement and play the first two sections without repeats. This movement is normally omitted from Concertos, the custom being to have three movements rather than four.

Forms are not rigid, and during the nineteenth and twentieth centuries many changes have taken place. We find the order of movements being changed, we find extra movements being added, we find symphonies in one movement, concertos without soloists, choral symphonies, symphonies for organ and so on. But only the most eccentric of composers will attempt to dispense with form entirely since it is not merely a framework for his ideas but an invaluable prop to the listener in his search for points of reference.

There are many books that devote far more space to the subject of Form than I have allocated here, but this brief survey should clarify the subject sufficiently for us to be able to embark on the voyages ahead with some of the necessary aids to navigation.

BACH
1685–1750

To pass a talent from father to son is common enough; but for that same talent to pass from generation to generation for a span of more than two centuries is altogether remarkable. Such was the case with the Bach family in the German province of Thuringia, for the first acknowledged musician to bear the name Bach was born around 1578 while the last died in 1846. Thus the musical inheritance continued unbroken for upwards of 250 years so that there was always at least one Bach – usually more – to carry on the tradition; yet for the concertgoer of today the name Bach needs no further identification, even the initials J.S. being superfluous. The eldest son, Carl Philipp Emanuel, may interest us for his historical importance in the development of a truly pianistic style of composition; Johann Christian, another son, may charm us with his anticipations of Mozart, on whom he had some influence when that prodigious child visited London; but among the multitude of musical Bachs Johann Sebastian stands a giant supreme, to be ranked amongst the greatest masters of all time.

As with most great and prolific composers, Bach's output falls into several categories, each of which makes different demands on the listener and which therefore should be approached in a frame of mind suitable to its purpose. First place must be given to the great religious works, the Passions, Masses, Oratorios and Cantatas, not only for their exceptional scale but also for their spiritual profundity. Secondly we find a number of orchestral compositions, the magnificent set of six Brandenburg concertos, the four orchestral suites, and a substantial group of concertos for one or more solo instruments of which some are admittedly transcriptions of compositions by Vivaldi while others are re-arrangements of his own work, as, for instance, the D minor keyboard concerto which is certainly a transcription of a violin concerto whose original version has been irrevocably lost. Thirdly comes the wealth of organ works, still unsurpassed by any later hand, to which, as a subsidiary if even larger category, we must add the repertoire for solo keyboard, the '48' Preludes and Fugues, the French and English Suites, the

Partitas, the Fantasias, Toccatas, the Inventions in two and three parts, the 'Italian' Concerto and the elaborate 'Goldberg' variations. Fourth would come the works for solo violin or cello, while a fifth category might be termed 'learned', and would include 'The Musical Offering' and 'The Art of Fugue'.

This last work, which the composer left incomplete, demonstrates his absolute mastery of the fugue as a musical form, a mastery which however brought him an undeserved reputation as a 'mathematical' and, by implication, an unfeeling composer. While it is true that certain works of his do presuppose an intellectual interest on the part of the listener, they represent a relatively small proportion of the total. Indeed if one were to search for a common factor in all the five categories I have suggested, it would be not the fugue but the dance. Even in such profoundly spiritual works as the *St. Matthew Passion* many arias are essentially dances in character, while far the larger proportion of the purely instrumental music is conceived in dance forms. The Allemande, the Gavotte, the Minuet, Sarabande or Gigue (Jig) came as naturally to Bach's pen as the Fugue, a fact which, once realised, instantly makes him far more accessible. The problem for the layman's ear lies in the multi-layered textures that Bach delighted in. Although he knew perfectly well how to write a long sustained melody over a simple accompaniment, he clearly preferred to give himself (and us) a greater challenge by weaving together a number of strands of more or less equal importance. It is the performer's duty to clarify the web of counterpoint, the listener's duty to accept that Bach is not a 'top-line' composer. However there are many works which are neither melodic nor contrapuntal, consisting as they do of harmonies broken up into undulating and, for the most part, unvarying patterns. A classic instance is the first prelude from Book I of the '48', which has no tune and no counterpoint, but whose repetitive patterns weave a hypnotic spell. Clearly we need to listen to such 'pattern' preludes in a wholly different way from a richly harmonised chorale, a festive chorus, or an elegiac sarabande for solo cello. More than with most composers we need to learn to accept Bach on the terms he offers us in his immensely varied compositions, for his textures may range from the huge complexity of a double chorus and orchestra to a single unaccompanied line, while his time-scale may vary from the immense span of the B minor Mass to a tiny minuet written for a beloved wife or child.

The Brandenburg Concertos

To his Royal Highness, Monseigneur Crêtien Louis, Margrave of Brandenburg.

Monseigneur,

As I had the honour of playing before Your Royal Highness a couple of years ago, and as I observed that You took some pleasure in the small talent that heaven has given me for music, and in taking leave of Your Royal Highness You honoured me with a command to send You some pieces of my composition, I now, according to Your gracious orders, take the liberty of presenting my very humble respect to Your Royal Highness, with the present concertos, which I have written for several instruments, humbly praying You not to judge their imperfection by the severity of the fine and delicate taste that every one knows You to have for music, but rather to consider benignly the profound respect and the very humble obedience to which they are meant to testify. For the rest, Monseigneur, I very humbly beg Your Royal Highness to have the goodness to continue Your good graces towards me, and to be convinced that I have nothing so much at heart as the wish to be employed in matters more worthy of You and Your service, for with zeal unequalled Monseigneur,

I am
Your Royal Highness's most humble and most obedient servant

Jean Sebastian Bach.[1]

So wrote Bach in unaccustomed French to the Margrave of Brandenburg in the spring of 1721. At the time he was at Cöthen where, since 1717, he had been in the service of the young Prince Leopold. It was one of the happiest periods of his life for the Prince had a genuine enthusiasm for music as well as a resident orchestra of eighteen musicians. Thus it was circumstance as much as inclination that caused him during the Cöthen period to devote his talents more to instrumental music than he had previously done. We do not know precisely how Bach came to meet the Margrave of Brandenburg – it was either in Meiningen or Karlsbad some time in 1719; what is certain, as the letter above reveals, is that Bach had played for him and in doing so had found another musical enthusiast among the aristocracy. Although it would be nice to believe that the so-called Brandenburg concertos were made to measure for the Margrave's own household orchestra, modern scholarship has established that this was not so; nor does the necessarily sycophantic dedication mention a specific commission. Perhaps the Margrave provided the incentive to write some of the concertos, but it seems that the set of six was a collection of varied works whose very different instrumentation would almost preclude their performance by one relatively small orchestra. Had they been written specifically for the Margrave's band, Bach would surely

[1]Albert Schweitzer, *J.S. Bach*, Vol. I, p. 404 (A.&C. Black, London, 1945).

have ascertained its composition and used a more or less comparable orchestration for all six works.

Although Bach himself called them concertos, they represent an evolutionary stage between the *concerto grosso* and the true solo concerto. The standard form in a *concerto grosso* was to establish a contrast between the main body of less skilled players (the *ripieno*) and a small group of more gifted performers capable of playing music that was technically more demanding (the *concertino*). The composer would control the performance from the harpsichord at his own discretion above a left-hand part that exactly corresponded with the orchestral bass (the *continuo*). The composition of the concertino group was largely dependent on a realistic assessment of the technical ability of the players available at the time; it might consist of three string players, or two oboes and a bassoon or even a mixture of wind and strings. What seems extremely unlikely is that if Bach was writing for the Margrave's resident orchestra he would have demanded so varied a range of potential soloists and yet employed them in such an inconsistent manner. Thus we find two horns, three oboes and a bassoon in the first concerto, of whom only one oboist is required further; the second concerto has an exceptionally demanding trumpet part, but the player is never used again; the third concerto is for strings alone, divided, uniquely, into three string trios of equal calibre; concerto no. 4 introduces two recorders, also for the only time, while the fifth concerto has an enormously important solo keyboard part in addition to a single flute and violin. As for the sixth concerto, it employs nothing but two violas, two *viole da gamba*, cello, double bass and continuo harpsichord, an exploitation of the lower string tones that surely has no parallel until Villa-Lobos wrote his *Bachiana Brasileira* for soprano and eight cellos.

In the conventional nineteenth-century use of the word Bach had little feeling for orchestration since, as we shall see, the blending of tone colours was not his prime concern. He seldom uses sustained chords on wind or brass to establish focal points of harmony as later composers did. For the most part his music is conceived in horizontal strands rather than vertical blocks; musical values were more important than mere colour; consequently we often find passages woven into a complex web of sound that is difficult for the untrained ear to disentangle. The harmonic framework of the music is perfectly clear but there is something of an excess of decoration strung across it. Whether he uses flutes or oboes or strings, they will all play the same material even if at different times, so much so that some parts are extraordinarily difficult to play since they pay little heed to the idiosyncrasies of the instrument concerned. For him a theme was a theme; its musical value would be unaffected whether it was played on a violin, a flute, an oboe or a trumpet. This is an attitude no nineteenth-century composer would have accepted. Even in Purcell's day instruments were seen to have a clearly defined character – the 'martial' trumpet, the 'tender, soothing' flute. While

Bach was certainly not indifferent to these characteristics, as his masterly choice of obbligato instruments in the Passions and cantatas shows, he seems to have felt that in purely instrumental compositions it might be entertaining for each instrument to bring its individual timbre to the same theme in turn, rather than to devise music appropriate to its inborn characteristics. To amplify the point a little, the choice of an obbligato instrument in a cantata will relate to the mood indicated by the text; a meditation on death might suitably be accompanied by an oboe d'amore, whereas the joyful news of the resurrection would call for a trumpet or, if it was a choral work, three trumpets. Such type-casting simply does not occur in the Brandenburgs.

Concerto No. 1 (in F major)

The first concerto of the set is enterprisingly scored for two horns, three oboes, bassoon and strings. There is an additional part for a *violino piccolo*, not, as is sometimes thought, the little dancing-master's fiddle, but a three-quarter size violin tuned a fourth higher than the normal instrument. The keyboard part is assumed though not written out. Although the bass line is usually shared by all those instruments capable of playing it — bassoon, cello, *violone grosso* (predecessor to the double-bass) and the harpsichordist's left hand — in this work Bach occasionally allocates passages specifically to the cello or bassoon alone.

The concerto begins with an exceptionally complex texture consisting of three distinct ideas: the horns have a fanfare whose occasional triplet rhythms are at odds with everything surrounding them, the oboes have a chattering semiquaver figure divided into three distinct parts; the bass instruments give characteristically sturdy support, albeit with a quite independent pattern. As for the violins, they quickly transfer their allegiance from the horns in bar 1 to the oboes in bar 2. Further complication is added by the viola and the third oboe, both of whom go their separate ways. Thus in bar 2 alone, where the horns are divided, there are in all seven different strands of music, none of which can be regarded as mere supporting harmony. After this initial free-for-all, lasting some eighteen bars, Bach begins to take his small orchestra apart so that we find a bar for strings, a bar for oboes, a bar for horns, then a brief *tutti*. The principle of blocks of sound is very evident here, but notice in this game of 'pass-the-parcel' it is not the identity of the instruments but the identity of the material that is preserved. Horns are no longer given the concession of conventional fanfares; they are expected to be as nimble as oboes or violins.

The movement continues with occasional though not substantial variations of material and it is here that we realise the huge difference between this and, say, a movement by Mozart or Haydn. There are no breaks, no half-bar silences before the presentation of a new idea, no double-bars with repeats, no cadenzas, no positive cadences to establish the dominant key (in this case C major). The music is woven into a continuous tapestry of sound but the rapid changes of sharply differentiated tone-colours, horns—oboes—strings, ensure that the ear is kept continually alert.

In the second movement we find something nearer to the conventional concept of orchestration, a melody at the top with a discreet accompaniment. The tune is given to the first oboe, the accompanying chords are on the strings with just the first beat underlined by the other two oboes. But in the fifth bar we find a swap round which would have been inconceivable to Mozart or Haydn: he gives the tune to the violino piccolo and transfers the accompanying chords to the three oboes. Oboes in those days were not unduly refined and although Bach marks them *p* and the violin *f* I cannot believe that the balance would ever have been satisfactory; it is hard enough to manage even with modern skills. In a third stage the tune is shifted down to the bass accompanied by sighing chords that alternate tenderly between oboes and strings. The musical content is sublime; the tone-colours are certainly crystal clear. However, the subtleties of balance are put firmly into the performers' court; Bach could not have been so unrealistic as to expect oboes to play as softly as violins; it seems therefore that the discrepancies in tone and volume between them did not perturb him, an attitude which a nineteenth century-composer would have found amateurish and inept. It is revealing that when he begins a long and elaborate canon between the first oboe and the violino piccolo (who follows a beat behind) the accompaniment is stripped bare so as not to obscure the contrapuntal interweaving of the two solo lines.

The movement ends with an intriguing dissolution of the orchestra, individual chords from the continuo group, the three oboes, the violins and viola in turn. This sudden fragmentation of sound is a striking effect, making a feature of the essentially differing tone-colours with an almost Webern-like economy.

The third movement, which surprisingly is not the finale, begins with the horns re-establishing their existence after their silence during the preceding adagio. However the first oboe and first violins are soon left in the clear, and the whole texture of this movement shows Bach letting in a good deal more air to the score than he did in the first movement. All the same, some combinations of sound are distinctly unusual as, for instance, when a solo horn, a solo violin and the bass line (without bassoon) play a trio that is distinctly uneasy in balance. The music is gloriously tuneful, though, and we are easily swept along by its rhythm, taking such oddities in our stride.

The two movements that follow, a Menuet and a Polacca, were probably added as an afterthought, a concession to the French taste which the Margrave was known to prefer. In some ways they are the most intriguing from the point of view of orchestration, in that Bach uses a genuinely full orchestral sound in the minuet without so much concern for counterpoint and using the horns far more conventionally. Certainly the virtuoso element so noticeable in the first three movements has been completely abandoned. As for the central Trio in the Menuet, it really is one, for two oboes and one bassoon.

Strangest of all is the second Trio (in the Polacca) where he puts three oboes in unison against two separate horn parts, presumably with the idea that three oboes equal one trumpet. It is a curious sound, certainly not to be found anywhere in Haydn, Mozart or Beethoven. Nor is the rhythmical structure of this Trio at all conventional, consisting as it does of a pair of three-bar phrases followed by a two-bar phrase. The horn parts throughout the concerto are frighteningly difficult, and Bach may well have learned from experience that they were too demanding since nothing like them occurs again.

Concerto No. 2 (in F major)

Although it is in the same key, the Second Concerto is surprisingly different from the first. The solo group, or concertino, is an oddly assorted mixture: trumpet, flute, oboe and violin. Such a selection brings home forcibly Bach's conception that even instruments so palpably different from each other could be regarded not merely as equals but as interchangeable. As in the first concerto, the opening bars (properly called a *ritornello* since they return a number of times) consist of a blend of several clearly differentiated themes. The trumpet spells out a straightforward if somewhat martial version of the notes of the common chord of F major, ending with a running ascent to the first of many high C's. (The trill on this sustained high note is sheer exuberance.) Meanwhile flute, oboe, solo violin and the first orchestral violins combine in unison to give rugged strength to the most important theme in the movement, a rustic dance tune with an irresistible bounce to it. As for the bass, it circles round in a surprisingly agile fashion for two bars, infecting the upper parts with a comparable rash of semiquavers in bars 3–4. With F major well and truly established, the solo violin breaks ranks and offers a cheerful little theme of rather more aristocratic breeding. After all, it is only right that the conversation of skilled soloists should be at a more elevated level than that of the common mob. But the common mob will have none of it and immediately return to their rustic cavorting. 'That was rather interesting – what you said just now . . .' says the oboe taking over the violinist's theme, while the violin has an accompanying figure that nods in agreement. But their conversation is again interrupted by the initial dance, bouncy as ever and given additional spice by a rush of semiquavers to the trumpeter's head. Flute and oboe now pick up the conversation where the oboe and violin had left it off, followed, after yet another rustic interjection, by the trumpet and flute. And so this marvellously logical construction is built up:

```
                                                                      ⎧ trumpet
                                                    ⎧ flute           ⎨
                                 ⎧ oboe             ⎨                 ⎩ flute
                                 ⎨                  ⎩ oboe
            violin               ⎩ violin

            2 bars               2 bars             2 bars            2 bars

Tutti 8 bars │ . . . . . │ 2 bars │ . . . . . │ 2 bars │ . . . . . │ 2 bars │ . . . . .
```

Ever present, of course, is the continuo — hence its name — providing the necessary bass and supporting harmonies via cello and harpsichord.

Up to this point each two-bar interpolation from the tutti or ripieno has been based on bars 1–2 of the movement, but now, the quartet of soloists all having had a say, Bach allows the ripieno a longer section based on bars 3–8 of the opening. From here on the tendency is for the solo parts to become more elaborate, introducing several new developments, while the ripieno, no longer content to sit back and listen for even two bars at a time, takes a continuously active part, even though it may not always be of great musical import. In due course, after some fifty-nine bars, a miniature fugue emerges, based on the elegant phrase introduced by the solo violin as far back as bar 9. The order of entries is flute, violin, oboe, trumpet; but no sooner has the trumpet finished its phrase than all four soloists are caught up once again in the general dance, this time in the unexpected key of C minor. Another extended section of some thirty-four bars ensues with the soloists showing off prettily while the ripieno either reminds us of the main theme or introduces interesting new elements ranging from organ-like sustained harmonies to mischievous syncopations. At last, in bar 103, there is a united agreement that it is time to restate the initial theme unadorned save for a cheerful variant on the trumpet. A brief and hushed excursion into a few foreign keys provides a moment or two of mystery before we emerge once more into the clear daylight of F major and the expected triumphant conclusion.

Not surprisingly the trumpet is omitted from the slow movement, partly for the practical reason that the player's lip will need a rest, but also because the instrument would be out of place in what is essentially a piece of chamber music since the main body of strings is also silent. Flute, oboe and violin share an exquisite trio, mostly in canon (exact imitation) while two cellos and harpsichord provide a constantly moving bass as well as such harmony as may be needed. This is minimal since the three solo lines are so interwoven as to provide both elegant counterpoint and expressive harmony.

The third movement has a truly arresting opening as the solo trumpet presents a brilliant fugue subject, pivoting around high C and even leaping daringly to a top F. Oboe, violin and flute pick up the ensuing entries but with no real hope of matching the exciting impact of the trumpet's clarion tones. A composer from a later period would surely have saved the trumpet for the fourth entry rather than the first so that it would provide a climax; as it is, Bach leads with his ace. The ripieno strings, awe-struck by the display of virtuosity from the concertino, delay their entry till the forty-seventh bar; even then it is a surprisingly tentative one and within ten bars they drop out again leaving the soloists to continue developing the fugue. In comparison to the bustling complexity of the first movement the ripieno has a relatively small contribution to make, Bach preferring to focus our attention on the brilliance of the quartet of soloists.

Before we leave this concerto a word should be said about the trumpet part which makes demands that find no parallel in Mozart, Haydn or Beethoven. It seems that there was a guild of trumpet players who had mastered the secret of playing very high and rapid passages on the valveless instruments of the day; for some inexplicable reason the secret was not passed on to succeeding generations. By comparison even Beethoven's trumpet parts are very unadventurous; in fact, even as recently as the 1930s Bach's writing was regarded as impractical and the part was often performed on a clarinet — not really an adequate substitute. The current preoccupation with authenticity in the preformance of Baroque music has produced a crop of players who have mastered the ancient skills and it would be surprising nowadays not to hear this exceptional piece played as Bach intended.

Concerto No. 3 (in G major)

At first glance the Third Concerto would seem to be the least interesting in orchestral colour even if the best blended since it is scored for a group of strings with no wind or brass to provide variety. A more careful look at the score shows that Bach devised a completely original, possibly unique disposition of his forces — three violin parts, three viola parts, three cello parts, plus the usual violone (double bass) and harpsichord to give support to the bottom line. While the work is often played by a string orchestra, eleven players would seem to be the ideal — even ten if the harpsichord is omitted as it frequently is in this work. The three-note figure with which the movement begins proves to be astonishingly fruitful, its passage from one group to another being like a sonic game which Bach plays with the greatest dexterity.

The first eight bars present the main theme in three-part counterpoint, violins, violas and cellos each grouped in unison as 'families' with the violas having a marginally less interesting part than their colleagues. The end of this brief exposition is made clear by a general agreement to converge on a descending scale of G major. No sooner is this done than the parties split up; a fragment of the initial theme (two beats' worth) is offered by the violins, accepted by the violas and then commented on by the cellos. It is a game that will be played a number of times in the movement though at this point it is cut short by a return to the second part of the theme which is agreed by all. Once more that fragment is passed from group to group but this time it leads to new developments culminating in a sturdy tune easily recognised by the three-fold repetition of its highest (and then its second highest) note. Suddenly the tone is reduced to *p* to allow us to hear a witty exchange between the lower and upper sections, tossing the tiny three-note pattern with which the work began between them like a ball. Other notable exchanges follow; for instance in bar 32 we find the opening theme in the bass in a new tonality — C major. The three violins greet this event with a chortle of delight, a bustling phrase all in semiquavers; but when the cellos restore their theme to G major it is the violas' turn to laugh. It is these constant interchanges that hold our attention since the thematic interest is continuously on the move. For instance, at one point (bar 47) the first violin decides to show off a bit with a miniature cadenza, causing the violas to mark time in admiration; but at bar 51 the second violin says 'I can do that as well, and what's more in a more awkward key'. In due course, after some further discussion of the three-note fragment, the third violin takes a turn at a similar passage, again causing the violas to stop in their tracks. The whole movement is full of such pleasantries. Three-quarters of the way through Bach has a joke at our expense; we have reached the point where we might legitimately expect a convincing return to the opening material (bar 78). Unsupported by anyone save the three viola players, the second violinist bravely sets out on theme 1 in its original form. Without warning the *first* violinist simultaneously embarks on a completely new idea whose first three notes (*doh-mi-soh*) remind us of the opening of the violin concerto in E major. The idea proves sufficiently attractive to divert the second violin off course, following his leader in fugal style. After a few bars of animated discussion they are joined by the third violin, supported by the third viola, and it looks as though the fugue is really going to develop. But it is not to be, and in one of the most memorable passages in the whole movement the fugue dissolves in a cloud of oscillating harmonies which descend to the alien world of B flat major. Here the first violin again embarks on a cadenza, reducing his colleagues to mere onlookers. More and more emphasis on the three-note fragment leads to an increasing desire to return to theme 1, which, after a murky passage through the underground, finally surfaces in triumph. 'Did you think "finally"?' says Bach and begins to tease us with the swiftest and most extensive juggling so far. One phrase, a single bar taken from the cadenza passages, appears on six different instruments in turn — Violin II, Violin I, Violin III, Viola I, Viola II, Viola III — all in the space of six bars. And then, for the first time, the cellos are allowed to gratify any ambitions they may have as soloists with an athletic cadenza five bars long which is finally released in a scattering of three-note fragments. At last the pieces converge and, after 125 bars, there is a genuine reprise of the opening theme to bring the movement to a close.

What follows has been the subject of much debate; can a single bar, marked *Adagio* and consisting of two chords, be regarded as a slow movement? Nothing has been lost, for this unique curiosity appears in mid-page in the manuscript. Was Bach really content to have this strange A-men and nothing more? Various solutions have been suggested, ranging from the interpolation of a slow movement from a trio sonata to the Draconian gesture of removing the bar completely. Majority opinion favours a cadenza either from the first violinist or from the unnoticed keyboard player, but one which would set out from the first chord and come to rest on the second. Bach, who it should not be forgotten was nearly as accomplished on the violin as the harpsichord, could easily have filled in with a spontaneous improvisation on either instrument.

The finale is a lively dance in which we initially get the impression that four couples take the floor in rapid succession, the circling semiquaver runs suggesting the girls' skirts swirling round while the strutting quavers evoke images of the proud male dancers. There are no pauses for breath and the two sections into which it is divided are both repeated, the first part being a mere twelve bars long, the second part three times as lengthy. The impetus never flags for a moment, though, while the basic figuration is maintained throughout, there are occasional moments of exhibitionism as there would be in any high-spirited folk-dance. Thus in bars 15–16 the first violin has a series of upward flips which have more than a suggestion of the excited squeals which girls traditionally give in folk-dancing when their partners lift them in the air. In bars 35–6 we find an exactly comparable display in the first viola part, the deeper timbre suggests that this time it is a male dancer who indulges in the high kicks while the others watch with bated breath. If the idea seems too fanciful, I would quote no less an authority than Professor Arnold Schering who in his introductory note to the Eulenberg score says without apology that the movement is a German *Ländler*, a peasant dance that has endured to this day.

Concerto No. 4 (in G major)

This concerto exists in two forms, either for violin solo, two recorders and the normal string ripieno or, in a less familiar version transposed down a tone to F major, with a keyboard replacing the violin. The idea of transcribing violin concertos onto the harpsichord did not seem at all strange to Bach and one could say with some degree of confidence that all the so-called solo keyboard concertos are transcriptions of violin works. Such an idea would have been virtually unthinkable in the nineteenth century even though Beethoven did make a piano version of his violin concerto at his publisher's request. It is also said that the scherzo of the Brahms B flat piano concerto originated from a sketch for a second violin concerto; even so one cannot imagine the music having anything like the same impact if it were to be transferred to the violin.

Bach specifies recorders (*flutes à bec*) rather than the normal flute (*flauto traverso*), a decision which dictates a marked difference of approach to the scoring. Compare the density of the opening pages of the First Concerto to the start of this work. In No. 1 we find two horns, three oboes and strings all playing at once in a complex web of sounds in varied rhythms; here the scoring is transparent, with the ripieno supplying soft dabs of harmony on each first beat to allow the recorders every chance of being heard. The music is light and airy, and the delicate tracery of the recorders (even when joined by the solo violin) stands out with wonderful clarity. As the movement develops we find long passages for solo violin, virtually unaccompanied, and it may well be that Bach found that he had taken economy too far here, prompting him to transfer the music to the harpsichord. However, despite its apparent light weight the first movement is very substantial in content, 427 bars in all as opposed to the mere eighty-three bars of the much more solidly orchestrated No. 1. The solo violin part is of true concerto dimensions with long passages demanding the utmost agility as well as an episode involving extensive use of double-stopping (pairs of notes played simultaneously a sixth apart.) Indeed this is as much on the way to being a violin concerto as the Fifth Concerto is to a harpsichord concerto. It is in such ways that these two works in particular may be seen as a transitional stage between the concerto grosso and the true solo concerto.

The second movement is a stately minuet in character if not in name. A notable feature is the way in which the quavers throughout are phrased in pairs. Knowing the Margrave's taste for French music this suggests that Bach was indicating that the players should observe a French style of playing known as *notes inégales* or unequal notes. It was an affectation designed to give extra grace to the music as much as to save the composer trouble in writing down a rhythm whose exact notation was anyway hard to indicate. (The written figure ♫♫♫ would be played somewhere between ♪♪♪ and ♪♪♪). Musically the most remarkable passages are to be found in the recorder parts, where a series of chromatic descents presents a severe test of intonation. Four bars from the end there is a brief cadenza for solo recorder which any player worth his salt would almost certainly have embellished. The movement ends interestingly enough with the identical two harmonies which constituted the enigmatic 'slow movement' of the Third Concerto.

The third movement is a vigorous fugue whose subject is presented boldly by the violas over a running bass. The order of entries is viola, second violins, first violins, cellos and lastly recorders, whose high D makes a thrilling effect. After some forty bars the solo violin and the two recorders are left on their own to delight us with a little fugue-within-a-fugue into which, after twenty-two bars, the violas trip decorously to usher in the supporting players. Before long the solo violin once again attempts to transform the work into a solo concerto with a lengthy display of virtuosity which reduces the recorders to silence. (One senses the strong influence of Vivaldi, whom Bach greatly admired.) Subsequently, when all the players have rejoined the fray, Bach begins to use his recorders and solo violin in an almost organ-like way, sustaining relatively slow-moving harmonies against a much more energetic contribution from the ripieno. Towards the very end of the work there is a dramatic piece of writing in which pairs of strong chords are followed by brief silences, as though the sheer effort of playing so forcefully demands a breathing space. The whole movement is a brilliant demonstration of Bach's contrapuntal skill, and although the display passages for solo violin may remind us of Vivaldi, there is nothing Vivaldi-like in the working-out of the fugue.

Concerto No. 5 (in D major)

If it seems probable that Bach would have played the solo violin part in the Fourth Concerto, it is virtually certain that he wrote the elaborate harpsichord part in this concerto with the intention of performing it himself. Not even in the solo keyboard concertos do we find so demanding a part, and the massive cadenza towards the end of the movement is conceived on a far grander scale than had hitherto been known. Bach had acquired a new and splendid harpsichord from Berlin in 1719 and he presumably wanted to exploit its capabilities to the full. The other two soloists involved, a flute and a violin, are inevitably overshadowed by the harpsichord, their most significant contribution being made in the slow movement, a genuine trio in which the main body of strings plays no part.

The work begins with a rousing tune built on first the arpeggio and then the descending scale of D major. It is a stirring ritornello which, though it recurs many times in truncated forms, the soloists completely disregard once its first statement has been made. As in the Second Concerto we gain a distinct impression that there are two levels of music here, commoners and aristocracy. The utterances of the soloists have a refinement and elegance that is denied to the ripieno as the frequent use of a playful triplet figure indicates; it is never given to the 'orchestral' strings.

The three soloists make their entrance in the ninth bar, violin and flute bland and suave while the harpsichord tends to chatter rather more busily. Twice the strings try to reintroduce the opening ritornello but their efforts are abortive. An elegant conversation between flute and violin makes much of the playful triplet figure already mentioned until, in bar 19, the strings make another attempt to bring back the ritornello, this time in the dominant key. (A major.) Once more they are interrupted by the soloists who skilfully transform the character of the theme by smoothing it out and removing the most recognisable feature of repeated notes. At bar 29 the ripieno strings try to make a more positive impression by producing the second part of their main theme though with little greater success. As before they are quickly reduced to a supporting role although mutterings of discontent can be heard in various interwoven fragments of the theme now transposed into B minor (bars 35–7.) Bach stays for a while in this key (known as the 'relative' minor since it shares the same key signature as D major), but soon the harpsichordist embarks on some dazzling runs that virtually silence the opposition. Although it is devoid of malice or of the heroic rhetoric we find in nineteenth-century piano concertos, there is an element of competition here and it is worth mentioning that the derivation of the word 'concerto' is from the Italian *certare*, to combat or strive and *con*, with. There are therefore implications of a struggle for supremacy even though a *concerted* effort implies a unity of purpose.

Towards the middle of the movement there is a passage of some thirty bars which provides a complete contrast, an almost static period which is devoid of the forward thrust so evident in previous sections. The music settles quietly into the key of F sharp minor, easily recognizable since the strings play smooth sequences of repeated notes, emphasising the static nature of the harmony. Meanwhile the flute and violin exchange time after time a somewhat melancholy phrase lasting only a single bar. For a long period the mood is curiously veiled until some weirdly dissonant trills usher a return to bright daylight and a triumphant reappearance of the opening ritornello. Once again it is cut off in mid-flight by the soloists who, having regained the home key of D major by a slightly devious route, do begin a virtually exact recapitulation of their opening material without even allowing the ritornello to take its proper place.

In due course the harpsichordist begins once again to demonstrate his agility in swift scale-passages until his increasingly brilliant playing demands our total attention. So begins the massive cadenza, over sixty bars in length and, apart from the final fireworks, largely relevant to thematic material already presented at the keyboard. After such a display there is little to be said and all the orchestra can do is round off the movement with a reprise of the opening ritornello, only the second time in the whole movement that it is heard in its entirety.

The slow movement is pure chamber music without even a supporting cello or gamba to duplicate the harpsichordist's left-hand part. Bach gives the indication *Affetuoso*, affectionately, implying a tender and expressive style of playing. Although each individual phrase is emotional in content, the texture is subjected to the contrapuntal discipline that came naturally to Bach, with the initial entry of any phrase invariably being copied by a second instrument. Thus the first main theme is presented by the violin and copied (though not pedantically) by the flute two beats later. In bar 5 the harpsichord leads off with the same theme, echoed in turn by the flute and violin in that order. In bar 10 the flute leads off, shedding new light on the theme by putting it into the major, a suggestion which the violin happily accepts two beats later and which is even briefly shadowed in the left hand part of the keyboard. There is no drama, no climactic point leading to a cadenza; the music is an eminently civilized discussion between three equals, too good-mannered to become involved in argumentative dispute.

The last movement is an unashamed dance based on a theme that (to English ears at least) bears a close resemblance to 'A frog he would a-wooing go'. The music is initially presented as a four-part not-to-be-taken-too-seriously fugue, by which I mean that its academic pretensions are soon abandoned. The solo violin leads the dance, the flute is next to take the floor, while the harpsichordist provides the next two entries, first with the left hand then the right. The three soloists continue in playful mood for twenty-eight bars before the accompanying strings are persuaded to join in. (Again the image of royalty leading off before the commoners dare participate comes to mind.) Bach briefly reverts to a fugal style with the ripieno entry but it is soon dispelled by some nimble runs in the harpsichord part. Shortly after, in bar 79, the flute introduces a substantially modified version of the original fugue subject; only the first four notes are clearly related and even they are given a new slant by being in a minor key. Although the tempo remains as lively, there is an undeniable change of mood which duly spreads to the other two soloists when they, in turn, take over the same idea. It is not long before once again they are left on their own, flute and violin providing a more sustained line than has been offered so far while the harpsichord continues its busy triplets. They are called to order by the ripieno strings with a reminder of the original subject, but an exciting ascending passage leads not to the expected reprise but to an orchestral take-over of the modification described above. The music bustles along happily for a considerable time, toying with fragments of the opening theme. At last, in bar 233 a genuine recapitulation of the initial fugue begins, the music pursuing an identical course for no less than seveny-eight bars before coming to a gloriously satisfying end. Some idea of the perfect proportions of the movement is revealed when we find that the exposition and recapitulation combined come to 155 bars while the central section consists of 153. It is extremely unlikely that Bach planned so close a correlation but it does show his intuitive feeling for a balanced form in music.

Concerto No. 6 (in B flat major)

Political revolutions may be accomplished overnight; musical ones take rather longer. New and improved instruments may be devised and made but it takes time for them to become generally available. Harpsichord and fortepiano existed side by side for some time before the former came to be regarded as obsolete; Haydn's trumpet concerto was written for a player who had acquired a new, more versatile instrument equipped with pistons; Mozart re-scored his late G minor symphony (No. 40) to include clarinets once they became available; Beethoven, in his Ninth Symphony, wrote a special part for the fourth horn-player, the only member of the orchestra to be the proud possessor of one of the first two-valved horns. Such developments are not irrelevant to a discussion of the Sixth Brandenburg Concerto since its most notable feature is the employment of instruments that were already obsolescent but which were still being played alongside their ultimate replacements. Purists will argue that the viola and cello are as different from the viola da braccio ('arm' viol) and viola da gamba ('leg' viol) as the harpsichord and spinet are different from the piano; they have substantially different body shapes, different numbers of strings, different types of bow and different techniques of playing. Yet in a historical and evolutionary sense they can be said to be related since, as with the harpsichord and fortepiano, they co-existed for some time before the greater tonal power of the viola and cello led to the virtual extinction of the earlier instruments. Blend also proved to be a factor since a 'consort of viols' consists of one family of like-sounding instruments whereas a viola da gamba is less satisfactory than a cello when it comes to mixing in with violins.

The historical interest of the Sixth Concerto lies in its use of instruments which were shortly to disappear from normal concert-giving, even though Bach might still use them in a solo capacity or as obbligato instruments in vocal music. (See St. Matthew Passion No. 66.) The viola da braccio is also known as the 'tenor' viol, the viola da gamba the 'bass' viol, yet Bach also specifies a cello, violone and harpsichord. Notice that he employs neither treble viols nor violins so that the music becomes the string equivalent of a male-voice choir. Naturally enough the somewhat archaic instrumentation has led scholars to assume that this, though numbered six, was the first of the set to be written. The case is not proven although the relative simplicity of the bass viol parts has led to the interesting suggestion that one of them was designed for Bach's patron and employer Prince Leopold to play.

The concerto begins with a stirring version of the arpeggio of B flat major with the second violas following the first in close canon a mere quaver behind. The extreme proximity of the two lines suggests argument rather than agreement, lending an intriguing tension to what might otherwise be a rather conventional statement, especially as the bass remains unusually static. After sixteen bars of this closely knitted texture the music breaks free and a more varied discussion ensues, still imitative, but involving the cello and gambas in what is essentially a four-part contrapuntal structure. However, after a mere eight bars of this, the first motif returns in the dominant key (F major) albeit in a substantially abbreviated version. In fact, despite its very different tone-colour the form is not dissimilar to that of the Third Concerto — an opening ritornello to which frequent partial references are made, punctuated by a number of excursions into new but congruent material.

Deeper musical values are to be discovered in the second movement, a serenely beautiful fugue in E major treated in such a way that there are usually three different metric units continuing at the same time, minims, crotchets and quavers. Particularly effective are the final entries of the fugue subject in the bass, above which the two tenor viols weave a decorative web of two-part counterpoint. The movement comes to rest on a less than final cadence (D major, the dominant of G minor), only to plunge us without warning into the third movement, a jig that shows Bach in his most bucolic mood. As in the first movement, he makes considerable use of syncopated rhythms which give a nice rustic bounce to the music. There are a number of more athletic passages, usually circling runs in semiquavers. Bach shows an obvious concern for balance here, ensuring clarity by thinning out a texture that by being confined to the lower register runs the risk of muddiness. This is particularly evident when some dashing arpeggios appear in a swift interchange between the two tenor viols; the sole accompaniment is a series of separated notes from the cello, implying that even the harpsichord should be silent.

It is certain that Bach never visualised all six concertos as a single concert programme; it is a mistake therefore to regard this work as something of an anticlimax after the more overtly brilliant Fifth. Each of the Brandenburgs has a markedly individual quality, showing Bach ever ready to experiment with different combinations of sound. Orchestration as we interpret the word today was an art that had to be learned once orchestras as such emerged. Bach never had what Beethoven would have called an orchestra, but he did marvels with what resources he could command.

St. Matthew Passion

This monumental work is unequalled as a musical testament to the Christian faith and even the most hardened agnostic must be moved by its profound beauty and the intense feeling with which Bach unfolds the story of Christ's betrayal and suffering. Although the forces called for seem on paper to be large — two choruses, two orchestras and a number of soloists — it seems that the performances Bach directed himself were not overwhelming in sheer numbers. It is unlikely that he had more than three or four singers to each part since for the whole work, including the double choruses, he copied out only eight voice parts. While it is true that further copies might have been made by members of the family or pupils, it seems unlikely; after all, if Bach knew that such help was to be forthcoming, why did he not content himself with one master-copy instead of going through the labour of making the eight? As for the soloists, they would have been drawn from the choir; not for Bach the highly-paid international stars of the concert-platform that we have grown accustomed to in modern performances.

It seems that Bach made several versions of the Passion but the only two to survive are the *St. John* and the *St. Matthew*. The *St. John* is shorter, more concentrated, but, despite its many qualities, it has been relegated to second place in public affection. Even so, it provided one of the greatest choruses in the *St. Matthew*, for Bach had originally ended Part I with an unadorned chorale; second thoughts (some twenty years later) led him to lift in its entirety the richly complex setting of 'O Man bewail thy grievous sin' and transfer it from the *St. John* to the later work. In fact the composition of the *St. Matthew Passion* appears to have come in two stages, an original but substantially shorter version having been performed in 1727, followed two years later by the more expansive treatment we are familiar with today. The text was provided by Picander, but Bach made a number of alterations to it to satisfy his musical requirements. The chorales make use of hymn tunes by earlier composers such as Hassler (1562–1612) and Isaac (*c.* 1450–1517), tunes that would have been familiar favourites to Bach's congregation in Leipzig.

Although there are seventy-eight 'numbers' in all in the vocal score, some are extremely short — a few bars of recitative to move the story forward or a chorale of a mere twelve or sixteen bars. The overall plan becomes clearer if we regard it as two 'Acts' containing twenty-four 'scenes', the twelve subsidiary ones being marked by chorales, the twelve more substantial ones indicated by arias. These arias are scored in such a way that a specially prominent part is given to one instrument (sometimes a pair) whose function is partly to provide the orchestra with a 'solo voice', partly to lend an individual tone-colour suited to the sentiment expressed. Such a part is called an 'obbligato'. Musically we can divide the work into four clearly defined styles; first, the simple telling of the narrative which is either recounted by a solo tenor (the Evangelist) or acted out by a few soloists such as Jesus, Peter, Judas or Pilate; second, the arias of contemplation in which it seems as though Bach himself pauses to reflect upon the full implications of any particular event for humanity at large; third we find the choir's reaction to the story, whether withdrawn from the drama (as in the chorales) or actually involved in it as the crowd or *turba*; fourth, and on quite a different scale from the rest, we find three monumental choruses, one at the beginning, one to end 'Act I' (and therefore serving as a centre point), and one at the conclusion. Of these, the first chorus is not only the most magnificent but also the most complex. In it Bach makes clear the function of his two choirs, one representing those who are actually involved in the story, the other standing for the questioning observer, unfamiliar with the events. In all probability they were placed at opposite ends of the nave, hence the need for two orchestras; it must be said though that at times Bach combines his forces rather than using them alternately.

Part One[1]

1   Prologue. Unlike Handel, Bach was never drawn towards opera; nevertheless the opening bars of this massive chorus, climbing step by gradual step through the span of an octave, give the impression of an immense curtain rising to reveal the scene we have come to witness; the impression is confirmed when in the sixth bar cellos and basses at last leave the key-note of E with a marvellous ascent covering an octave and a half. Although the tempo is not fast, Choir I suggests a milling crowd converging from all directions to see some momentous event, though one that fills them with anguish in anticipation of tragedy. Like recent arrivals unaware of the situation Chorus II interpolate monosyllabic queries — 'How? Whom? When?'. The music is restless and uneasy, but suddenly a new strand appears, serenely confident in faith, the treble voices Bach would surely have used suggesting purity and innocence.

> O Lamb of God most holy
> Who on the cross didst languish
> O saviour meek and lowly
> Who suffered bitter anguish.

The measured tones of this great Lutheran hymn symbolise unswerving faith; it may even be that Bach, visualising the crowd of spectators thronging the narrow streets, saw in his mind's eye the figure of Christ walking, heedless of the mob, and used this sturdy tune to convey that image. The idea is not too far-fetched since his religious music is filled with vivid symbols, as we shall discover.

2   The first huge chorus having ended, Bach immediately establishes two important conventions — that the Evangelist as narrator should set the scene virtually unaccompanied so that every word shall be clear, and that the utterances of Jesus shall be accompanied by soft string chords, a musical 'halo'. Note also the extended distortion of the word 'Crucified', already suggesting the agony of the cross.

[1]The translations of the text are taken from the Novello edition edited by Ivor Atkins and Edward Elgar, as are the numberings of individual sections.

3   The first chorale, sung by both choruses expressing incredulity that such a fate can lie in store for the Saviour.

4–5   The Evangelist tells of the conspiracy of the priests to kill Jesus. With almost cinematic brevity we 'cut' to the gathering of the priests who in a confusion of voices argue 'Not upon the feast lest haply there be an uproar.'

6–7   The scene changes to Bethany where the woman anoints Jesus with a precious ointment; now it is the disciples' turn to protest and we hear them ask indignantly 'To what purpose is this waste?' After the huge span of the opening chorus these interpolations, whether of priests or disciples, are notable for their dramatic timing, concise and to the point.

8   Jesus rebukes the disciples and commends the action of the woman.

9–10   The first aria of contemplation, sung by a contralto so as to identify with (though not portray) the woman. The preceding recitative 'My Master and my Lord' is accompanied by two flutes who, throughout, repeat a pattern that is a symbol of lamentation much used by Bach and his contemporaries. The ensuing aria, also accompanied by the flutes, is the first example of Bach's remarkable use of dance forms in a profoundly spiritual context. An initial reaction may be to feel that there is something almost pagan about this, for did not priestesses dance in the temples of Delphi or Luxor? It is impossible to believe that Bach had such an analogy in mind. To him, as to all Baroque composers, Faith was a cause for rejoicing. (Pergolesi's *Stabat Mater* is a remarkable example of joyous music married to an essentially harrowing text.) Therefore, even though the contralto sings of grief rending the guilty heart, belief in ultimate salvation defeats despair. Even the tears depicted by a delicate arpeggio figure in the flute part sound more like a scatter of droplets from a fountain; the music would not be out of place in a gentle pastoral scene.

11–12   The mood darkens as Judas names the price of treachery. The ensuing soprano aria 'Break in grief' is a true lament, the paired notes in the orchestral part eloquent of sighs. The middle section has some vivid examples of musical word-painting, circling phrases for 'around' and a sinuous writhing figure for a 'serpent'.

3–14–15   The Preparation of the Passover.
Jesus prophesies that one of the disciples will betray him. Incredulously they ask 'Lord, is it I?' With a dramatic subtlety that might easily pass unnoticed Bach poses the question eleven times in all. The twelfth disciple, the betrayer, has no need to ask.

16   A marvellously harmonised chorale in which both choruses identify themselves with Judas. ' 'Tis I whose sin now binds Thee.' Should they not share Christ's suffering in atonement?

17   The first Communion at the Last Supper, the most openly lyrical music given to Jesus in the whole work.

18–19   A recitative and aria of contemplation for soprano that perfectly balances 9–10 for contralto. In place of flutes we find two *oboi d'amore* but in other respects the match is remarkable in its similarity. Both recitatives are accompanied by constantly repeated patterns symbolising lamentation; both arias are essentially dances. Here the soprano seems to step forward eagerly to offer her total commitment to Jesus. 'Jesus, Saviour, I am thine; come and dwell within my heart.'

21–4   At the Mount of Olives Jesus foretells Peter's denial of Him. The action moves at an almost operatic pace but is interrupted by two deeply moving chorales. Jesus comes to Gethsemane and bids the disciples to watch with Him.

25   For the first time Bach combines a soloist with the chorus. There is a wonderful contrast between the anguished phrases of the solo tenor and the restrained grief of the choir. Their music is a decorated version of the chorale first associated with the crucifixion (No. 3), here transposed down from B minor to the much darker-sounding F minor. One has the impression that they are stunned by their impotence to intervene whereas the tenor is filled with a passionate desire to go to Jesus' aid.

26   In one of the most beautiful arias in the whole work the tenor expresses the wish that he might be a member of that watching group surrounding Jesus in Gethsemane. Meanwhile the chorus sings a slumber song that might be said to lull the disciples to sleep. Here again soloist and chorus have markedly different kinds of music.

27   Christ prays in the garden: . . . 'Let this cup pass from Me: yet not as I will, but as Thou wilt.'

28–9 The first bass recitative and aria. As before we find a 'pattern' recitative followed by a dance aria. Note the drooping phrases in the strings to symbolise 'the Saviour low before His Father *bending . . .*' The voice in the aria is, we feel, Bach's own:

> Gladly would I take upon me
> Cross and cup and all His burden
> Could I follow Christ my Lord.

Time and again in this work we have an impression of Bach turning his eyes away from the drama unfolding before him, unable to look any more until he has had time to meditate upon its full implications for humanity and in particular for the devout Christian.

30   Jesus finds the disciples asleep and gently rebukes them, an action that prompts the ensuing chorale (31).

32   The Betrayal and Arrest of Jesus: one of the longest sections of pure action, the Evangelist sustaining the narrative with occasional interpolations from Jesus or Judas. Notice the restraint with which Bach refrains from introducing the chorus when Judas arrives with 'a great multitude with swords and staves.' A set-piece here would be out of place.

33   Christ is bound and led into the city. Here we find a wonderful example of Bach's ability to combine two completely opposing types of music. Flute and oboe begin with a forlorn descending scale, gently syncopated so as to intensify the impact of the dissonant notes, while beneath them the violins have a restless uneasy figure betokening agitation. Soprano and contralto soloists bewail in turn 'My Saviour now is taken'. This is a duet of contemplation; in their imagination they see Christ being led bound through the streets but they are helpless to intervene. However, every now and then their lament is almost swamped by furious shouts from the chorus: 'Loose Him! Leave Him! Bind Him not!' These abrupt interjections seem to belong to a different time dimension, as if part of the actual event, whereas the two soloists disclose Bach's own distress at the contemplation of the scene across the centuries. At the words 'They lead Him hence, with cords they bind Him' notice the two descending scales in measured and weighty crotchets, symbolising the guards leading Jesus down into the prison cell. Without pause we are launched into a chorus of extraordinary violence:

Have lightnings and thunders their fury forgotten?

The fugal entries in the order bass, tenor, alto, soprano give an impression of accumulated anger that the elements themselves do not intervene; a rapidly circling figure in the bass gives a graphic depiction of the continuous rumble of thunder, while pairs of sharply accented chords, always descending, suggest lightning spitting from the clouds. A dramatic silence in the middle — the eye of the hurricane? — is broken by a dramatic change of key (G major to B major). The whole chorus is operatic in conception, a strikingly graphic example of Bach's descriptive sense.

34 After the tumult and turbulence a scene of calm, the serene string chords surrounding the words of Jesus serving as a point of repose before the great chorus that concludes 'Act' I.

35 This truly monumental piece was added to the St. Matthew Passion some twenty years after the original performances. It was taken from the earlier St. John Passion, either because Bach felt that it was on too large a scale for the earlier work or perhaps because he felt that the St. Matthew would inevitably supplant the St. John in public esteem. (Composers of the day had little thought for posterity and were eminently pragmatic when it came to transplanting and re-using material.)

The orchestral introduction is based almost entirely on paired semiquavers, played in such a way that the second note is slightly shortened. They appear in flutes, oboi d'amore and violins, or in cellos and basses, who move either in parallel with the upper parts or alternating with them. This figure continues virtually unbroken for ninety-eight majestic bars; it is completely independent of the voice parts who pursue their own course with a richly contrapuntal treatment of one of the greatest of all chorale tunes, 'O Man bewail thy grievious sin'. (*O Mensch bewein' dein Sünde gross.*) It is easy enough in hindsight to understand that Bach felt that this masterly movement made a more fitting end to the First Part than the simple thirteen-bar chorale he had originally used; but it should be remembered that the Passion was intended to be performed as a church service on Good Friday with an inevitably lengthy sermon given between the two parts. Incidentally, on the same Good Friday which saw the first performance of this supreme religious masterpiece, at the same hour, a Passion by Gottlieb Frober was performed. He was candidate for the vacant post of cantor at the New Church, and for the Leipzig public this event was the more novel and therefore the more important.

Part Two

36   Prologue. Here we find not, as we might expect, another large-scale
      chorus but a contralto solo whose sentiments are reflected and
      shared by the second chorus. Once again the music is basically a
      dance with a light first beat and a stressed second beat (3/8).
      'Whither is thy beloved [Saviour] gone?' asks the chorus, and the
      introductory music suggests not only anxiety but also the actual
      motion of searching through a crowd, looking from side to side and
      occasionally turning to hurry in a new direction. The initial con-
      tralto note, sustained for more than four bars, may well be intended
      to depict the searcher standing still at some vantage point before
      mingling with the throng. The search is in vain for Jesus has been
      taken to the house of Caiaphas the high priest, as we are told in the
      ensuing recitative (37). A chorale condemning the injustice of the
      accusations laid against Him (38) leads to the depositions of the false
      witnesses (39) and Christ's refusal to answer their allegations.
      Unusually this is described not by the Evangelist but by a tenor
      from Chorus II, as though he himself had been present at the
      interrogation (40).

41   The same voice embarks on a tortuous aria, notable for its impor-
      tant cello obbligato. The first bar of the instrumental part consists of
      eight quavers, smoothly paired, symbolising the word 'Endure!'.
      The following three bars exploit jagged intervals and a sharply
      dotted rhythm, clearly designed to suggest the vicious malice of
      'lying tongues and taunting'. (Handel uses the identical rhythm,
      albeit less adventurously, in his '*Messiah*' beneath the words 'All
      they that see Him laugh Him to scorn'.) The word-painting in the
      voice-part is especially vivid with the jerky elongations of the word
      'taunting' suggesting sardonic laughter.

42   The high priest questions Jesus and denounces His reply as blas-
      phemous. Five aggressive bars suffice for the chorus's shout of
      agreement — 'He is worthy of death'.

43   A brief recitative describes the wrath of the crowd as Jesus is
      buffeted to and fro. The writing is deliberately chaotic with terse
      phrases tossed rapidly from one choir to another as the unfortunate
      victim is cuffed from side to side.

44   Bach turns his eyes from the scene in horror and anger in the chorale
      'O Lord who dares to smite Thee?' There is a tradition amongst
      English choirs that this should be sung in hushed tones, but it seems

more proper dramatically to begin it as an outraged protest. There is always a danger that the chorales may be treated too sentimentally.

45–6 Peter is discovered in a courtyard and is accused, first by a couple of girls and then by a group of curious bystanders, of being a disciple of Jesus. He denies it angrily . . . 'And immediately the cock crew . . .' Ordinarily, the Evangelist should sing with a certain detachment, as though reading from the Bible. Here though he is allowed a deeply expressive phrase as Peter 'wept bitterly'. The peak of this cry of agony (A–G♯–F♯) is transformed in rhythm and pitch into the opening phrase of the ensuing aria. (D–C♯–B).

47 Here for the first time, as though to emphasise the expressive quality of the music, the obbligato instrument is a solo violin. The instrumental introduction could easily be mistaken for the slow movement of a violin concerto in the style of a Siciliano. So graceful a dance seems scarcely in keeping with the contralto's plea, 'Have mercy Lord on me', yet the apparent incongruity is justified as soon as we realise that its purpose is to reassure us that mercy will be forthcoming. The woman may weep but God smiles upon her through the music.

48 A chorale of humility, 'Lamb of God, I fall before Thee'.

49–50 Judas admits his guilt, but the priests and elders express their indifference; he casts down the thirty pieces of silver, 'the price of blood', and in bitter remorse hangs himself. Bach shows him no pity; his suicide is simply reported, not dramatised.

51 The ensuing bass aria, again with violin obbligato, seems at first hearing to be almost frivolous with decorative ascending scales and athletic passage-work across the strings. However, knowing Bach's delight in musical symbolism, it is not far-fetched to interpret the rapid ascending scales as the movement of Judas's hand tossing the coins in the air while the ensuing figures show them bouncing and rolling across the floor of the temple. Inevitably, for musical reasons, the passage is extended for far longer than realism would require, but it serves as a springboard for one of the most immediately appealing arias in the whole work.

52 Christ is brought before Pilate; the scene is presented without drama, reflecting His refusal to answer the accusations against Him.

53 A chorale of faith, 'Commit thy way to Jesus'.

54   Pilate offers the people the choice — should he release Jesus or Barrabas? With a dramatic stroke that one might more readily expect to find in a twentieth-century work Bach gives the combined choruses a single dissonant shout of 'Barrabas'. It is an unforgettable moment, the more striking for its shocking abruptness. Asked what shall be done with Jesus they reply 'Let Him be crucified'. The first syllable, cru- is extended through four bars of 4/4 time with twenty-three notes so shaped that the phrase seems literally to writhe in torment.

55   One of the Passion chorales reappears for the third time (cf. Nos. 3 and 25). It is a compound of amazement that Christ should be willing to suffer so for mankind and incredulity that mankind should so betray Him.

56–8   A contemplation of the essential goodness and compassion of Christ. The format is now well established: a brief recitative from the Evangelist, followed by an accompanied recitative for the soprano with, as in Nos. 9, 18, 65 and 69, a pair of instruments providing the obbligato (oboi da caccia). Then comes the aria, in which the two oboi da caccia are reduced to a more subsidiary role, their plangent sound giving a harder edge to the dulcet tones of the flute — needless to say wooden in Bach's time and therefore less penetrating than the metal instruments of today. Notice the word-painting, the extension of the word 'love' into an encircling embrace and the chromatic fall on 'dying'. (Here Bach and Purcell share a common mastery.) As in all the arias of contemplation time stands still so that the ensuing outcry, 'Let Him be crucified (59) seems like a direct continuation of the closing bars of 54. Bach underlines the point musically by ending 54 with a chord of B major (having started in A minor!) and then beginning 59 in B minor. The cru- syllable of 'crucified' is extended still further to twenty-six notes, while the higher pitch makes the voices seem more shrill and menacing.

60   The Scourging. Bach distances himself (and us) from the full horror; relentlessly we hear the lashes fall with dreadful regularity but the sound is distant, its harshness softened by being given to strings — those same violins that earlier had consistently provided a halo whenever Jesus spoke. The dotted rhythm is the same as that used in *Messiah* for 'He gave His back to the smiters' though Bach's harmonies are far more intense than Handel's. Both composers use the contralto to describe the scene though again with Bach we have the impression that she is looking back helplessly across the gulf of centuries.

61   The aria that follows continues the rhythmic pattern of the scourg-
      ing even though it is written out in a different notation. Frequently
      there is a short rising phrase culminating in a sharp accent on the
      second beat of the bar. It is surely a cry of pain as the lash cuts ever
      more cruelly. (The aria tells of 'the sacred wounds bleeding'.)

62   Virtually unaccompanied even by the conventional keyboard con-
      tinuo, the Evangelist tells of the mock coronation of Jesus with
      scarlet robe and crown of thorns. In jeering tones the chorus hails
      Him as King of the Jews.

63   The chorale 'O Sacred Head sore wounded'. The chorales not only
      provide an emotional commentary with which the congregation
      could readily identify; they also serve to give musical unity to a
      work on this vast scale. This tune has already appeared as 21, 23 and
      53; it will appear again as 72. In every case Bach provides a different
      harmonisation.

64   The Evangelist tells of the Via Dolorosa and of how Simon of
      Cyrene was chosen to carry the cross.

65–6 In the brief preliminary recitative for bass solo we should notice the
      pathetic three-note phrases on paired flutes that graphically depict
      Christ's steps as He stumbles exhausted beneath the weight of the
      cross. In the aria that follows the obbligato is provided by a viola da
      gamba and though it is obvious from the dotted rhythm that even
      the strong and youthful Simon walks a trifle unsteadily he strides
      out proudly, rejoicing that he can ease the Saviour's burden.

67   The arrival at Golgotha is again described in an exceptionally
      austere recitative, almost without emotion; the ensuing jibes from
      the chorus seem the more hooliganish by comparison as they yell
      'Save Thyself, come down!'

68   Even the thieves crucified beside Him abuse Him, or so the
      Evangelist tells us.

69–70 Again we find the formula, recitative with a pair of instruments
      providing the obbligato (oboi da caccia), followed by an aria
      accompanied by the same instrumental colouring. As in the scene of
      the scourging it is the contralto who is chosen to express the
      universal grief.

      Ah, Golgotha! Unhappy Golgotha!
      The Lord of Glory here 'mid shame and scorn must perish . . .

The reiterated figure in the accompaniment may be intended to represent the mournful tolling of church bells though it could as well be the wringing of hands in sorrow.

The aria returns to the dance format with an almost lilting bass and a gently rocking shape to the melody that suggests a beckoning motion as Christ's hands seem to draw us towards Him. (The notion is not fanciful; the original text reads, in translation, 'See, Jesus holds out His hand to give us strength . . .') 'Come, come' He seems to say, and the second chorus, as though in recollection of their bewildered enquiries in the very opening chorus, again interject 'Come where?' There is an extraordinary tenderness about this episode, a release from the surrounding pain.

71   The Death of Christ. With brief interruptions from a still hostile chorus the Evangelist tells of Christ's last hour. The string 'halo' surrounding Jesus's words is withheld; at this dying moment He is the nearest to being mortal man.

72   The Passion chorale 'Be near me Lord when dying'. The most extreme example of Bach's use of chromatic harmony as a means of intensifying emotion.

73   And now, in comparison to the austere economy so notable in all the narrative passages leading to the crucifixion, we suddenly find an intensely dramatic recitative, vividly descriptive of the rending of the veil of the temple, the earthquake, and the resurrection of the saints. It is shortly followed by what many regard as the most sublime phrase in all music:

'Truly this was the Son of God.'

Within the space of two bars and one beat we find a matchlessly beautiful *melody* in the soprano part, supported by superlative *counterpoint* in tenor and bass, all clothed in *harmony* of memorable richness. It is not merely an affirmation of faith but a perfect fusion of the elements of music itself. It is perhaps worth remarking that in Bach's time it was probably sung by eight singers rather than the hundred or more we have grown accustomed to.

74–5   To a gently murmuring accompaniment of strings the bass soloist tells of the evening hour and the lowering of Christ's body from the cross. As usual in these accompanied recitatives one pattern prevails throughout in the orchestral part. The aria — yet another dance! — has a pastoral air not unlike 'He shall feed His flock' in Handel's *Messiah*. However it is longer and introduces more elaborate figuration in the central section.

76   A brief recitative describes the entombment of Christ. A chorus of
       priests and Pharisees demands of Pilate that the tomb shall be
       properly sealed; the music is pompous and self-righteous, becom-
       ing indignant in the closing bars.

77   Prior to the final chorus Bach places this masterly little scene in
       which each of the four soloists in turn is given a farewell phrase
       interspersed with gentle murmurs from the second chorus — 'Lord
       Jesu fare Thee well.'

78   The final chorus, for all its expression of tender grief, is a sarabande,
       not a funeral march. It has neither the dramatic intensity of the very
       opening chorus nor the majesty of the end of Part I (35). It creates a
       very personal relationship with the departed Christ, of whose resur-
       rection no mention is made in this Good Friday work. 'Lie Thou
       softly here' is the culminating phrase and the whole chorus is
       designed to give a sense of peace. Whitman's 'Come lovely and
       soothing death' captures something of Bach's philosophy and the
       feeling we have at the end of this immense work is not one of bleak
       despair but rather a sorrow that is warmed by a true love of Christ.

BÉLA BARTÓK
1881–1945

Though he was frequently reviled and subjected to malicious and ill-informed criticism during his lifetime, Bartók is now securely established as one of the greatest and most significant figures in twentieth-century music. It is hard to believe that there was a time when one of the most esteemed music critics of the day could seriously write, 'In shunning sentiment Bartók has lost beauty, in shunning rhetoric he has lost reason.' Since Bartók's music is so well organised that every note is meticulously placed, to say that he had lost reason was about as stupid a criticism as it was possible to make; but then every cheap jibe about excruciatingly wrong notes, torturing dissonances and so on was hurled at Bartók, even though he was a superb pianist and a composer whose music had been enthusiastically endorsed by some of the greatest musicians of the 1930s. On the other hand, it would be foolish to deny that some of his compositions do present a daunting challenge to the listener; he was not one to make compromises and it could well be that the very hostility he was forced to endure made his music more openly aggressive than it might otherwise have been. Certainly the work he produced towards the end of his life shows a mellowing that could reflect the increasing esteem in which he was held.

If his music seems strange to us, a prime reason must be that it is derived from a literally foreign source, the genuine folk-music of countries which, centuries ago, were affected by the invasion of Turks from the East. As a young man Bartók made a number of tours of Hungary, Romania and even North Africa in search of authentic folk-music. He amassed a huge collection which made a deep impression on his creative psyche, leaving a fondness for asymmetrical rhythmic patterns, unconventional scales and curiously angular melodic intervals. These attributes spring not from perversity but from a strongly felt identification with peasant music. (It is worth mentioning that in exactly the same period that Bartók was walking through the countryside rescuing music which he believed to be endangered by the encroachment of urban civilization, Vaughan-Williams and Holst were engaged in a similar quest in England.) During those long walking tours Bartók must often have found himself in remote country places at night and he developed an obsession with the nocturnal sounds of nature, the strange noises of insects and birds, the cry of the nighthawk, the almost inaudible rustle of tiny creatures whose restless activity was concealed from the eye by the calm all-enfolding night. His sense of hearing was abnormally acute and it was said that he could pick up sounds from a mile away that a normal person could only hear from a few hundred yards.

The introduction of folk-music as an exotic element within the context of organised compositions is nothing new. Haydn and Mozart frequently incorporated elements of Austrian folk-music into their works, Beethoven could build a string-quartet movement on a Russian folk-song to gratify one of his patrons, while Brahms and Liszt were fascinated by Hungarian folk-music. But even Liszt, himself a Hungarian, tended to present such borrowings in their Sunday best, washed clean, well-mannered, and clad in very fancy dress. Bartók preferred to treat folk melodies and rhythms as truly raw material, emphasising their primitive elements with strongly accented dissonances that, especially in the piano music, help to take the instrument out of the drawing-rooms of high society into a more rustic environment.

Like so many of his fellow-students in the late 1890s Bartók was initially overwhelmed by the influence of Wagner, although in his case Liszt proved equally fascinating. In 1902 he came across Richard Strauss's music for the first time and at once became so fired with enthusiasm that he made brilliant piano transcriptions of some of Strauss's most formidable scores. His first impact as a professional musician was as a quite outstanding pianist; for two years he hardly composed a note. It was as though in his search for a truly Hungarian identity he was trying to shake off the essentially Germanic tradition his pianistic studies had inevitably enhanced. His declaration of musical independence came with a vast symphonic poem called *Kossuth* (1903) whose ten movements were based on the exploits of a Hungarian revolutionary leader of the mid-nineteenth century. Although by no means characteristic of mature Bartók, it was a significant step away from the mainstream of European music. However, his ability to absorb folk idiom without allowing it to become his master enabled him to compose with complete confidence in even the largest forms and his works include three piano concertos, a violin concerto,[1] an unfinished viola concerto, the concerto for orchestra, the splendid 'Music for string instruments, percussion and celesta', the Divertimento for string orchestra, a one-act opera, a major ballet, a dance suite for orchestra, two sonatas for violin and piano, a piano sonata, innumerable folk-song arrangements and transcriptions and, in some ways his most significant contribution to the repertoire, six string quartets. That

[1]An early violin concerto exists, but Bartók incorporated most of its music into the first of the *Two Portraits for Orchestra* Op. 5.

such a man should die in enforced exile and genuine poverty is a sad commentary on an age in which popular entertainers were already able to become multi-millionaires by the exploitation of rather less enduring talents.

Music for String Instruments, Percussion and Celesta (1936)

This truly unique work serves as an excellent introduction to Bartók's music since it contains virtually all his most distinguishing characteristics, folk-derived melodies and rhythms, a consistent exploitation of patterns based on somewhat angular intervals and an intensely imaginative use of tone-colour. If one asks 'How then can it be unique?' the answer lies in its combination of instruments, a double string orchestra, a considerable battery of percussion instruments including side drum, bass drum, cymbals, tam-tam (gong), xylophone, timpani, a harp, a celesta and a piano. Because the latter instrument has an important part to play it may seem surprising that it is not mentioned in the title, but Bartók, ever logical, no doubt argued that since it has a large number of strings and hammers it falls comfortably into either of the two categories specified, string or percussion. The work as a whole is a perfect example of his ability to balance intellect with emotion; although it is constructed with a notable economy of material, its impact at all times is primarily emotional. Parts of it sound like music for a ghost-story, other sections could be taken for a description of a mist-enshrouded dawn by some remote forest lake, while the finale is an orgiastic gipsy dance.

The first movement combines the classical discipline of fugue with the impressionist technique of tone-painting, for although Bartók gives us no specific clue as to the subject-matter, it is easy to imagine it to be a description of a dawn in which the shapes of trees, rocks and mountains gradually become visible as the sun disperses the early mist. It begins with a single thread of music, almost inaudible on muted violas, its brief phrases rising and then falling by narrow intervals that have a vaguely Eastern flavour.[2] The ensuing entries give an almost pedantic impression of adhering to the academic concept of a fugue, yet the subject is undefined in its tonality while the differing phrase-lengths defy any attempt to enclose the music in a conventional time-scheme such as 6/8, 3/4 or 4/4. Gradually but logically Bartók weaves more and more threads into the texture until it becomes a spider's web of sound. Just as a spider's web is geometrically satisfying so is this music, for each of its lines is built from the same material and all the instruments[3] discuss and explore the same shapes. The growth is slow and

[2] Its second, third and fourth phrases are shown at the first, third and fifth examples on page 41.

[3] Strings only for the first thirty-three bars.

imperceptible, but gradually the great arch of the movement takes form, like some mountain appearing through the morning haze. At the central climactic point, briefly heralded by crescendo rolls on cymbals and timpani and precisely marked by a single stroke on the bass drum, all the strings converge on a single vibrant note (E flat). Beyond the peak of any mountain lies the descent, and so this music must unwind to its ultimate disintegration. The prevailing theme is now inverted, the logical antithesis to the previous ascent, yet the whole concept of the movement is surely imaginative despite the intellectual control of the material. Towards the end the celesta makes its first appearance with a rippling figure that inevitably suggests water. At exactly the same moment the first and fourth violins, three octaves apart, present the original and the inverted versions of the initial theme, a slightly distorted mirror image that surely represents reflections on the surface of a lake. The ripples die down; the movement ends in utter stillness on a single held note.

The second movement is a dance, much more physical in its appeal. The music is designed to be carried on the strong tide of its rhythm in direct contrast to the nebulous shapes that drift through the first movement. From the layout of the music it seems that Bartók may have visualised two groups of dancers since we find many swift interchanges between the two string orchestras. Occasionally the piano assumes a role comparable to a leading male dancer, though not to the degree that it does in Stravinsky's *Petrushka*. The folk element is evident to even the most imperceptive listener, although anyone who attempts to tap their toes in time to the music will have a mortifying experience since the rhythmic patterns are not merely syncopated but increasingly asymmetrical as the movement progresses. Rapid alternations between 2/4 and 5/8 give a strangely lurching gait to the music which, despite the suggestion of happy inebriation, never falters in its forward drive. Even so, Bartók uses all the most masterly tricks of classical musical construction; instruments echo each other's phrases, often in strict canon, they invert them, overlap them and so on, almost as though the composer was openly challenging the critics, daring them to accuse him of academic incompetence when, despite its thrillingly physical impact, the music was so intellectually controlled. One can even detect the basic structure of sonata form with an Exposition, Development and Recapitulation. The end of the Exposition is clearly signalled by two loudly stamped out beats from the timpani (F$\sharp$–C$\sharp$) followed by a silence. The ensuing Development begins quietly with a considerable exploration of the potential of the more 'feminine' second subject. After some time the pianist introduces a new and forceful idea, quickening the tempo as he does so. Some loud explosive chords of G major (!) followed by a few bars of solo drumming lead to an easily recognisable development of the first subject, a fragment of which soon settles into a machine-like *ostinato* (a multiple repetition of a five-note pattern) while above, piano and pizzicato violins introduce positively jazzy rhythms whose melodic outline proves to be based on the initial groping phrase of the *first* movement, now transformed almost beyond recognition. The excitement gradually dies down through a long passage for plucked strings until the music is reduced to a quiet reiterated drum-beat with an occasional grumble from cellos and basses. Suddenly a solo cello, playing very quietly, introduces a slithering sinuous theme that would serve nicely to illustrate a nature film showing a small eel wriggling out of the muddy bottom of a pond. A little thought reveals that it is a much compressed version of the virile dance theme originally heard in bars 5–7, orchestra I's opening gambit of the movement. Bartók treats this transformed idea as a strict fugue whose academic rectitude is only slightly disturbed by urgent restless drumming from the timpanist. The music gains in tension and excitement as it grows progressively louder, the two orchestras throwing phrases at each other with heightening antagonism. A victory of sorts for orchestra I ensues, marked by a series of rapid descending scale-passages, contracting by a note at a time and ultimately diminishing in tone as well. For a brief moment it seems as though the energy is spent save for a strange whirring trill on the lower strings. With an abrupt broadening of the tempo and a dramatic crescendo we are suddenly precipitated into the Recapitulation, no longer in dispute between the two orchestras, but shared in a combined unison that gives it a tremendous impact. Freely decorated though it may be, it is an unmistakable landmark.

Sweeping *glissandi* in harp and piano signal the arrival of the Coda which, at ever quickening speeds, makes clearly recognisable references to the main themes of the movement. With a touch of humour the music seems to be on the verge of disintegration, only to finish with an abruptly skidding descent.

The third movement is one of Bartók's most remarkable creations, seeming like an improvisation yet tightly organised. So atmospheric is the music that the listener is unlikely to be aware of the overall structure which can be conveyed by this very simple diagram

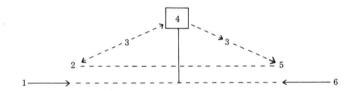

There are six sections in the movement; one and six correspond with each other: section five is a variant of section two, but influenced by (and therefore seeming also to resemble) section three. The fourth section is the centrepiece from which (at bar 49) section three moves away in reverse (retrograde) motion. Six is also a reversal of One even if Bartók is not so fettered by his plan as to make such relationships inflexible. In addition to this ingenious but convincingly symmetrical structure we find several subtly disguised links with the first movement; for instance, bar 2 of the work —

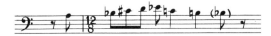

reappears as a simple unison phrase in bars 33–4 of the third movement:

bar 3 of the work —

reappears in equally simple guise in bars 60–3

while the fourth phrase of the work —

appears on celesta and piano at the end of a rippling passage on the celesta which itself recalls its memorable entry in the first movement. Here, more than eighty pages later, is this further reference to the very opening page.[4]

As if these disciplines were not enough, there is also a fugue whose subject is split up and used to introduce the various sections shown in the pattern of numbers on page 40.

Once the music is subjected to structural analysis of this kind there is a danger that our attention may be diverted towards a search for the dry bones; in doing so we may try, quite wrongly, to resist the intensely emotional impact the music is intended to have. The structure is really the composer's concern, a necessary prop for ideas that might otherwise be mistaken for pure impressionism. From the very first notes it is clear that Bartók's prime purpose is to engage our imaginations; the percussion instruments are used with extraordinary inventiveness, suggesting any number of nocturnal

---

[4]In spite of the curious differences of notations in these pairs of examples, the melodic contours are identical.

visions. Crickets and bullfrogs can easily be perceived, while the passage between bars 20–34 is one of the most spine-chilling examples of ghost music ever written. (According to Bartók's own timing the 'ghost' appears after 1 minute 45 seconds of music.) After the ghost has walked, harp, celesta and piano combine in shimmering *glissandi* that suggests the glitter of moonlight on the troubled surface of a lake. If ever music demanded to be listened to with the imagination at full stretch this is it; read into it what visions you will.

The finale is a complete contrast, a wild gipsy dance whose driving rhythms give the music an intensely physical quality. The form, such as it is, is a rondo, the main theme a bouncy trip down-and-up a scale with a catchy if elusive rhythm. Thrumming pizzicato chords on massed strings suggest guitars, while some of the writing for the piano is surely meant to convey that the player is too drunk to be capable of playing octaves without splitting every note. As is often the case in folk dances there are a considerable number of variations of tempo, episodes where individual dancers show off their particular skills. In such noisy and exuberant company the celesta is out of place and for much of the movement the player joins the pianist to form a piano duet. In addition to the 'gipsy fiddler' tunes there is a hilarious dialogue at one point between the pianist, trying to play a popular song, and the strings who, as one man, decide for no particular reason to practise their scales.

A slower central section, the girl dancers perhaps, leads to a brief but impassioned cello solo; if it is a male courtier, he fails in his intent for the music takes flight in swift upward scales whose irregular rhythms remind us of the opening theme. Suddenly there is a moment of calm as harp and celesta do indeed play that theme, its syncopations ironed out so that all the notes are equal. Did Bartók have in mind the extra careful deliberation with which the really drunk will enunciate every syllable in order to prove their complete sobriety? Perhaps, for the revels resume as wildly as before only to terminate in a general collapse.

Concerto for Orchestra (1943)

In the autumn of 1940, after an arduous and frustrating journey, Bartók and his wife (a former pupil) arrived in America with the hope of settling there permanently. His health was already a cause for concern and such work as he was able to obtain was not too well paid. The best part of a year was spent researching and noting down a huge collection of Yugoslav folksongs that had been amassed by an American enthusiast and scholar called Milman Parry and which was lodged in the archives of Columbia University. The work was not uncongenial but inevitably it left him little time or energy to compose. A mysterious illness sapped his strength; grants began to run out, and, although he was honoured by various universities, he felt the understandable despair of an unwilling exile.

1 March 1942

> . . . And now the bad knews. (sic) Our situation is getting daily worse and worse. All I can say is that never in my life since I earn my livelihood (that is from my 20th year) have I been in such a dreadful situation as I will probably be very soon. To say dreadful is probably exaggerated, but not too much . . . I am rather pessimistic, I lost all confidence in people, in countries, in everything . . . Until now we had two free pianos, a baby grand and an upright. Just today I got the news the upright will be taken from us. Of course we have no money to hire a second piano. So we will have no possibility to study two-piano works. And each month brings a similar blow . . .[5]

(The 'we' refers to his wife Ditta with whom Bartók had given some successful two-piano recitals.)

In 1943 his health deteriorated seriously with nightly fevers and such pain in his joints that he could scarcely walk. Soon he was confined to bed in hospital. In such circumstances he must have found a visit from Koussevitsky the famous conductor a welcome surprise, the more so when Koussevitsky offered him a commission of a thousand dollars to write a work for the Boston Symphony Orchestra. Bartók had some doubts about his ability to cope with such an invitation but the conductor left him a cheque for five hundred dollars and promised that he would receive the rest on completion. Amazingly, Bartók managed to write the 'Concerto for Orchestra' (as he chose to call it) in the space of two months. The decision to call it a concerto rather than a symphony was a compliment to the virtuosity of the Boston players and the work has proved to be a magnificent showpiece for any orchestra that tackles it.

The concerto begins mysteriously with a slow-moving theme on cellos and basses, a quiet shimmering figure from the violins and a faint suggestion of a tune from flutes. It is a formula that one might legitimately compare with the opening of Schubert's 'Unfinished' symphony even though the effect is very different. Schubert's initial theme is designed to be memorable as a tune, 'laid down' to be fully matured in the central development section where it is transformed to dramatic purpose. Bartók's music is a perfect example of the fundamental change of attitude that we find in a twentieth-century composer. His opening phrase is not really a theme in the Schubertian sense; it is

---

[5]From Halsey Stevens, *The Life and Music of Béla Bartók* (O.U.P., 1953).

deliberately vague, ambiguous in its rhythm, a shape rather than a melody. Certainly it is evocative, suggesting darkness and mystery; but its true purpose is to establish the fundamental importance of an interval, the fourth. (Intervals are measured from the lower note to the higher: thus A—D, B—E, C♯—F♯ are all fourths.) Here, at the very start of the work we find four of them in the first six bars, two rising, two falling.

Ex. 1

The ensuing rustle from the violins is pure tone-painting, a suggestion of a faint breeze stirring the leaves in the dawn mist; two flutes imitate a bird-call — a not too fanciful interpretation since Bartók's love of nature is well documented. Gradually the opening phrase from cellos and basses is extended, still emphasising the fourths as the most important interval. A solo flute offers a vaguely Oriental melody which creates quite a stir in the lower strings. Three muted trumpets accept the flute's suggestion a trifle uncertainly, hesitating at the end of each little group of notes. Suddenly, to thrilling effect, divided violins introduce a passionate melody, derived from, but by no means copying, the flute's first theme. The gipsy influence is very strong here, though not for long; bassoons, followed in turn by all the woodwind, initiate a machine-like repetition of a five-note fragment, consistently rising and whipping up the tempo as it goes. (It is a twentieth-century version of a technique used by Beethoven in his *Egmont* overture, repeating one small pattern a number of times until enough tension has been wound up to cause a break into a new and quicker tempo.) Using the rising five-note pattern as a springboard, Bartók's theme explodes into action.

Ex. 1a

Notice that although this appears to be totally different from the dark opening theme (Ex. 1), there is still a predominance of fourths; bar 1 covers an 'augmented' fourth, bar 2 has C—F followed by the join into bar 3, E♭—A♯; bar 4 is bar 1 inverted, bar 5 has yet another fourth, E♭—B♭. Increasingly in this movement we will find Bartók exploiting this way of establishing 'family relationships' between themes. Ex. 1a proves to be very adaptable and he frequently breaks off one small part (segments 1, 2 or 3) and toys with it, tossing it from one section of the orchestra to another. In amongst the fun and games a single trombone introduces a rather more severe idea, although this too makes extensive use of fourths.

Ex. 1b

This should be tucked away into the listener's memory as it is destined to have a very exciting future.

A contrasting note is proffered by an oboe with a curiously innocent little tune that rocks gently to and fro between one note and its next-door neighbour. It creates an oasis of calm from which we are rudely aroused by a sudden return to the vigorous five-note passage which broke out of the introductory section. (Ex.1a/bar 1) This sweeps through the score with tremendous energy, only to give way to a forceful discussion of Ex.1a/bars 2–3. A clarinet tries to quieten things down with a degree of success, but once again the impatient strings throw in the little five-note phrase, breaking the spell. We have reached the climax of the movement, a marvellous fugue for the whole brass section based on Ex.1b. This is music fit to blow down the walls of Jericho and it culminates with a huge sustained chord that literally seems to burst apart. The little two-note tune returns, this time on a clarinet instead of an oboe; but after a delicately scored interlude followed by a few false starts, Ex.1a makes a very positive reappearance, sweeping all before it. A last outburst from the brass (Ex.1b) brings the movement to an end.

The second movement is called '*Giuoco della Coppie*', or 'Joke with couples'. Is it possible that Bartók may have been inspired by the vision of a sort of musical Noah's Ark? We know he was fascinated by animals, birds and insects so the idea is not wholly frivolous. After a few bars from a side-drum to establish the pace,[6] two bassoons lead off with a pawky little tune in which they consistently stay a sixth apart. Next we have a pair of oboes a third apart, a pair of clarinets a seventh apart, a pair of flutes a fifth apart and then a pair of trumpets a second apart. The intervals are preserved constantly with each pair and I have sometimes wondered whether the different intervals, a third, a fifth, a seventh, and so on, might perhaps represent the different bulk of the animals — wider or narrower as they are. It is a fantasy that has no grounding in scholarship, but Bartók must have had a reason for deciding to arrange the

---

[6]Crotchet = 94, not 74 as shown in the printed score.

music in this unique fashion. One can of course argue that it was a way of showing off the virtuosity of the wind-players in the Boston Symphony, but the music is not really a vehicle for technical display. Britten does that much more consciously in his 'Variations on a Theme of Purcell' ('Young Person's Guide'). The instruments appear in a different order but there too we find a pair of flutes (albeit with a piccolo added), a pair of oboes, a pair of clarinets and a pair of bassoons. However, the differences of character are much more sharply defined, and Britten, especially in the flute and clarinet variations, certainly aims to show off the virtuosity of the players.

In the centre of the movement there is a brief chorale for brass, a few moments of solemnity that only make the side-drum fidgety. But then my Noah's Ark fantasy suffers a blow, for the woodwind procession begins again, this time with *three* bassoons. Next we find paired oboes and clarinets playing together as a garrulous quartet. Bartók rings further changes as the movement draws to its close, the final touch consisting of a delightful fusion of all the various intervals into one harmonious chord. The side-drum beat dies away to nothing: the movement is ended.

The central movement of the five is called *Elegia*. It begins rather as the first movement did with double-basses playing a shadowy theme in which fourths are again conspicuous. Then the ripples start, little fountains of notes on clarinet or flute with a surrounding haze provided by the harp. A piercing high D flat on oboe and clarinet freezes all movement, and then, after a pause, the ripples begin again but this time as though seen in slow motion. Suddenly the mood changes completely as Bartók springs a major surprise on us. Plucked from page two of the Concerto and transplanted onto page fifty-three we find the very phrase that muted trumpets had once offered tentatively before the first passionate outcry from the violins (see page 44). Now violins and clarinets join in this Orientally-slanted melody, dramatically accompanied by sweeping downward scales and massive thumps from the lower regions of the orchestra. The mood grows increasingly agitated and vehement until a huge climax is reached with the return of the gipsy lament that the violins had played so passionately in the introduction to the first movement. Indeed the motto for this central Elegy could well be 'By the waters of Babylon we sat down and wept' for there can be no mistaking the impressions of water nor of a dreadful despair.

That despair melts away in the ensuing movement, the '*Intermezzo Interrotto*', or Interrupted Intermezzo. After a peremptory clearing of musical throats from the entire string section, a solo oboe embarks on a shy little tune with a minimal accompaniment. It has the slightly irregular lilt characteristic of Bulgarian folk-music though there is no reason to believe it is not Bartók's own creation. It is developed in several ways, sometimes by fitting itself against its own image, mirror-fashion. Its character is clearly feminine even though rather demure. Not so the violas who, standing in for an imaginary tenor, sing an ardent love-song. The impression of a serenade is heightened by the harp accompaniment; here, one feels, is a truly operatic conception, but one which is destined to have a rude interruption. A brief reprise of the shy maiden's song slyly disintegrates into a vamping accompaniment of the most banal kind. A solo clarinet introduces a tune composed entirely of descending sequences, each one a little more absurd than its predecessor. As if losing control, the tune begins to tumble over itself only to be greeted by a Rabelaisian 'raspberry' from muted trumpets and shrill woodwind, followed by a cackle of laughter from the clarinets. Two monstrous farts from the trombones form an even more derisive comment.

The significance of this grotesque passage is lost on many a listener today since the object of its mockery is seldom heard any more. It appears that while working on this Concerto Bartók heard Shostakovich's '*Leningrad*' Symphony for the first time. (It was still wartime and the work was being performed quite often to inspire us with admiration for our Russian allies.) Bartók found the prevailing theme of Shostakovich's symphony ludicrously inept in the context of so much human suffering and could not resist the temptation to lampoon it in this admittedly rather childish way. The joke is soon over, and as the musical laughter dies down the 'tenor' theme reappears, gorgeously harmonised. A tender wisp of the 'girl's' tune leads to a brief flute cadenza, surely a nightingale singing to the young lovers; they bid each other good-night and the movement ends as they tiptoe away into the darkness. Purists will no doubt argue that such an interpretation is not supported by any documentation, yet so much of Bartók's music is descriptive, so much is based on folk situations that I feel we are perfectly justified in seeing such images if they seem apposite. Bartók collected innumerable folk-songs describing the joys and pangs of village courtship; the themes in this movement are clearly pastiche folk-songs, the 'voices' of oboe and viola are surely symbols for girl and boy. Indeed, the movement would make a delightful ballet; by calling it an Intermezzo Bartók is certainly inviting us not to take it too seriously.

A short arresting fanfare from four horns in unison shatters the mood; its final note, reinforced by trumpets, gives us a moment to absorb it into our memories since, in due course, we will discover that it has a more important role to play than a butler's announcement that the finale is about to be served. Guitar-like, the violas and cellos start thrumming away energetically, increasing their pace to match the urgent scurry of the violins. The gipsy influence is strong indeed and for quite a time the music relies on the sheer excitement of speed to sweep us along in its wake. Suddenly a single bassoon is exposed in a brief solo, clearly derived from the opening horn fanfare. Other woodwind instruments take up the idea with the intention of launching a decently respectable fugue, but just as it seems to be getting under way there is a complete change of mood. A romantically inclined flute turns the fugue subject upside down, playing capricious tricks with its rhythm; violins, divided into six parts, play a descending sequence of text-book harmonies that suggest we are entering an oasis of calm. It is not to be however, and, goaded on by the woodwind, we are soon swept away into the helter-skelter rush of the opening pages once more. But now a new element appears, so important that its first entry has to be on a trumpet. Beginning with three very positive notes (D^b—A^b—D^b) it grabs our attention even more insistently with an eight-fold repetition of the central A^b. This theme is the real substance of the movement, a fugue of truly classic dimensions even though it may seem far from classical in its presentation. Despite the mad whirl of semiquavers with which he surrounds it, Bartók treats the fugue subject with all the skill of an eighteenth-century contrapuntist; the theme is inverted, it is played in notes of double the value; it is played in notes of half the value; it is treated in *stretto* (with the entries overlapping); it is even developed so as to shed new light on its character. Yet though this is truly a demonstration of academic skills at their best, the enduring impression of the movement is its demonic energy. Even when the fugue subject appears in its final augmentation it is shot through with hurricane scales on strings and wind. To play the work at all taxes the skills of the finest orchestras; for a sick man to have written it in seven weeks is something of a miracle.

Violin Concerto No. 2 (1937–8)

Bartók was first attracted to the idea of writing a violin concerto in 1907; however, he was entering a period of change at the time and was growing increasingly dissatisfied with the frankly romantic idiom — a state of mind shared equally by such contemporaries as Stravinsky and Hindemith. In the end he salvaged what he considered the best portion of the work and incorporated it in the first of the 'Two Portraits for Orchestra', Op. 5. Thirty years passed before he tackled the medium again and then it was only as a commission from the Hungarian violinist Zoltan Székely. Although he was asked to write a violin concerto, Bartók said that he would much prefer to write an extended set of variations, presumably on a Hungarian theme. Székely insisted that as he was paying for the work he had the right to specify its nature; he wanted a concerto, not a set of variations. In the end he got both, for, not liking to admit defeat in an argument over artistic matters, Bartók with some deviousness produced a concerto that is in fact an extended example of variation form. Being a composer of infinite technical resource he disguised his intentions very cleverly. At first hearing, or even on looking at the score, there doesn't seem to be much resemblance between the opening phrases of the first movement and of the finale. The one consists of quiet and somewhat isolated pizzicato notes on the lower strings placed beneath some remarkably simple harp chords — unadulterated B major for the most part. The other has all the strings in unison playing an aggressive phrase that has a kick like a mule. Yet, as we can easily see if we superimpose one on top of the other, the bare bones are identical.

Ex. 1

It is easy enough to dismiss those initial pizzicato notes as a mere preamble, but the violin's entrance clearly brings a theme of considerable importance. Its broad lyrical line is admirably suited to the violin, but then so too is the cheerful dance tune with which, quite unaccompanied, it makes its appearance in the finale. By slightly more Procrustean methods we discover that these two themes, so unlike in character, are brothers under the skin.

The transformation of themes is an old trick and one of which Bartók's great Hungarian predecessor Liszt was particularly fond. It would be laborious to trace the other thematic relationships which exist, but the fact is that there are also similarities of structure between the outer movements of this concerto, similarities of which we may only be aware subconsciously but whose existence gives a satisfying unity of design. One of Bartók's greatest strengths is his feeling for musical structure; whatever the intricacy of detail he never loses sight of the shape of the movement as a whole. In almost every work we find a fascination with shapes, mirror-images, back-to-front versions of themes, arches — they all appear time after time in his music, so much so that one is sometimes amazed that music of such burning intensity can be so meticulously organized.

Considering that it was written in the late 1930s this concerto is a remarkably tonal work. In spite of the harp's initial chords of B major, the

Ex. 2

true key is B minor, a key which both Elgar and Walton also chose for their violin concertos. Like them, Bartók obviously believed that the violin is essentially a melodic instrument for all its brilliance and agility. The opening theme extends for twenty-one bars of which only the first four are shown in example Ex. 2. But then a slightly more restless figure establishes itself, bringing with it an increase in pace; an element of virtuosity becomes apparent leading to the first real climax. Almost as though rebuking the soloist for this bout of exhibitionism, the orchestral violins restate the first theme, or as much of it as suits Bartók's purpose, which is not merely to re-establish the original tempo but to provide a firm reminder of the opening. The soloist seems to accept the hint in the nicest possible way but then, without warning, starts to goad the orchestra with a waspish little phrase which brings increasingly anxious and fluttering reactions from wind and strings alike.[7]

A sequence of crotchets wafting out of the heights brings a period of calm that lulls us into a false sense of security, for suddenly there is a sort of

[7]For those sufficiently interested, this passage too has its counterpart in the finale, as a comparison between bars 56–8 from I and bars 87–93 of III will show. The later version is 'stretched' by a chromatic ascent in the woodwind, but allowing for the differences in rhythm, the two passages are closely related.

screech from the orchestra and, like a falcon swooping down on its prey, the violin has a fierce descending chromatic scale which leads into an agitated episode that only a savage trill on two trumpets can effectively quell.[8] Calm is restored by harp chords reminiscent of the opening; a new theme, a surrogate 'second subject', appears in guileless simplicity. But is it so 'new' after all? Although new in character, the notes themselves were laid down at the very start of the work with the pizzicato bass shown in Ex. 1. Here it assumes an importance that has never been hinted at. It is echoed, after a fashion, by a cor anglais and, a little later, by cellos and basses. For more than forty bars (115–59) peace reigns, the meandering scales on the violin being no more than a twentieth-century equivalent of the type of passage-work found so often in Mozart and Beethoven. Then, just as the orchestra shows signs of total somnolence, 'Enough!' cries the soloist, and awakens everyone with a vigorous finger-exercise straight out of Everyman's Advanced Violin Tutor. This 'practising' passage ('sawing away regardless' to use Sir Henry Wood's unforgettable phrase) continues for some time, even though first a horn and then a cor anglais offers lyrical reminders of the opening theme.

A curious dialogue ensues between the strings — with distant memories of the opening tune in the violins casting a shadow in the basses — and the wind, whose syncopated rhythms have quite a jazzy flavour (182). The soloist seems to want to join the wind and offers some energetic triple-stopping (three-note chords) in exchange. Then, as if realising that such a display of strength is not really needed, the violin embarks on a perfect inversion of the original theme against a quietly shimmering background of harp and celesta. (Notice that the 'finger-exercise' figuration is now given to violas and second violins in turn, an opportunity for a little basic practice that can do no harm.) The soloist breaks off in mid-flight with a terse pattern of three rising notes — actually the lead-in to the first theme — which becomes the basis of an animated discussion in the orchestra. An abrupt halt and a momentary silence lead us to a classic recapitulation with the soloist now presenting the theme two octaves higher than it had been originally and also with some subtle changes in the orchestral accompaniment. As recapitulations go it is fairly strict though there is a characteristic fondness for turning some of the music upside down. A sequence of rapid tightly-knit chromatic groups leads to the substantial cadenza which, in its first stages, is accompanied by lyrical references to the opening theme from bass clarinet to solo horn. It is an easily recognised landmark for, having settled like a particularly vicious wasp on the open string D, the violin experiments briefly with microtones, flattening or sharpening the note by less than a semitone. As might be expected the cadenza is challengingly difficult. It is followed by a

---

[8]Since the preceding passage (bars 73–91) has flirted with the serial technique of a twelve-note row in both violin and orchestra, this outburst may justifiably be regarded as a scathing rejection of Schoenbergian methods.

condensed summary of the main themes — the jazzy one on bassoons, the lyrical first subject on a solo horn, and other fragments of which one catches only a brief glimpse as they flash by. The movement ends with a solid unison B, reaffirming Bartók's conviction that tonality is not dead. (The thought comes — does so positive an assertion of B serve as a signature for Bartók?)

Székely's wish for a concerto and not a set of variations is openly defied in the second movement which is unashamedly a set of six variations on a theme; there is even a double-bar in the score to show the demarcation between each variation. The theme, a series of short phrases that suggest derivation from a folk-song, is in a slightly distorted version of G major, the fourth note of the scale tending to be sharpened. Variation I is an elegant elaboration of the tune with a minimal accompaniment from pizzicato double-basses and timpani, mere dabs of sound to mark the time. Variation II is virtually a duet for violin and harp, whose rapidly turning figures seem literally to 'run rings' around the soloist. The woodwind provide a relatively static accompaniment. Variation III shows the violin at its most aggressive, goaded by sharp dissonances from a pair of horns. Variation IV adopts a slower tempo with the cellos and basses playing a simplified version of the theme while the violin weaves sinuous coils of notes above. The closing bars create a contrasting mood of absolute calm with the soloist initiating a simple pattern of notes that is imitated in canon by violas, cellos and double-basses in turn. Variation V is a miniature scherzo in which harp and woodwind play a prominent part, while even a triangle and side-drum are enlisted to enhance the distinctly playful character of the music. Variation VI must surely be added to the catalogue of Bartók's 'insect' music with the solo part suggesting the rapid beat of tiny wings. Gradually the movement slows to a halt; with the utmost simplicity the soloist recalls the original theme in a higher octave. The final bar is more like a disappearance than a conclusion.

We have already seen how the third movement begins in Exx. 1 and 2. Although the cheerful little dance tune presented by the soloist leads us to expect a Rondo, the music is actually a large-scale sonata-form movement which is also a variation on the first movement. This it resembles quite closely in structure; for instance the first break into a quicker tempo comes in bar 22 in the first movement, bar 29 in the third. (Since the movements are in 4/4 and 3/4 respectively this means 88 beats as opposed to 87!) References to the first movement become more obvious when the second violins, accompanied by pizzicato strings and harp, launch into a lyrical singing theme which is at once taken up by all the woodwind in unison. It is shortly after this that the variant already mentioned in footnote 7 on page 50 occurs. Not surprisingly there are more opportunities for the display of sheer virtuosity in this movement, but one notably quieter moment is worth mentioning. Easily recognised with its simple accompaniment of triangle, cymbal and harp, it appears to be a totally new theme, lyrical in character even if eccentric in its intervals. On closer examination this too proves to be a remarkably close relation to a theme from the first movement, the flirtation with serialism that was then so rudely received. This time it merely evokes a sort of *frisson* in the strings.

Later in the movement the opening dance tune is converted into a carillon by the brass to tremendous effect, an idea which is picked up quite captivatingly by the soloist towards the very end. Speaking of endings, Bartók's original intention was to finish with a purely orchestral playout but Székely persuaded him that no soloist would really feel happy about this; an alternative was duly forthcoming though both versions are printed in the score. It is curious that similar alternatives are provided at the end of the *Concerto for Orchestra*. Bartók would seem to be the last composer to have had doubts about his music; he had pursued his own path heedless of biting criticism from those who should have known better. Yet in these two cases he clearly had second thoughts; it was characteristic of his integrity that he did not attempt to suppress the original versions but rather to leave posterity to judge.

Piano Concerto No. 3 (1945)

Bartók's first two piano concertos, dating from 1926 and 1931 respectively, were certainly written to suit his own style of playing and to provide him with what Stravinsky would have called 'visiting cards' — works with which he could introduce himself to a wider public as composer and pianist. In this respect he was following in a long line of tradition embracing such varied figures as Mozart, Beethoven, Chopin, Liszt, Rakhmaninov and Prokofiev. Both works treat the piano as essentially a percussion instrument and there is a raw ferocity about much of the writing which antagonised critics and public alike. Nowhere do we find the openly seductive melodies that have brought Rakhmaninov such popularity; the audience is battered into submission rather than cajoled. Although he was a solo pianist of the first rank, this tendency was not particularly apparent in his recital programmes. His repertoire included Scarlatti, Bach, Couperin, Mozart, Beethoven, Chopin, Liszt, Debussy, Ravel as well as his amazing piano transcriptions of Richard Strauss's major orchestral works. Not surprisingly he also included works by such contemporaries as Kodály, Stravinsky, Hindemith and even Schoenberg (despite his pronounced scepticism about serial methods); yet it seems that he did not feel that he had a Messianic role to play with regard to modern music in general. It was his own work, naturally enough, that interested him most, and the fact that his 'official' Opus 1 is a Rhapsody for Piano and Orchestra shows that from the first he visualised himself as the most persuasive advocate for his cause. However, he did not make his task easy whether by the musical idiom he developed or the technical demands he made on himself. The first two concertos in particular are fearsomely difficult to play, calling for exceptional rhythmic precision and steely strength in wrist and finger.

The private life of a composer is not always of any great significance with regard to his art but Bartók's case has a relevant interest. Like many musicians at the start of their careers he was forced to do a certain amount of teaching to earn an adequate living. In 1907 he gained a professorship for piano at the Budapest Academy of Music; although he detested teaching he found himself much attracted by two girl students. The first, Stefi Geyer, was a talented violinist to whom he not only wrote long and revealing letters but also dedicated the abortive violin concerto whose first movement he later adapted as the first of *Two Portraits* for violin and orchestra (Op. 5). It seems that she must have felt that they were too incompatible for a deeper relationship and in February 1908 she wrote him a parting letter. The day he received it he wrote a sad little piano piece called 'Elle est morte'. The heartache was superficial, though, and he found solace in the company of a pupil who had first appeared in his class at the tender age of fourteen. Her name was Márta Ziegler and in the following year (1908) Bartók was already dedicating quite important compositions to her including the aptly named 'Portrait of a Girl'. In the autumn of 1909, when she was in her seventeenth year, they were married; a son, Béla, was born the year after.

In 1923 there was an almost uncanny repetition of the same situation. Once more Bartók became emotionally involved with a piano student in his class. Inevitably the age-gap between them was even wider but he found her charms so irresistible that a divorce was arranged and quickly followed by his second marriage. Ditta Pásztory was a talented pianist and was to remain with him for the rest of his life, giving many concerts with him as a piano-duo.

More than twenty years later, in 1945, Bartók began work on the Third Piano Concerto; this time he was writing not for himself but for Ditta. Although America was not proving to be quite the Promised Land they had both hoped for, there was much to lift Bartók's spirits that year. Not only was Nazi Germany defeated; Bartók was nominated as an honorary member of the new Hungarian parliament and restored to the various official musical posts from which he had resigned when he left his homeland. The Third Concerto is clearly influenced by these crucial events; its opening pages radiate a sense of gentle content, a feeling of 'All's right with the world' that is absent from its two brittle and harsh predecessors. Ironically Bartók did not live to hear it; indeed the final seventeen bars had to be orchestrated from a shorthand score by a devoted disciple of Bartók's named Tibor Serly. (He was also responsible for constructing the Viola Concerto from a number of sketches that the dying composer had been unable to finish.)

The Third Concerto is one of the most classical works that Bartók ever wrote, classical in spirit and in form. In the opening bars the strings set up a gentle undulation of harmonies not unlike the shimmering introduction to Stravinsky's *Petrushka*, though somewhat lower in pitch. Two timpani quietly etch in the dominant and tonic notes of E major (B—E) thereby proclaiming that the music is truly committed to a positive tonality. With both hands in unison, two octaves apart, the pianist begins a long and elegant tune with some elaborate, almost rococo, decorations. Its style resembles a Romanian dance called a *doïna*. Towards the end of the tune the notes seem almost to tumble over themselves, giving an impression of quickening pace even though the tempo remains constant. As is so often the case in Bartók concertos the orchestra takes over just enough of the theme to establish its identity but then proceeds to turn it in new directions.

A striking feature of the piano-writing in this movement is the extensive use of parallel motion between the two hands, whether in single unison notes, octaves or chords. At the twenty-seventh bar the pianist introduces a note of rhetoric that is almost Brahms-like in texture leading to a passage in octaves in which the left hand presents a delayed mirror-image of the right. Bar 54 sees the introduction of a true Second Subject which frequently exploits pairs of falling notes and fluttering trills. A charming dialogue develops between piano and solo clarinet who cuckoo happily at each other as the exposition ends.

The structure could scarcely be clearer for the ensuing Development begins with boldly declaimed arpeggios in A flat major from the pianist and a long extension of the opening theme, now on all the woodwind in unison. This is followed by a more fragmented version for piano solo in B flat major upon which the strings have a few cogent comments to make. Soon the charming second subject reappears (unison in the piano again) its trills setting the woodwind all a-flutter. A sustained and gradually diminishing trill from the violins leads us to a classic Recapitulation, the pianist's hands still moving in parallel but now in paired notes instead of simple unison. Every feature of the original Exposition is recognisable in some form and the movement ends enchantingly in what might almost be described without offence as a sort of cloud-cuckoo-land, so often does that most identifiable of bird-songs seem to appear.

It is unlikely to be pure coincidence that the second movement begins (and ends) with what I have termed the 'cuckoo' phrase. In this new context it serves a very different purpose, no longer a playful frivolity but the beginning of a serenely beautiful phrase of disarming simplicity. Bartók gives the instruction *Adagio religioso*, the only time he uses such a word in all his works; the religious feeling is one of monastic austerity, a warning against an over-sentimental approach for the string-players, who are divided into five-part polyphony without the double-basses. Their opening phrases, fifteen bars in all, die away to silence. The piano enters with a theme that is like a hymn; its reticence can only be compared to the entry in the comparable movement in Beethoven's Fourth Concerto, though Beethoven's music is tinged with a profound sorrow that is quite absent here, as is the sense of conflict between strings and piano that Beethoven exploits to such dramatic effect. So far as I know nobody has ever proffered an explanation for Bartók's decision to write this chorale-like movement. Two possibilities occur to me; first, that it may be a literal hymn of gratitude that the war was ended and his country freed from Nazi domination; second, that he knew he was dying of cancer and that the music, if not exactly a prayer for his own soul, is a reconciliation with the approach of death. Certainly the strings' closing phrase is like a gesture of benediction (54–7).

There follows an extraordinary interpolation, a whirring sound from the strings that suggests the flight of innumerable insects. Oboe, clarinet and piano fill the air with tiny fragments of sound, the nocturnal cries of birds and the little creatures that seldom venture out in daylight. Some of these darting patterns of notes are based on actual bird-calls that Bartók had noted down in Asheville, North Carolina in 1944. Nearly twenty years previously he had written a suite of piano pieces called 'Out of Doors' which he had dedicated to Ditta when they had been married for only two years. Was this movement intended to stir memories for her too? This whole central section is a classic example of Bartók's identification with nature, quite different from the soft 'water-colour' impressions we gain from Delius or Vaughan-Williams, sharply etched but no less deeply felt.

In due course the pianist's opening chorale returns, this time on wood-wind, with an almost Bach-like two-part accompaniment on the piano that now and then dissolves into shimmering runs and trills. There is a moment or two of passion towards the end of the movement but the closing bars again seem like a benediction, the last two chords even saying a peaceful Amen.

The last movement brings an abrupt awakening with a whirlwind rush up the keyboard leading to a strongly syncopated theme. This is the most familiar and popular aspect of Bartók, the stamping rhythms and sheer animal vitality that he exploits better than any other major twentieth-century composer. Yet even in this movement there is an unashamedly classical element, for after the initial energetic dance rhythms have exhausted themselves in a timpani solo, the pianist sets out on a strict fugue, a whim which the orchestra seems happy to follow. This is developed at some length until the pianist introduces another dance tune in octaves, loud and clear. A second solo passage for timpani leads to a new episode, gentler in character and marked *grazioso*. Yet another theme, rather more foursquare in character, appears in the orchestra, provoking the pianist to frenzied scale-passages of great brilliance. After further exploration of the 'gentle' theme, this time on horns to emphasise its pastoral nature, an exciting chromatic scale from wind and piano leads us back to Theme I, more exuberant than ever. A breathless silence precedes the final *Presto*, beginning gruffly on the piano but growing ever more exciting. Bartók was still working on the manuscript score in bed, five days before his death. In his desperation to finish he made a shorthand version of the final seventeen bars, lacking the time or strength to make a full score. The finale gives not the smallest hint that his life was ebbing away fast; it is truly a dance in the face of death, a triumph of the human spirit.

BEETHOVEN
1770–1827

Speculation about who is the greatest composer is a fairly fruitless exercise but it is undeniable that Beethoven was one of the most significant; he it was who extended and developed such major musical forms as the sonata, symphony, string quartet and concerto; he it was who liberated music from classical restraints and opened the way for the Romantic Movement in which composers expressed emotions in personal terms rather than as abstractions. Early Beethoven works take over from Haydn; late Beethoven leads towards Schumann, Brahms and even (in the slow movement of the Ninth Symphony) towards Mahler. To accomplish such a revolution in musical taste required an immensely powerful creative personality; to accomplish it despite the handicap of deafness needed exceptional moral courage.

Although the bulk of the music written by Beethoven in his early years gives little evidence of genius, one work stands far above the others, a work which ironically he was never to hear performed. It is the 'Funeral Cantata on the death of the Emperor Joseph II' composed in 1790. Performances had twice been cancelled owing to the uncooperative attitude of the players who found the music altogether too difficult. A similar fate met the cantata that Beethoven wrote to celebrate the accession to the throne of Joseph II's successor, Leopold II. Surprisingly we have no record of Beethoven's re-action to this considerable setback at a crucial period in his life. He certainly realised that the Funeral Cantata in particular represented an enormous step forward towards artistic maturity; in fact he used a substantial portion of the material in the second finale of his opera Fidelio, a sure acknowledgment that he realised its worth. (The Cantata itself was not performed until 1884.)

It seems quite probable that this double rebuff brought a psychological block in its wake. The effective rejection of two substantial works in the course of a single year must have hurt Beethoven's self-esteem; certainly he continued to compose, but not for orchestra. Apart from the first two piano concertos, a form in which his own mastery of the keyboard assured him of success, all the works written during the last decade of the century were sonatas or chamber-music of some kind. This reluctance to embark on a major orchestral composition is surprising and uncharacteristic. The concept of the symphony as a form had been clarified by such early masters as C.P.E. Bach, Wagenseil, Gassman and Stamitz; it had then been developed with wonderfully inventive powers by Haydn. One would have expected Beethoven to welcome the challenge with enthusiasm, yet even a period of tuition with Haydn in 1792 failed to give him the necessary confidence to do so. He made some sketches for one in 1795 but they proved abortive. If the lessons with Haydn had planted symphonic seeds, they appear to have lain dormant for seven years; with apt historical timing they were to flower with the dawn of a new century in the year 1800, the year of the First Symphony, Op. 21.

Symphony No. 1 in C Major
Op. 21

Following a precept set on many previous occasions by Haydn and his contemporaries, Beethoven begins this symphony with a slow introduction. Although the opening bars may seem undramatic to a modern ear, they are sufficiently unorthodox to have elicited a great deal of comment over the years. It should be understood that the standard way of beginning any major work, whether symphony, concerto, sonata or quartet, was to spell out a sequence of notes or harmonies that would establish a 'home' key, or tonal base. For example, each Mozart symphony begins with a clear declaration of tonality. 'This music,' he seems to say, 'is *in* the key of D major or G minor or C major', as the case may be. Such a declaration is not a mere technicality of interest only to theoreticians; it is vital to the understanding of all the larger musical forms in Western civilisation for a period of at least a century (1740–1840). The 'home' key, or tonic to give it its proper name, served both as point of departure and as ultimate destination. The listener was supposed to be able to appreciate the import of journeys into new tonal centres that contradicted the tonal implications of the original one as well as to savour the satisfaction of returning 'home' after such adventures. At the very start of this symphony Beethoven leads the listener astray by suggesting other 'homes' than the proper one of C major so that when the music does break into a quick tempo we sense a twofold release. Not only is the sustained tension of the Introduction resolved, but also the enigma of uncertain tonality. However, if the Introduction seems to pose the riddle 'What do these pairs of chords signify?' the subsequent *Allegro con brio* supplies an answer. Careful listening reveals a close relationship between the slow opening and the quick music that emerges from it even though the character seems very different.

If the first main theme of the *Allegro* strikes a slightly military attitude with its crisp precision, the second theme is almost operatic in flavour with flute and oboe engaging in a delightful dialogue. The ghost of Mozart hovers in the air, soon to be exorcised with peremptory rhythms that suggest the rapid beat of a side-drum, even though such an instrument was not to find a regular place in the symphony orchestra for the best part of half a century. Out of this brief clash of arms we are suddenly shifted into a world of shadows and mystery. Cellos and basses lead the way, while the strings above offer an accompaniment of gently throbbing harmonies that briefly touch on tonal centres as yet unvisited. The air of mystery imparted by this passage is not simply achieved by playing quietly. The music is mysterious because it ventures into tonalities that contradict the basic components of C major, moving far from 'home'.

During the eighteenth and nineteenth centuries the repetition of the
various sections of a composition was standard practice. If the music was for a
soloist he would regard the repeat as an opportunity to introduce spontaneous embellishments of his own; if it was for orchestra such an element of
caprice could scarcely be allowed, but it is perhaps not too cynical to suggest
in those under-rehearsed days that a second try might have been welcomed
by all. In such a symphony as this the repeat would be taken from the start of
the *Allegro*, dispensing with the slow Introduction. The aesthetic value of the
convention was to establish the 'home' key firmly in the listener's mind.

The so-called Development section, the central part of any movement
constructed on these lines, begins with three reminders of the first main
theme divided one from the other by restless syncopations that give an air of
insecurity. Furthermore, the 'home' key of C major is deserted in favour of
new tonal centres which shift so rapidly that not one is established with any
permanence. Among the most fundamental differences between Western and
Eastern music is the exploitation of such changes of tonality and its resultant
effect. Eastern music tends to be conceived as a single (even if elaborately
decorated) line, whereas Western music is more concerned with harmony
and the play of relationships between one tonal centre and another. Hard to
understand if one is not a composer is the subtle balance between the
conscious and the subconscious processes during the composition of a work.
Thus Beethoven's conscious self makes a purely intellectual decision to move
further and further away from the 'home' key during the Development by
introducing an increasing number of notes foreign to it. However, once these
notes begin to appear in actuality they breed a reaction in the subconscious
which dictates an emotional response, which in turn will affect the next
intellectual decision. To draw a very simple analogy, suppose that one
decides for no particular reason to write down the word 'horse'. One then
decides (consciously) to add the word 'galloping'. The inner response to the
image the two words 'horse galloping' evokes is an emotional one, essentially
dramatic, which provokes the next conscious choice of word. If on the other
hand one were to decide to add the word 'sleeping' to the 'horse' image, it
would evoke a quite different emotional response, and in consequence a
different sequel. Comparable to this, although far more complex in detail, is
the process by which Beethoven arrives at the considerable 'storm' that takes
place in the centre of the movement. By consciously deciding to shift from
the 'home' key to remote tonal centres he breeds an emotional (subconscious)
response that produces the storm. The point is so significant in comprehend-
ing symphonic thought that it needs to be made at this early stage.

The central crisis resolved, the composer re-assembles the original
material in the third main section of the movement, the Recapitulation. This
should never be regarded as mere repetition for the sake of academic convention; it is a reassessment of the themes in the light of experience gained during
the Development. As to the final bars of the movement, they are designed to

emphasise the restoration of the 'home' key of C major, as if to assure us that it is no longer at risk.

The second and third movements give a clear indication of Beethoven's transitional state as a composer since the slow movement looks back towards the formal dance-style of the eighteenth century while the ensuing Minuet (so-called) totally discards such conventions. The movements offer a contrast between the academic and the unorthodox, the *Andante* beginning with a demure theme that is treated as a miniature fugue, the following *Allegro molto e vivace* setting off like a whirlwind. Anything less like a Minuet could hardly be imagined and the title must be taken as a joke. The whole conception is totally original; it is in effect the first symphonic scherzo and is the largest comparable movement that he was to write for some time.

As for the finale, it begins with an impressive gesture that turns out to be a hoax, for, like a bevy of hesitant beginners the first violins make no less than five abortive attempts to play a scale, progressing one note further each time. It is a characteristic example of his musical humour that Beethoven would have hated us to take seriously. When at last the movement gets under way it sparkles with wit and vitality. In particular the rising scale that initially seemed to frighten the first violins proves to be a fruitful source of material, whether ascending or descending. Towards the end there are two massive pauses that lead us to expect some great event. Again it is a leg-pull, an amusing exploitation of the effect of anti-climax. The final march, garlanded with scales from the woodwind, is like a children's game. There were no clouds in Beethoven's sky when he wrote this delightful symphony.

Symphony No. 2 in D Major
Op. 36

Sketches for the Second Symphony were begun in 1800 but Beethoven was a slow worker and the germination of any of his major works was a laborious process involving much rejection of preliminary ideas, ideas which often seem incredibly banal but which were ultimately forged into great music. Perhaps the most remarkable thing about the Second Symphony is that it was written during a period of intense personal despair. In October 1802 Beethoven wrote a lengthy letter now known as the 'Heiligenstadt Testament'. Addressed to his brothers, though never sent, it expresses in eloquent terms the composer's misery at the onset of deafness; the following is a quotation of less than a quarter of this remarkable document.

> . . . not yet could I bring myself to say to people 'Speak louder, shout, for I am deaf.' O how should I then bring myself to admit the weakness of *a sense* which ought to be more perfect in me than in others, a sense which I once possessed in the greatest perfection, a perfection such as few assuredly in my profession have yet possessed it in — O I cannot do it! forgive me then, if you see me shrink away when I would fain mingle among you. Double pain does my misfortune give me, in making me misunderstood. Recreation in human society, the more delicate passages of conversation, confidential outpourings, none of these are for me; all alone, almost only so much as the sheerest necessity demands can I bring myself to venture into society; I must live like an exile; if I venture into company a burning dread falls on me, the dreadful risk of letting my condition be perceived. So it was these last six months which I passed in the country, being ordered by my sensible physician to spare my hearing as much as possible. He fell in with what has now become almost my natural disposition, though sometimes, carried away by the craving for society, I let myself be misled into it; but what humiliation when someone stood by me and heard a flute in the distance, and *I* heard *nothing*, or when someone heard *the herd-boy singing*, and I again heard nothing. Such occurances brought me nigh to despair, a little more and I had put an end to my own life — only it, *my art*, held me back. O it seemed to me impossible to quit the world until I had produced all I felt it in me to produce; and so I reprieved this wretched life — truly wretched, a body so sensitive that a change of any rapidity may alter my state from very good to very bad.'

Such inner torment in a Romantic composer would undoubtedly have produced an equally harrowing piece of music, a literally Tragic symphony. Beethoven, it seems, was able to exorcise despair by the act of composition for the Second Symphony is an exuberant and optimistic work that bubbles over with high spirits. Only in the slow introduction do we find the occasional sorrowful phrase; even so, it appears to be more a conventional expressive gesture than a revelation of private grief.

Many Haydn symphonies begin with a slow introduction, a convention that Beethoven copied in four of his symphonies, including the first two. Here the introduction to the opening movement is very much more elaborate than that in the First Symphony. Although it begins in D major Beethoven soon plunges into alien keys, taking us into a different world where eerie horn-notes stab through the darkness and rapid ascending scales suggest great winds blowing through echoing caverns. An eloquent phrase on violas and cellos seems like a deep sigh, expressing a sorrow that is singularly absent from the rest of the work, considering that it was written at a time when the onset of deafness had put the composer into a suicidal mood. After sundry fluttering trills from flutes and violins, a long sustained A builds the tension until, with a sudden downward swoop, the first movement proper appears out of the murk. The main theme is given to the cellos but the swift flurry of notes that flashes through the first violin part from time to time is an important feature that prevents the music from sounding at all pedestrian. A similar interpolation is to be found in the Second Subject, an almost Mozartean march to begin with, though it is subsequently treated in a deliberately rowdy manner. As in the First Symphony there is something of a storm in the middle of the movement but it is clearly not to be taken as serious. More important as an indication of the direction Beethoven was going to take is the Coda, the final section of the movement in which cellos and basses share a majestic ascent that recalls 'The Heavens are Telling' from Haydn's *Creation*. It was a work Beethoven much admired and the passage may even be a conscious tribute.

The idyllic Larghetto which follows seems so relaxed and serene that it is almost impossible to believe that it was written at the same time as the despairing document known as the Heiligenstadt Testament. Here we find the same lyrical character that often appears in Schubert, though he would have been a child of five or six at the time Beethoven composed this. In addition to the wealth of tunes, one of the great delights of the music is its scoring. Trumpets and drums are omitted; clarinets and bassoons in particular lend the movement its special colour. Apart from two ghostly dialogues between the lowest strings and plangent woodwind there is no sign of sorrow.

The ensuing scherzo is crisp and compact, notable for its very individual scoring. The rapid alternation between strings, horns or woodwind is like a practical joke designed to catch the players off their guard, while a comparable trick is played on the audience when, in the central section, the strings come to a complete halt only to be aroused again by a bellowing unison note on wind and brass which should take us all by surprise.

The finale, too, is full of humour, from its initial hiccup to the tiptoe games in the closing pages. With our instinctive feeling that symphonies are meant to be taken seriously it may be hard to accept that even a substantial outburst of orchestral fury proves to be a hoax, but Beethoven's deflation of his own rhetoric is unmistakable. However, the symphony as a whole shows a remarkable unity of themes, not so much four independent movements as a truly organic whole. The scale of the Symphony as a form was ripe for development; the 'Eroica', (No. 3), reveals a remarkable increase in stature.

Symphony No. 3 in E flat Major (The 'Eroica') Op. 55

In the spring of 1804 Beethoven completed his Third Symphony. On the title-page were inscribed two names, his own and (Napoleon) Bonaparte's. The work was meant to be dedicated to the great French revolutionary leader, although it is misleading to take it in any way as a portrait. (One does not write a funeral march for someone who is still alive.) However, when news came that Napoleon had assumed the title of Emperor, the composer flew into a rage and tore the title-page in half, so offended were his republican sentiments. In the end it appeared as 'Heroic Symphony; composed to preserve the memory of a great man, and dedicated to his Serene Highness Prince Lobkowitz' — one of Beethoven's aristocratic patrons. It is ironic that a symphony designed to celebrate a man who stood for revolutionary freedom should ultimately be dedicated to a prince.

After two massive chords of E flat major proclaiming the 'home' key, the most significant theme of the first movement appears in the cellos. Its confirmation of the key is undermined by a disturbing alien note (C sharp) that immediately spreads a feeling of unease to the violins. The almost pastoral mood of the opening is deceptive, as though a sculptor were caressing the stone before striking the first hammer-blow which will hew it into shape. By the twenty-fifth bar we find strongly accented chords that disrupt the even flow of the music; order is re-established with a full-blooded repetition of the first theme. The opening movement is particularly rich in material; the mood changes frequently and yet there is a convincing unity to the conception. Ideas that should be mentioned include an elegant 'conversation' between oboe, clarinet, flute and violins based on a three-note phrase, a leisurely rising tune played by clarinets, a strongly rhythmic and athletic passage for strings and a contrastingly gentle theme in the woodwind that begins with no less than nine repetitions of the same note.

During the Development section the opening theme is transformed in character partly by being shifted into a minor key, partly by being combined with the athletic pattern in the strings. At one point a fugue of sorts begins but it is soon engulfed in a violent storm whose dissonances shake the very foundations of Harmony. The other really outstanding moment in this wonderful movement comes just before the return home to the Recapitulation. The orchestral texture is reduced to a mere whisper from the violins, seeming for the moment to lose all impetus. Faint and evocative, a distant horn-call reminds us of the very opening theme. The suggestion is accepted joyfully by the full orchestra.

A major structural feature of the movement is the extension of the Coda, normally something of a formality. Beethoven launches into it with two strange side-slips in the harmony that must have seemed like a musical earthquake to listeners in 1805. The shock of the unexpected harmonies is emphasised by extreme dynamic contrasts between soft and loud. New light is then shed on the opening theme by a playful counter-melody in the first violins. Only real familiarity can bring a full appreciation of the magnificent architecture of this movement in which order and unity are imposed from within rather than by the application of academic rules.

The second movement is a funeral march suitable for a mythical hero. Note the avoidance of the use of drums, the double-basses supplying a sound that is comparable to the rumble of muffled drums but which is musically more interesting. The immense span of the phrases coupled with the very slow tempo means that the movement is very long, but for those who are prepared to adjust themselves to its measured tread there are ample rewards. Periodically the feeling of grief is softened by episodes in major keys, like warming rays of sun on a grey afternoon.

The Scherzo which follows could hardly be more different, bustling along without a care in the world, its rhythmic vitality unflagging. Excitedly the strings set the rhythm ticking; after six bars of quiet staccato chords, the oboe offers us a cheerful little tune beginning with seven repetitions of the same note. It is taken up in turn by a flute, but for no fewer than ninety-two bars Beethoven avoids a positive affirmation of the 'home' key of E flat major so that when it is finally reached it seems an event of great importance. In due course we arrive at the central Trio, a term that is more apt than usual since it is mostly scored for three horns, one more than he uses in any other symphony except the Ninth where there are four. Although for the most part the mood continues to be exuberant there is, towards the end of this section, a hushed dialogue between horns and strings that establishes a feeling of twilight different from anything else in the symphony. The quiet ending to the central Trio simplifies the transition back to the Reprise, but just when we are liable to feel that Beethoven is merely observing an established convention there is a sudden disruption of the rhythm that takes us by surprise. The whole Scherzo is roughly twice the size of any comparable movement by Haydn, not that direct comparison can be made, so unique is its conception.

The theme of the finale must have been an especial favourite of Beethoven's as he used it in several other compositions including the ballet-music for *Prometheus*. The opening torrent of notes suggests high drama but there are rather different things in store. The strings pluck out a curiously fragmentary little tune punctuated by sudden three-note outbursts from wind, brass and timpani. There are two possible interpretations of this enigmatic passage. It seems that in the Prometheus ballet, the hero breathed life into statues that then took their first faltering steps. One can imagine such a scene to this music but, in the absence of any such programmatic explanation, it is more likely that Beethoven is once again playing a joke on his audience. As the great musicologist Donald Tovey wrote, 'we can almost see Beethoven laughing at our mystified faces'. What we hear is not in fact the real theme of the movement but the *bass* of the theme, a servant wearing the master's clothes. When at last the proper tune appears above this enigma all falls into place.

Soon, as if to apologise for playing such tricks upon us, Beethoven settles down to some severe counterpoint, embarking on a fugue. However, this more serious mood does not last for long. Against a background of swiftly running scales the woodwind present a delightful variation on the main theme. Listeners who look for security will be at a loss in this movement since it shifts from serious to frivolous without warning. For example at one point there is a march, but it cannot be taken to refer to Napoleon since it is soon deflated by a very light-hearted version of the main tune. At another point the fugue-subject is turned upon its head against a comically running counterpoint from the first violins.

Perhaps the biggest surprise in a movement that is full of surprises comes near the end when there is a fundamental change of tempo. A choir of woodwind instruments initiates a slow variation on the main theme. Gradually the orchestra seems to take on the semblance of a great cathedral organ with the main theme transferred to the pedals while the organist improvises an elaborate Postlude above. Then with a sudden memory of the opening flourish we are whipped into a final Presto in which the horns present a hunting version of the main theme. If the final repetitions of the 'home' chord seem too many, Beethoven clearly felt they were needed to establish security after a movement so full of caprice.

Symphony No. 4 in B flat Major
Op. 60

In 1806 Beethoven had already started work on the Symphony we now know as Number Five when he was approached by Count Oppersdorf with a commission to write a symphony, almost certainly with the proviso that it should be in the style of Number Two, which the Count greatly admired. Unwilling to miss the chance of earning a fee of 350 florins, the composer put the C minor symphony aside and wrote the Fourth, seemingly with greater ease than usual. Thematic relationships between the two symphonies offer clear evidence that both works were in his mind at the same time. The first such clue appears in the very opening bars despite the great difference in mood and tempo. The same musical concept, two falling thirds, is to be found in the two symphonies, veiled in mystery in the Fourth, defiant and intractable in the Fifth.

While a number of such similarities may not be immediately apparent, the differences need no emphasis. The two works are a world apart in emotional significance, so much so that the Fourth has always tended to be overshadowed by its mighty neighbours. Nevertheless, the Fourth has magical qualities, and is perhaps the best orchestrated of all the nine. The opening in particular is unforgettable for the beauty of its sound. During the slow introduction the music seems to be feeling its way towards a destination only dimly perceived. At last, after long deferment, a series of brief ascending scale-fragments, crisp and sharp as the crack of a whip, leads us into the main *Allegro*.

The principal theme alternates swift detached notes on the strings with a smooth *legato* phrase on the woodwind. It is like emerging into bright sunlight after the mysterious shadows of the Introduction. As a contrast we find a second group of themes, cheerful little tunes allocated almost entirely to the wind and cleverly (if not obviously) inter-related. Many subtle new developments occur in the central section of the movement of which the most remarkable is the passage leading into the reprise. The violins hover uneasily on two notes for four bars at a time before an ascending flick which evokes a warning grumble from the timpani, a process which is repeated but which ultimately opens the way back to the Recapitulation.

The second movement begins with an important rhythmic figure against which the violins unfold a deeply expressive melody, later to be elaborately decorated. After a second main theme has been introduced by a solo clarinet and then taken up by the full woodwind choir, the double-basses remind us of the initial rhythmic figure; in due course it comes to dominate the scene leading to an astonishingly dramatic descent with each note heavily accented by explosive cannon-shots from the timpani. Out of the tumult emerges the gentlest of phrases, coiling sinuously through the violin-parts. It has been described by a great authority as 'one of the most imaginative passages in Beethoven'. Soon a solo bassoon reminds us of the opening rhythm, though Beethoven might have preferred a horn at this point. (The notes would have been unobtainable on the instrument used in his time.) The closing pages of the movement have a romantic beauty that is virtually unsurpassed in the whole canon of the nine symphonies.

The next movement is vigorous in its rhythmic drive, alternating strongly accented chords with strange ribbons of unison notes in woodwind and strings. As a contrast, the central Trio is mincingly elegant, a parody of the refined conventions Beethoven had clearly lost patience with.

The finale is as exuberant a movement as he ever wrote, almost a study in perpetual motion. Like Mozart and Haydn before him, Beethoven was a more than adequate violinist and there are passages in this symphony that suggest that he was recalling hours of technical practice spent in mastering the instrument. There are also notoriously difficult passages for the double basses as well as a famous bassoon solo. The whole movement bubbles over with good humour and high spirits.

Symphony No. 5 in C Minor
Op. 67

The opening bars of this symphony have become a musical symbol of the image we tend to have of Beethoven, rugged and uncompromising; yet it should be remembered that once the first two phrases have made their dramatic impact, the ensuing passage is more notable for pathos than drama. The music is curiously ambiguous, the falling pattern of each paired interval implying a deep sense of grief, while the driving rhythm seems to forbid such emotional indulgence. There is an almost continual conflict between a cry for pity and the refusal to grant it. Gradually the rhythm generates more and more force until the battering sounds seem literally to disintegrate in a single explosive chord. Horns in unison announce the imminent arrival of the Second Subject, a graceful tune whose poise is destroyed by the all-pervading rhythm with which the cellos and basses doggedly persist. Abrupt chords signal the end of the Exposition, which should be repeated.

The Development section is notable for its fierce concentration on the material so far exposed to us. There is scarcely a note that cannot be traced back to some fragmentary idea in the Exposition. The demonic energy of the rhythm gives a special character to this remarkable movement whose impact is such that it is the most immediately recognisable of all Beethoven's works.

The second movement provides a welcome release from tension. It is a set of variations on a sublimely simple theme which is presented to us by violas and cellos in unison with a few bass–notes sketched in *pizzicato* by the double-basses. The last segment of the tune is lovingly extended by the woodwind, an extension which is at once taken up and amplified by the strings. An unusual feature is the inclusion of a quite independent second theme, a smoothly gliding woodwind tune whose accompaniment in triplet figuration makes us assume that it is the start of a variation on Theme I. The assumption is wrong; the second theme has a clear identity of its own, particularly when trumpets, horns and drums give it a martial air. Doubting phrases on the violins dispel this new confidence, leading us ultimately to the first variation on Theme I. It takes the form of an unbroken stream of notes for the lower strings. Further variations follow, easily discernible even to the untrained ear. Beethoven's original plan for this movement was far more conventional in layout. In rejecting past custom he showed how assured he had become in devising new and yet logical forms.

In all nine symphonies there is not a scherzo more individual than the one we find here. It suggests an improvisation for orchestra, a prophecy of things to come rather than an extension of dance movements from a previous era. Dark and mysterious, the initial theme seems to grope its way forward, uncertain of its destination. Violins bring the music to a complete halt. A second start by the lower strings progresses a little further but is again brought to a standstill. In just such a way will an improviser seem to search for an idea. Suddenly Beethoven strikes out boldly in a new direction, hammering out the theme on unison horns supported by chunky chords from the strings. Even though it is confirmed by the full orchestra this tune also falters, coming to rest on a chord whose waning strength dwindles to nothing. The ghostly opening phrase returns, the music continuing to alternate uncertainty with resolution. In the centre we find a section that combines the scholarly pretensions of fugue with an almost impish sense of humour. Cellos and basses, filled with a confidence so absent at the start of the movement, briskly set the fugue on its way. Later, as though telling us that such academic devices are no longer valid, Beethoven allows the fugue to come apart. Twice the cellos and basses make false starts in an endeavour to get the music back on course. A return to the opening material seems far from secure with various woodwind instruments playing tentative fragments of the previously bold horn theme over an almost inaudible accompaniment. Suddenly all movement is stilled save for the quiet beat of a drum, strangely sinister. In response to its hypnotic throb the violins initiate a weird dance, groping their way upwards step by step. It is an ascent from darkness to light, an ascent that has been hinted at from the very first bars of the movement but which is only accomplished at the last.

The sheer impact of the finale that emerges is enhanced by the addition of three trombones, a piccolo and a contra-bassoon. Perhaps the blaze of sound coming out of a sort of 'aural fog' symbolises a psychological victory over the composer's deafness. Certainly the pure and straightforward harmonies seem to clarify the harmonic vagueness of the preceding passage. For some time the music continues upon its triumphant way, building towards a climax that surely presages some great event. Instead there is a sudden break followed by a hollow ticking sound from the violins; as though a ghost has entered, we hear a spectral version of the horn theme from the previous movement. It is an unforgettably dramatic interruption. Order is restored with the return of the majestic march theme with which the movement began. Towards the end of the symphony the tempo quickens to a headlong rush in which dignity is sacrificed to brilliance, the final affirmation of C major being perhaps over-emphatic in its repetitions.

Symphony No. 6 in F Major (The 'Pastoral') Op. 68

The first movement of this symphony is described in the score as 'The cheerful impressions excited by arriving in the country'; the second is called 'By the stream'; the third is 'A happy get–together of peasants', the fourth is 'Storm', and the fifth 'The Shepherds' Hymn, gratitude and thanksgiving after the storm'. The title 'Pastoral' was sanctioned by Beethoven, though in calling it a 'Pastoral Symphony, or a recollection of country life' he warned against a too literal interpretation with the phrase, 'More an expression of feeling than a painting'. It seems probable that this admonition not to take the pictorial content of the work too literally was prompted by the fear that listeners might misinterpret his intentions. Descriptive pieces were much in vogue at the time but they were mostly trivial and naive, words that can scarcely be used of this delightful but major composition.

It begins with a bare fifth in the bass, the traditional drone-bass of rustic music; above, the violins spell out a simple melody from which much of the material is derived. A notable characteristic of the first movement in particular is the exploitation of the repetition of patterns that we find throughout Nature. The symmetry of leaves on a tree, of flowers, or even of the ripples on the surface of lake or stream, these may well have been in Beethoven's mind as he penned notes that seem to reflect both the infinite similarity and the infinite variety of nature's patterns. After the distraught energy of the Fifth Symphony the mood here is extremely relaxed, a clear symbol of the inner peace the composer found when alone in the country. The harmonies are often sustained over many bars at a time, giving a feeling of a slower pace than the actual pulse of the music would appear to indicate. Long sustained notes in first or second violins shine through the texture like beams of sunlight. The score, like the forest, teems with life, yet the impression we gain is of a great stillness. Towards the end of the movement clarinet and bassoon anticipate the arrival of the little village band which Beethoven parodies so delightfully in the third movement.

Before the peasants' gathering we spend a lazy afternoon by a meandering stream (second movement), unusually scored with two muted cellos lending depth to the sound. The first main theme is notable for its recurring silences, seeming to be literally breathless at the beauty of the scene. The music flows continuously even allowing for these breathing spaces. Despite its length the movement is concentrated in its form, having clearly recognisable First and Second Subjects, a Development section and a Recapitulation. There is an uncharacteristic concession to the purely descriptive on the last page of the movement when flute, oboe and clarinet echo the song of nightingale, quail and cuckoo.

Although it contains an amusing parody of a small village band, much of the third movement is scored with a delicacy that would not seem out of place in more aristocratic surroundings. The opening phrase tiptoes its way in unsupported by harmony; it is answered by a smooth and gentle tune in a contrasting key. Soon a new theme is introduced, rough-hewn, with heavy accents. High horns bellow their approval as scooping figures in the strings suggest the sort of dance where men toss the girls into the air. There is a feeling of robust horseplay far removed from the delicacy of the opening. In due course we hear the little band, depicted with delightful humour, the oboist rhythmically insecure, the clarinettist more accomplished, the horn-player rashly confident in his approach to dizzy heights, the bassoonist cautious and inept. An increase of tempo leads to a second dance-tune, accompanied by droningly primitive harmonies. The movement ends in a panic rush as the peasants realise a storm is about to break.

Without even a final cadence to the preceding music the storm makes its presence felt with a quiet but ominous rumble from cellos and basses. An agitated little figure from the second violins suggests the first drops of rain. Suddenly the storm breaks in its full fury with flickers of lightning in the woodwind and thunderclaps from the timpani. At last it dies away; an oboe sings out a simple melody derived from the first agitated raindrops, now smoothed out into a musical rainbow. An ascending scale on a flute leads without break into the finale. The initial 'hymn' is soon transformed into an ecstatic paean of joy. The movement is part Rondo, part Variations, culminating in a marvellous climax in which shimmering strings convey an impression of blazing sunlight while the wide-reaching phrases in cellos and basses suggest the trunks of great trees, their branches stretching towards the sky. A long descent leads to a quiet statement of belief, more prayer than hymn. A last whisper of breeze stirs through the strings, a distant horn sounds an almost inaudible curfew.

Symphony No. 7 in A Major
Op. 92

After completing the 'Pastoral' Symphony Beethoven was to wait more than three years before embarking on the Seventh (1811). As in the First, Second and Fourth symphonies, he begins with a slow introduction from whose massive first chord a solo oboe tune emerges. Further strong chords mark a gradual accumulation of melodic strands until, in the tenth bar, a rising scale in the strings makes its first appearance. By bar fifteen it has been transformed into an awe-inspiring counterpoint to the initial theme. Soon the woodwind choir presents us with a grave march, almost ritual in character. For some time this and the opening theme seem to compete for our attention until at last the music settles onto the note E natural which is repeated speculatively over seventy times within ten bars. The increasingly wide spacing of these repetitions indicates that Beethoven is teasing us rather as he did at the start of the finale to the First Symphony. At last release comes as flute and oboe delicately mark out the rhythm which is to be the mainspring of the movement. The point made, a solo flute gives us the First Subject, a lilting and joyous tune in very different mood from the Introduction. The movement is notable for its rhythmic drive, there being few moments of repose. Quiet passages there may be but they never lose their forward impulse.

One of the most striking features of this symphony is the unity of rhythm in the various movements, none more insistent than that of the slow movement. Although the rhythm is all-pervading, the harmonic structure is rich. The solemn tread of the opening theme continues for some time until a glowing counter-melody illuminates its dark harmonies from within. The effect is of a grand procession passing by as the full orchestra is increasingly employed. Suddenly the mood changes as clarinet and bassoon introduce a new sustained melody accompanied by gently flowing triplets. It is in the key of A major (after A minor) and seems like a ray of sunshine in a grey sky. Cellos and basses continue to pluck out the initial rhythm but it is relegated to the background as this radiant theme unfolds. The spell is dissolved by a great descending scale through nearly four octaves, plunging us harshly back into A minor. Soon we find a ghostly little fugue in which the players seem to grope their way forward uncertainly. An intense crescendo duly leads back to the first theme, which, after a restatement of the lyrical clarinet tune, brings the movement to a strangely disintegrated close.

The Scherzo sets a new standard for vitality and humour, excelling all its predecessors in rhythmic vigour. The rapid shifts from one tonal centre to another are designed to keep the listener guessing, never able to predict what is going to happen next. The movement falls into five sections, the brisk opening material being interleaved with a rather more static theme derived from a traditional pilgrims' hymn. Woodwind and horns sustain the tune in organ-like tones while the violins hold a bagpipe drone that even has to be stoked up from time to time as the imagined 'pipers' run short of breath. After the hectic scramble of the Scherzo these long-held notes give a sense of great spaciousness.

The last movement displays tremendous energy, with strong accents on the second beat of the bar pounding out the rhythm. There is hardly a moment's respite for the players, Beethoven showing immense intellectual stamina in maintaining such intensity throughout. The final pages must rank as one of his most brilliantly conceived passages for orchestra; the notes seem to fly off the page as we are carried on the flood-tide of his inspiration.

Symphony No. 8 in F Major
Op. 93

As with the Second Symphony, one would never guess from the musical content that this work was written during a period of emotional disturbance — in this case a family row between Beethoven and his brother Johann (1812). It caused much bitterness, yet to judge from the music one would think that the composer was in an exceptionally good humour. The symphony begins without introduction or preamble although at one time a majestic prelude was contemplated. The first theme is almost old-fashioned, a look back perhaps before venturing on into the unknown. However its solid confidence is most wittily undermined as the music grinds to a halt. Preceded by a few apologetic chords and some faintly comical bassoon notes, the Second Subject begins in the distinctly alien tonal centre of D major, a key unrelated to the 'home' key of F. As though admitting to an error, the tune falters, turns awkwardly and arrives deviously at the proper key of C. (Violins play the tune in the 'wrong' key, woodwind put it 'right'.) The movement is full of such musical surprises, Beethoven clearly delighting in catching his audience unawares. One figure based on two notes an octave apart is of particular value in the Development even though it first appears as a most conventional gesture. It is interesting to compare this quietly insistent yet curiously static idea with the dynamic energy displayed in the first movement of the Fifth Symphony. In both works three swift repeated notes lead towards the ensuing strong beat yet the effect is totally different.

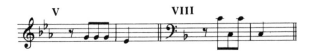

During the development the character of the opening theme undergoes a considerable change, becoming quite tempestuous. Surrounded by hostile chords in the wind and angry figuration in the violins, a fugue of sorts gets under way, though it is far from academic. The tension increases until at last the reprise of the opening theme blazes out in triumph. There are a number of surprises before the movement ends, not least the ending itself which recedes to a mere whisper.

The second movement has a clockwork quality that alludes directly to the inventor of the metronome, an ingenious friend of Beethoven's called Mälzel. The repeated chords give an impression of mechanical regularity, though the melodic fragments that dance to the rhythm are placed in a wittily capricious fashion. There is even a little phrase to illustrate the winding-up of the clockwork spring. Two passages in parallel thirds also deserve mention; they sound suspiciously like a mechanical organ — another manifestation of Mälzel's ingenuity. At the end of the movement the metronome appears to disintegrate in a passage that shows Beethoven's delight in musical humour.

The third movement pays homage to the spirit of Haydn, a deliberate regression on Beethoven's part that makes a striking change from his whirl-wind scherzos. A bland central section is notable for an unusually demanding horn-part.

The finale begins with a swift rustling figure from which emerges a nimble dancing tune, beautifully understated. After two brief silences there is a sudden ferocious unison on a wildly unexpected note, not just a joke as it happens but also a seed destined to bear fruit more than 350 bars later when it is used as a pivot to take the music into a distant tonal centre. The whole movement is a brilliant demonstration of how to use a conventional form to prepare traps for the listener. For instance, the so-called Second Subject appears without warning in the 'wrong' key (A flat instead of C). Then during the Development there are several halts followed by false starts as though the players lose all sense of direction. An elaborate Coda, or tail-piece to the movement, makes much use of a slower-moving theme based on five consecutive notes of the scale. It fits against itself in contrary motion, yet any intellectual analysis seems out of place in a movement so full of high spirits. There is not a trace of despair or self-pity in the whole movement; the composer seems completely reconciled to the cruel blow Fate had dealt him.

Symphony No. 9 in D minor (The 'Choral') Op. 125

The idea of setting Schiller's 'Ode to Joy' had come to Beethoven as early as 1793 although the Choral Symphony which incorporates it was not to be completed until the winter of 1823/4. Preliminary work on the symphony was spread over a period of years during which a number of major works were written. In 1808 he had composed the Choral Fantasia, a significant pointer towards the symphony. Not only does its main theme bear a close resemblance to the setting of the 'Ode to Joy'; the ground plan of the work anticipates that of the Ninth Symphony's finale to a remarkable degree. The long piano introduction (which Beethoven improvised at the first performance) might aptly be described as the 'Symphony', using the original meaning of that versatile term. Cellos and basses then offer a theme (as the orchestra does in the Ninth) which is rejected several times (as it is in the Ninth). In the Fantasia the solo piano seems to aspire to the condition of the human voice, precisely what the lower strings attempt to do in the dramatic unison passages that introduce the finale of the symphony. After a period of puzzlement and contradiction, the theme at last emerges pure and simple, again a moment that has its exact parallel in the Ninth. Whether Beethoven consciously realised it or not, the Choral Fantasia is an experimental version of the later work, though only of its finale. The first three movements are purely symphonic in conception.

In all the preceding symphonies the proclamation of a tonal centre has been of prime importance in the opening bars. Here the music begins as though in a void, the positive affirmation of D minor not arriving until the seventeenth bar. When it does appear the main theme is awesome in its rugged grandeur. It is presented in two versions, minor and major, the North and South faces of the same mountain-peak. Although the movement is conceived on a very large scale, the essential features are very clear. As in the 'Pastoral' Symphony, though to very different effect, the pace of harmonic change is often very slow, giving immense breadth to the music. Much of the material is tragic in mood, while in the Development lies the intellectual core of the movement in the shape of a triple fugue. More than is usually the case the themes of this movement are subjected to emotional changes.

One of Beethoven's most significant contributions to symphonic form was his expansion of the Coda. As we might expect, this movement shows him to have a huge amount in reserve, so much so that (as in the 'Eroica') the Coda is comparable to an entire new development section. Perhaps most remarkable of all is the closing passage, in effect a funeral march. Its foundation is a chromatic wailing bass above which brass and wind proclaim funereal fanfares.

The Scherzo begins abruptly; note the ingenious use of timpani in the fifth bar, the two drums tuned an octave apart — an experiment he had tried in the Eighth Symphony. After two bars of stunned silence a whispering fugue begins, utilising the dramatic octave leap with which the movement began. For no less than thirty-six bars the volume is kept under tight restraint; then a long sustained note on horns and clarinets signals a crescendo. Within seconds the full orchestra is playing at full stretch. Suddenly a radiant new theme flowers, bringing a moment of relaxation. The movement is substantially longer than any of the other scherzos but the material is easy to absorb. Most beguiling is the central section, the so-called Trio, which bears an intriguing resemblance to the comparable passage in the Second Symphony.

The elaborate Adagio which follows is one of Beethoven's most romantic utterances, anticipating Mahler in its profoundly expressive manner. Tender sighs begin the movement, leading to Theme I in which clarinets and bassoons seem to express their approval of each string phrase as though saying 'wasn't that lovely'. These echoes give great spaciousness to the theme which, once it has run its full span, melts into a new tonal centre in which we find Theme II, surely one of the most immediately appealing tunes Beethoven ever wrote. There follow several variations on Theme I, one of which has a particularly elaborate part for the violins. Brief and distant fanfares fail to disturb the immense calm of this sublime movement.

The transition from orchestral to choral music in the finale caused the composer much trouble. The discovery of the solution is revealed in a miniature scenario he jotted down in a notebook.

> · This is a day of jubilation, worth singing about . . . (Theme of the first movement) O no, that won't do, I want something pleasanter . . . (Theme of the second movement.) That is no better, merely rather more cheerful . . . (Theme of the third movement.) That's also too tender. Must find something more rousing like the . . . I'll sing you something myself . . . (Theme of the fourth movement.) That will do! Now I have found a way to express joy.

Here, in essence, is the 'plot' of the finale, the actual transition from instruments to voices being facilitated by giving the lower strings a number of quasi-operatic phrases that suggest the inflections of the human voice. The movement begins with a passage of extraordinary violence, a tonal crisis demanding a resolution. Like an operatic hero suddenly appearing on stage, the lower strings declaim their first dramatic phrase. For a second time the orchestral clamour breaks out, for a second time cellos and basses reply. The music then follows exactly the plan Beethoven sketched above, offering us brief snatches of the three preceding movements, each of which is rejected. At last a semblance of the true theme appears to be greeted with an orchestral 'shout' of acclamation. Unruffled, smoothly flowing, the tune finally unfolds, duly to be repeated in triumph.

The process is now repeated with a solo baritone taking over phrases comparable to those previously given to the lower strings. As a suitable verbal introduction to Schiller's Ode, Beethoven chose a simple injunction:

> O friends, not these sounds; let us tune our voices more acceptably and
> more joyfully.

Gradually the chorus is incorporated into the texture, along with a quartet of soloists. From here on the structure of the movement becomes somewhat complex although it is basically a set of variations on the main theme. One of these is a march, with triangle and cymbals adding the clank of swords and the jingle of spurs. Against its steady tread the tenor soloist sings of 'Brothers like heroes to conquest flying'. It is an essentially operatic passage which however is followed by an orchestral fugue of some complexity, itself a variation on the song to joy. After a further affirmation of the main theme there is a silence out of which emerges a great Hymn of Brotherhood:

> O ye millions, I embrace ye —
> Here's a joyful kiss for all!

There follows a vast section of great solemnity, in effect a slow movement within the finale. It ends abruptly with the simultaneous return of the two principal themes, the 'Song of Joy' and the 'Hymn to Brotherhood'. The two are combined in a brilliant fashion. From a huge climax the music suddenly disintegrates. Strangely fragmented phrases express the feeling of awe in the presence of the very Creator of the world.

The start of the final Coda suggests the running feet of happy children and it may well be that Beethoven had a stage presentation in mind. One of his preliminary notes for the baritone's text reads, 'Today is a day of celebration; let it be celebrated in song *and dance*'. It is a clue not to be lightly disregarded. Certainly the solo quartet has an operatic theme near the end whose innocent gaiety recalls Mozart at his most enchanting. Proclaiming the ideal that all men should be brothers, the symphony draws to its close, an epic ending to a gigantic conception.

(For a more detailed analysis of all the Beethoven symphonies, see A. Hopkins, *The Nine Symphonies of Beethoven*. Heinemann, London, and University of Washington Press, 1981, and Pan, 1982.)

Piano Concerto No. 1 in C Major
Op. 15

Beethoven's earliest public success was as a pianist rather than as a composer; we should remember, though, that the concerts he gave as a young man would have been given on a fortepiano (as it was originally called) hardly different from the instruments of Mozart's day. During his lifetime pianos underwent considerable development, enabling him to enlarge the scope of his keyboard writing so that the musical 'language' of his late works has a far wider range of expression, not to mention more sheer power than anything from his early period. The point is well demonstrated by the five piano concertos, in the first two of which he was compelled to use Mozartean stratagems to solve the problem of balance between soloist and orchestra. Not until he came to write the Fifth concerto did Beethoven have an instrument which, even though he was deaf, he sensed was strong enough to dominate the orchestra. To have written an opening cadenza as forceful as the 'Emperor's in 1795 (the date of Op. 15) would have been quite impractical since no piano of the period could have achieved the desired effect. That Beethoven was well aware of this is shown by the fact that he wrote three cadenzas for this particular concerto, the third of which is in a 'heroic' style that is far more demanding than anything in the original score. Since concerto and cadenza are separated by a gulf of some fourteen years the difference is understandable, even though in performance the cadenza inevitably seems out of proportion.

In 1784 Beethoven made his first attempt at writing a piano concerto, a work in E flat which can most charitably be regarded as a stage in his apprenticeship. Eleven years later, in March 1795, he was asked to play at a charity concert in aid of the widows and orphans of the Society of Musicians in Vienna. It was to be an important occasion, incentive enough to goad him into completing a piano concerto he had been mulling over in his usual painstaking way for a year or more. With only two days to go before the concert the finale had still not been written and it seems possible that it was the urgency of the situation that brought on a painful attack of colic. Beethoven took to his bed and with a doctor at his side and four copyists in the next room began the frantic rush to get the last movement down on paper. As each sheet was completed it was passed through to the copyists so that a set of orchestral parts could be made simultaneously. When the exhausted composer arrived at the hall to rehearse he found that the piano was half a tone flat. With the resourcefulness of a truly great musician he transposed the entire concerto up a semitone, playing it in B major instead of B♭, a feat that was all the more remarkable when we consider that he could not have actually practised the solo part at all. It is hardly surprising that the experience caused him to take a slightly jaundiced view of the work;[1] he put it aside, revised it a couple of years later, and published it as his Piano Concerto No. 2 in B flat major, Op. 19. The change of numbering was forced on him since meanwhile he had written another concerto, the one which to this day is still referred to as No. 1 in C major, Op. 15.

That Beethoven himself considered the C major concerto to be of greater substance than the one in B flat is indicated by his employment of a slightly larger orchestra, an increase of five players — two clarinets, two trumpets and timpani. The first movement is a march in character even though it begins quietly with strings only. The initial motif of a rising octave provides an instantly recognisable feature, while the swift ascending scale joining the first two phrases also proves itself to be more than a cliché when he makes extensive use of it later. After fifteen bars the full orchestra takes up the march theme with dramatic impact. The influence of Haydn is easily sensed particularly when the horns ascend to a perilous high C, but once he has established a solid cadence on the dominant (G major) Beethoven has a surprise for us. After a moment's silence the second violins murmur a gently rocking figure that suggests G minor; however, the subsequent entry of the first violins (supported by the lower strings) switches deftly into E flat major, a very unorthodox key for a second subject's first appearance. (It would normally be in the dominant.) As if aware that he has committed an indiscretion, Beethoven drifts through various keys, offering us a taste of F minor and G minor in turn before deciding to leave the second subject for the time being. He reverts to the first subject, taking it out of the parade ground and into the classroom by subjecting it to a course of counterpoint. Horns and oboes find this not to their liking and introduce a crisp little march that might have stepped straight out of the pages of a Mozart opera. A stern reference to the initial rising octave from bar 1, now four times repeated, brings this splendidly martial tutti to an end.

[1]When he sent it to be published, the accompanying note said 'I do not consider it to be one of my best'.

A full orchestra with trumpets, horns and timpani would put the small tones of the fortepiano at a considerable disadvantage; Beethoven therefore adopted the solution Mozart had devised, disregarding the orchestral material entirely and giving the soloist a gentle theme that the orchestra is never allowed to touch. Their insistence that the proper matter for discussion is the initial rising octave is met with a brilliant clatter of arpeggios from the soloist; indeed the first acknowledgment of the rising octave theme that we find in the piano part sounds almost derisive, the upper notes deliberately smudged.

The introduction of the second subject enables the soloist to participate on more equal terms, and he accepts it joyfully, adding playful elaborations that interestingly go up to a top F sharp, a note that was unavailable to Mozart. Soon the wind remind us of the Mozartean march tune, an idea which the soloist treats with some energy before embarking on a descending sequence of rotating figures. These, alternating with a more aggressive pattern in chromatic triplets, keep the music humming along in a somewhat facile way until an ascent to a high E, four times repeated, leads us into a different world, expressive and poignant. The spell is broken by a syncopated pattern in strings (and then woodwind) to which a sharply accented rising scale brings a touch of asperity. It is a formula he was to develop to more dramatic effect in the Fifth Concerto:

A sustained double trill from the pianist ushers in a substantial orchestral section in which the First Subject is again treated in a way that shows signs of Haydn's tuition; according to orthodox precepts it comes to a halt with a solid cadence in G, the dominant. There follows the heart of the movement. Encouraged by an orchestral modulation into the unexpected key of E flat, the pianist embarks on what seems like a free extemporisation incorporating flowing arpeggios that range widely over the keyboard as well as lyrical passages in parallel chords. Occasional orchestral reminders of the first few notes of Theme I do nothing to check the element of fantasy that gives the piano part a quite new character. The most magical moment comes just before the Recapitulation when there is a hushed dialogue between horns and piano, an uncanny anticipation of a corresponding duet between timpani and piano in the very closing pages of the 'Emperor'. However, after the truly inventive developments just described, the Recapitulation pursues an orthodox course and the movement ends in the Mozartean convention, that is to say with the orchestra alone playing the final thirteen bars after the cadenza. (I suspect that the convention arose because contemporary audiences almost certainly applauded at the end of the cadenza, just as they still tend to do when a singer triumphantly concludes his or her contribution to an operatic aria.)

The slow movement follows the Mozartean pattern closely, treating the piano as a surrogate soprano with an exceptional technique and range. The conception is essentially vocal even though it frequently goes beyond the compass of any mere mortal. One phrase especially, played as single unaccompanied notes, is lifted almost identically from the sublime *Et incarnatus est* in Mozart's Mass in C minor. However, the main reprise of the opening theme is quite unlike Mozart in its layout. Introduced by a trill that descends chromatically through three notes, it has an almost waltz-like accompaniment that must have seemed quite a new sound at the time. Notable too is the expressive duet between clarinet and piano near the end of the movement.

The finale, a Rondo, is set on its way with a delightfully witty theme stated with delicate precision by the soloist. The orchestra duly repeats it in a boisterously rowdy fashion. After some rapid passages from the piano it is the orchestra's turn to introduce the next episode, a tune whose efforts to sound suave are defeated by hobbledehoy accents on the last quaver of each bar, a gaucherie which the soloist does little to discourage by transferring the theme to the gruffest bass register. An improbable modulation to F minor allows the pianist to introduce yet another theme whose many 'crushed' notes may well be designed to suggest drunkenness, to judge by the violent attack of musical hiccups which immediately follows. (Beethoven's sense of humour was not noted for its subtlety.) Order is restored with the return of the initial theme; as before, it is repeated noisily by the orchestra. The central episode of this outstandingly witty movement is a tune in A minor that sounds strangely Latin-American to modern ears though Beethoven probably thought of it as 'Turkish', the standard term for anything exotic in Mozart's day. (One of the variations in the finale of Beethoven's 'Choral' symphony would have been considered 'Turkish' simply because of its use of percussion.)

The rest of the movement shows Beethoven amusing himself with further discussion of these varied materials, but the listener should look out for a delightfully novel twist just after the cadenza; a long trill manages to wind itself up a semitone so as to land in the totally alien key of B major, a situation from which Beethoven skilfully extricates himself before the last orchestral version of the Rondo theme. The coda starts with a witty exchange of scales and fragments of the Rondo divided between piano and wind. The last joke is a mock solemn Amen from oboes and horns, a gesture which is greeted with noisy derision in the final six bars.

Piano Concerto No. 2 in B flat Major
Op. 19

A great number of eighteenth-century piano sonatas begin with a formula consisting of a brief 'masculine' phrase, establishing the tonality, followed by a slightly longer 'feminine' response leading to a suggestion of the dominant. The 'masculine' phrase will then be repeated in the dominant and the response, probably somewhat modified, will lead back to the 'home' or Tonic key. The Second Concerto follows this pattern exactly with a 'heroic' first phrase, a 'tender' reply, a fresh statement of the 'heroic' phrase and an equally ingratiating response. A little surprisingly the tender mood seems to prevail, albeit with a new theme. The heroic theme is then transformed into a quasi-operatic duet between violins and cellos; the feeling here is suppressed but nervous and is soon countered by strong off-beat accents. An excursion into F minor brings the music to a dramatic halt on the dominant (C), thrice repeated *ff*. There is a moment's silence. So quietly that it suggests incredulity, strings and flute offer three D flats, *pp*, as an alternative. A graceful new theme appears in the unexpected key of D flat major, a tonality so outside the conventional scheme of things that it should arouse our surprise. Though it may appear to be the second subject it could prove to be an imposter. Some uneasy murmurings in B flat minor tend to confirm that all may not be well, and there is a certain sense of relief when, after a long and sinuous ascent we reach the 'heroic' opening phrase once more, this time without his female escort. Beethoven develops this brief idea at some length before bringing the tutti to a positive close.

As in the First Concerto, the soloist's entry follows the Mozartean tradition by refusing to enter into competition with the orchestra. The material is in the most fragile area of the early pianos and is quite unrelated to what has gone before. A brief interlude from the orchestra (whose pattern of repeated notes provides an intriguing premonition of the Fourth Concerto) leads to a more positive display by the soloist. This time he does accept the initial 'heroic' phrase, extending it at some length; the passage finishes with a long ascending scale which ushers in the true Second Subject, an ace that was well worth holding back till this moment. Orchestra and soloist discuss it in a very civilized manner until a trill on the piano takes us into an inspired diversion, a free episode in D flat major — the same key that had been planted unexpectedly in the Exposition. More fiery developments ensue in what is pianistically the most challenging passage in the concerto, but the storm abates as a long protracted modulation into the 'proper' dominant key (F) brings us to a powerful orchestral tutti. Here we find the 'heroic' theme in the bass with a new countermelody in the violins.

The pianist re-enters with the same material with which he had begun, though now in the dominant key (F) and sounding the better for it. A quite long development ensues, making clear references to the opening tutti, but to quite different effect now that the soloist is involved. The woodwind make much play with a repeated note theme which increasingly seems as though Beethoven is laying the foundations for the first movement of the Fourth Concerto. At last, as though impatient with the soloist's meanderings, we hear distant reminders of the 'heroic' theme in the strings heralding the actual Recapitulation. From here on matters proceed more or less according to expectation though Beethoven's cadenza, written at a much later date, makes substantially greater demands on the pianist than we find elsewhere.

The slow movement is a true *Adagio*, an extension of Mozart's language rather than a rejection of it. The orchestra has the first statement of the main theme which would not seem out of place in a setting of the Mass. The introductory phrases end with a string unison B to a peremptory rhythm out of which the soloist makes a cunningly contrived entry. The solo passages seldom have a greater density than we would find in Mozart though a reprise of the opening theme in the wind is accompanied by a very individual rippling figuration divided between the hands. The most noteworthy feature of the movement comes near the end. Marked *'con grand' espressione'*, it might be described as an *anti*-cadenza, a passage in single notes of the utmost simplicity yet possessing a spiritual profundity which is the mark of true genius.

Such spiritual matters are banished entirely in the final Rondo, which, if it resembles at all the finale Beethoven dashed off in his sick bed, represents a triumph of the human spirit over bodily ills. The pianist sets off with a gaily syncopated theme, a practical way of setting the tempo if, as I suspect, Beethoven intended to direct the work from the keyboard. As in the First Concerto, the orchestra voice their approval rather noisily; this done, they introduce a more solemn tone to which the pianist pays scant respect. In due course he introduces a rum-ti-tum-ti tune that sounds like a children's game, the more so when the orchestra put in some cheeky 'wrong' notes. The sheer happiness of the movement should dispel for ever the image of Beethoven as a frowning giant. There is even a section whose jazzy syncopations seem like a distant anticipation of boogie, while the ending is one of the best musical jokes Beethoven ever made, so much so that in the final bars we can hear him laughing uproariously at the way he has caught us out.

Piano Concerto No. 3 in C Minor
Op. 37

The Third Piano Concerto is as decisive a landmark in its way as the Third Symphony; both works show the composer widening his musical horizon and stretching established forms in a way that his predecessors had never envisaged. The first two concertos are clearly influenced by Mozart, and do not really extend the demands made on the soloist by all that much. But in this work, written in 1800, one feels that Beethoven is turning his back on the past and looking positively and with new authority into the century that lay ahead. While one might argue with some conviction that both the opening theme and the closing pages of the first movement show some indebtedness to Mozart's great C minor concerto, the scale of the work is substantially larger. Here, for the first time, we find the soloist beginning to assume the 'heroic' role that was to become the hallmark of the virtuoso concertos of Chopin, Liszt, Brahms or Rakhmaninov. The instrument for which Beethoven was writing was not yet capable of the physical domination that we find in the 'Emperor' concerto some ten years later but the aspiration to such dominance is certainly there.

Although we rightly think of Beethoven as a composer whose works were subjected to a long and arduous period of gestation, in the case of the Third Concerto he appears to have carried most of the solo part in his head right up to the time of the first performance as the testimony of a young musician called Seyfried reveals.

> At the performance of his Third Concerto, he asked me to turn the pages for him; but — heaven help me! — that was easier said than done. I saw almost nothing but empty sheets. At the most on one page or the other a few wholly unintelligible signs that could as well have been Egyptian hieroglyphics, scribbled down to serve as clues for him. He played nearly all of the solo part from memory, not having had time to put it all on paper. He gave me a secret glance whenever he was at the end of one of the invisible passages, and my scarcely concealed anxiety not to miss the decisive moment amused him greatly, and he laughed heartily at the jovial supper which we ate afterwards.

(Another unfortunate had a similar experience with Mozart who blithely played the piano part of a violin sonata from a score that showed what the violinist had to do but gave hardly any indication of the pianist's contribution.)

At least Seyfried was kept busy during the orchestral introduction which is the most extensive of all those in the Beethoven piano concertos. Without so much as a preliminary chord it goes straight to the heart of the matter with a theme of almost forbidding austerity.

Notice especially bars 3–4 whose staccato rhythm can easily be taken over by the timpani, instruments which Beethoven liberated from more military chores in a number of works including this concerto, the 'Emperor', the Violin Concerto and the scherzo of the Ninth Symphony.

The opening phrase on strings alone brings an immediate response from the woodwind, equal in length but poised on the Dominant (G) and harmonised with some pathos. Violins now introduce an expressive phrase which appears to be new but which Beethoven almost certainly conceived as a more lyrical version of bar 2; meanwhile cellos and basses give support by stretching the opening three notes so that they read C–E♭–A♭ instead of C–E♭–G. This skilful fusion of two elements of Theme I occurs three times in a rising sequence before falling neatly back onto the tonic chord of C minor. There is a silence. In fact during the next eight bars no fewer than sixteen beats are marked as 'rests'. It is a trick Beethoven had learned from Mozart's example; the gaps are left so that they may be filled in by the soloist in due course. The orchestral Exposition (or *tutti*) in a concerto must differ from the Exposition of a symphony since the composer must avoid showing his hand too openly. While it is important that he reveals the main themes, he must hold back on their development or there will be little left for the soloist to do. In extending the span of the opening tutti to the extent that he does here, Beethoven runs the risk of getting too involved with the material so that he is in danger of writing a symphony with a piano part stuck on to it as pure decoration. (The Second Concerto of Brahms has sometimes been described as 'a symphony with a piano part' by critics who feel that Brahms fell into this trap.) As an instance of what I mean I quote a dramatic episode beginning at bar 36. It is a truly symphonic development of the second bar of the whole work; to make the relationship clearer I have transposed the phrase from E minor to the 'home' key of C minor.

So forcibly is this stated by the orchestra that the soloist cannot really compete; when his turn comes he can only resort to elegant decoration.

Similarly the Second Subject is developed at some length by the orchestra, appearing first in E flat major in the woodwind; the violins seem willing to take it over but then have second thoughts, modulating unexpectedly into C *major* and allowing the flutes to continue with it in that key. A stern reminder of Theme I comes from the bass, is transferred to the upper strings and then confirmed by the wind. An abrupt and positive cadence into C minor leads us to expect the entry of the soloist, eighty-five bars surely being ample by way of introduction. Instead, the woodwind introduce a new and expressive theme beginning with four repetitions of the same chord.[2] Slightly hesitant pairs of notes in the bass bring a suggestion of the 'drum-beat' rhythm from bar 3; once again there is a cadence in C minor. Will the soloist enter this time? 'Not yet' says Beethoven. After a few more moments of apparent indecision he suddenly hurls Theme I at us *fortissimo* in canon; three forceful unison Cs bring the Exposition to an abrupt close.

In a comparable situation, with the orchestra ending so loudly, Mozart would not have dreamed of expecting the soloist to compete. His solution was to establish the piano's identity with a new theme, the soft answer that turneth away wrath (see his concertos in C minor K 491 and D minor K 466). This would not suit Beethoven's new 'heroic' concept; three terse rising scales suggest that the sleeping giant is suddenly aroused; they lead to a powerful statement of Theme I, clearly designed to establish who is master now.

If I seem to have devoted excessive space to the opening tutti, it is not only because of its exceptional importance in this work; all too often the uninformed listener tends to regard the orchestral exposition as a somewhat boring classical formality that defers too long the eagerly awaited entrance of the International Star he has come to hear. (How often do we find ourselves saying 'We're going to hear Pollini tonight' instead of specifying the work he is billed to play.) It is very noticeable that in the post-Beethoven period composers almost invariably brought in the soloist early in the movement as though tacitly acknowledging the audience's frustration at being kept waiting. Even Beethoven did so in his Fourth and Fifth concertos, and he was not a man to compromise. The fact is that the ideal listener should virtually know the opening tutti by heart before hearing a note of the solo part since only then will he appreciate the close relationship that exists between the orchestral exposition and what might be termed the secondary exposition that involves the soloist. In this concerto the Second Subject appears in bar 50; omitting the rhetorical gesture of the three rising scales, there are also exactly fifty bars between the soloist's presentation of Theme I and his version of the Second Subject — this despite a free unaccompanied passage which seems to break the mould completely. Not until more than 190 bars have passed does the music depart radically from the groundplan originally laid down by the orchestra; the moment is clearly sign-posted by the first sustained trill to

---

[2]It is an interesting precursor of a subsidiary theme in the 'Eroica' Symphony, I, bars 83–91.

occur in the solo part and a modulation into the remote key of G flat major, territory which has been significantly avoided up to this point.

From here onwards the piano part becomes increasingly garrulous, the orchestra being confined for the most part to fragmentary reminders of bar 3. A rushing downward scale extended over four-and-a-half octaves leads to a substantial episode for orchestra closely related to the original tutti. It is cut short by a gesture similar to that with which the pianist had made his initial entry, three rising scales. They appear to be in D major, a key which causes a faint query in the orchestra and a skilful diversion to the more acceptable key of G minor. We have reached the expressive heart of the movement in which the pianist, having reminded us of the opening theme in the simplest way, proceeds to improvise some touching variants on Bar 2.

This whole development is noteworthy for its reticence. In the orchestra we hear constant though subdued references to the rhythm of bar 3 around which the pianist, both hands in unison, weaves elaborate but unostentatious decorations. At last a sudden crescendo and another downward-swooping scale leads to a powerful reprise of Theme I from the full orchestra.

Although this is technically the Recapitulation, within eight bars Beethoven introduces delightful variants such as the mysterious little dialogue between orchestra and strings that is one of the most magical moments of the entire concerto. Even so, a Recapitulation it is and all the important landmarks reappear. As one might guess from Seyfried's nightmare experience turning the pages, Beethoven did not bother to write a cadenza at the time though he did produce one approximately nine years later. It offers a less than perfect solution to the problem but does not lessen the sheer magic of the subsequent orchestral passage. Quiet sustained harmonies from the strings give a nocturnal air while soft reminders of bar 3 are muttered by the timpani. Veiled arpeggios from the piano add a moonlight glitter to the scene. Almost imperceptibly a sense of urgency creeps in until a sudden outburst from the full orchestra elicits a torrent of notes from the keyboard culminating in rising scales through four octaves, an extension of the initial rhetorical gesture that is perfectly placed.

The Largo which follows is remarkable in many ways. First, the key (E major) is almost as remote from C minor as it is possible to be, instantly taking us into a different world; secondly, it begins with an extensive meditation for solo piano, a device that Beethoven uses in no other concerto; thirdly the movement is complete in itself, whereas the slow movements of the Fourth and Fifth concertos are linked by subtle means to the finales; lastly, not only is it the most highly developed of all the concerto slow movements but it is also the most elaborate in ornamentation.

The opening theme, densely harmonised in a way that we would never find in Mozart, is especially notable for a strange *tremolando* effect in the left hand, something we might expect to find in Liszt rather than comparatively early Beethoven. Having been offered a theme of such serene beauty the orchestra take it to themselves, turning it in new directions before giving way again to the pianist. There follows a passage which might almost be mistaken for early Chopin so florid is the writing; an elaborate passage in thirds is succeeded by a highly ornamental run (both hands in unison) which, despite the number of notes packed into each bar must never sound hurried.

A central section gives the thematic interest to the wind in the form of a quasi-operatic duet between bassoon and flute. The piano accompanies with cloudy arpeggios that create an almost impressionistic background. In due course the opening theme returns, this time split between piano and orchestra and with new and even more elaborate embellishments. These ultimately flower into a brief and expressive cadenza. Quietly orchestra and soloist fold the movement away, only to surprise us all with the final chord, a sudden explosion that shatters the dream.

Its function is to plant the third of the scale, G sharp, firmly in our minds, for by a process that can only be described as a musical pun, Beethoven wittily turns it into an A flat and uses it to set the last movement on its way. It is a rondo whose theme is obligingly presented by the soloist and then repeated by the orchestra. After thirty-two bars the orchestra is allowed a substantial tutti during which, at one point, a playful attempt is made to put the theme into C major instead of the minor. The proposal is vehemently rejected, and brass and timpani hammer out a parade-ground rhythm that calls everyone to order. The pianist obliges by practising arpeggios the easy way and then, as if indeed to ask whether this Czerny is really necessary, launches into a deliciously frivolous tune that shows that even a descending scale of an octave and a half can be made into sheer delight.

A little later some Scarlatti-like leaps in the piano part lead the orchestra to attempt to inject a more serious note. While it could not be called a fugue, it is a brief essay in academic counterpoint. The pianist's response is a swift passage in triplets that sound suspiciously like a musical fit of the giggles, out of which a dizzying chromatic run leads us back to the Rondo theme.

It is some time before anything fundamentally new appears but when it does it is worth the wait. Clarinets introduce a lyrical tune in A major which the pianist seizes at the first opportunity. A swift ascending scale leading to a long sustained trill signals the end of this episode. It is time to earn critical respect with a display of honest craft; in suitably hushed tones the cellos begin a fugue giving an air of propriety to the cheeky little rondo tune. Although the other strings take up the subject with proper seriousness, progress is halted as the music marks time on a repeated G — a fugal catastrophe. The G changes to an A flat which the pianist then repeats no less than sixteen times. Suddenly realising that the note can also be regarded as a G sharp, the pianist switches into E major, thereby reversing the 'pun' by which Beethoven had extricated himself from the slow movement. The rondo theme takes on a beguiling new aspect in this alien yet somehow recollected tonality. There follows a typical example of Beethoven's humour which has its equivalent in three other concertos. Using only the first three notes of the rondo theme he makes a number of abortive attempts to get it started again, all to no avail. A derisive cascade of notes from the pianist silences the orchestra, whereupon he shows them how it should be done.

A more or less conventional recapitulation follows leading to a brief cadenza which ends with the same joke that we find at the start of the finale of the First Symphony — a series of ascending scales, climbing a step further each time until, after a fraught pause, the music spills into a happily vivacious tune. Here it is obviously derived from the initial rondo yet the change of character is remarkable and the movement ends in a mood of wild exuberance, the notes spilling over each other like champagne overflowing.

Piano Concerto No. 4 in G Major
Op. 58

It was in March 1807 that Beethoven took his place at the piano to give the first performance of his Fourth Concerto.[3] The audience undoubtedly expected the normal convention of an orchestral exposition or '*tutti*' to be observed, and it is hard for us today to realise what a genuine shock it must have been when he put his hands to the keys and began the work on his own with a phrase of such simple and unaffected beauty that it has remained a landmark in music ever since. A second shock was to follow, for the orchestral entry is not only surprisingly hushed but is also in the 'foreign' key of B major. Echoing but not duplicating the repeated-note theme which is such a feature of the movement, the strings find their way back to the 'proper' key of G major with the minimum of drama; once settled there, they can begin the real exposition. The opening theme is made into a duet between violins and cellos, the lower instruments following the upper line like a shadow — and with the distortions that shadows inevitably bring. The gradual involvement of the full orchestra leads to a tautening of the rhythm and the first climax. The

[3]Tovey gives 22 December 1808, but modern scholarship disagrees.

tones seem to melt away and a new theme appears with an accompaniment of repeated notes in triplets; it is in A minor and might easily be taken for the Second Subject were it not that Beethoven has other ideas. At this stage, apart from its rather poignant melodic interest, he uses it mainly as a modulating device enabling him to move smoothly from A minor to E minor, from C major to B minor and from G major to F sharp minor. Returning to the repeated-note pattern of the opening, he begins a slow and beautifully graduated ascent whose purpose is to re-establish the home key of G, a moment that is signalled by a new and much more positive theme proclaimed in some triumph by the full orchestra. Two sustained chords check the forward impulse of the music just when it is in danger of becoming more stormy than the situation really demands; flute and oboe introduce an elegant new turn of phrase based on segments of descending scales which the strings duly copy. Quietly the wind reintroduce the initial theme, to which the violins add an expressive little commentary. A sudden crescendo leads to a strong and dissonant chord in which dominant and tonic are locked in conflict, a conflict which is interrupted by one of the most magical solo entries in all music. Since it is a trick Beethoven plays several times in this movement it is worth explaining in more detail. It is a particularly subtle exploitation of a favourite device among so-called 'classical' composers, by which I mean those to whom tonality, the identity of keys and their relationships one to another, was still an important concept. (It was a concept that was to be gradually eroded in the Romantic era as an increasing use of chromatic — and therefore enigmatic — harmony led to more fluid and rapid shifts from one tonal centre to another.) In this concerto, in which the soloist plays the role of Gentle Persuader rather than Dominant Master, there are several entries which reject the implications of the preceding orchestral phrase, sometimes even directly contradicting it. At this point, the end of the tutti, the orchestral dissonance demands to be resolved; instead, the pianist perpetuates the tension, though in the gentlest manner, by coming in on the note *below* that offered by the orchestra. The phrase climbs teasingly to a playful alternation between C sharp and D, leaving the orchestra to provide its own resolution of the dissonance some four-and-a-half bars later. It provokes a fleeting display of agility from the pianist which is almost instantly turned into a more caressing motif.

A brief reminder of the opening theme from the orchestra is taken up in decorated form by the soloist who then embarks on a quicksilver passage of rapid triplets. The supporting chords in the orchestra might be taken for a mere formality were it not for the fact that they continue to suggest the repeated-note idea that dominates the movement. It is remarkable how, even when the soloist seems to enter into passages that appear to have the spontaneous freedom of improvisation, the orchestral part tethers the music to the opening theme. For instance, an almost Chopinesque flight of fancy in B flat major in the highest register of the keyboard is accompanied by quiet sustained chords in the strings which spell out the repeated-note theme at half speed. In due course, after some glittering passages from the soloist, the strings introduce the true Second Subject which Beethoven has kept in reserve for this special moment of repose. The theme is repeated with slightly prickly decorations from the pianist. Sustained trills with thunderous arpeggios in the left hand lead us back to the material of the orchestral exposition and it is here that Beethoven shows his mastery of concerto form. Bars 29–58 (orchestra only) correspond almost exactly in content and structure with bars 134–64, the essential difference being that from bar 141 onwards the pianist participates with steadily increasing brilliance. Rapid chromatic scales and a double trill sever the link with past procedures, allowing the soloist a brief and expressive meditation on a theme that the orchestra had originally presented as a triumphant paean; soon, however, the orchestra takes charge with a virtually exact transposition of the closing nineteen bars of the initial tutti. This time their dissonance *is* resolved on to a chord of D major (the dominant).

It is at this point that the soloist opens the door to the Development with a magical touch, a soft but absolute contradiction of the previous orchestral chord. Out of the strong orchestral assertion of D major emerges a gently reiterated F *natural*, a denial of D major's most essential attribute (F *sharp*). It leads to a wonderfully mysterious passage whose drifting downward scales reach into a series of unexpected keys. These scales are then transferred to the violins, though nowadays their contribution is often drowned by the pianist's rapid arpeggio figures. On Beethoven's piano they would have seemed a silver lining decorating the much more important orchestral texture, but the modern concert grand has given pianists a weapon with which they can fire more lethal salvoes.

It would be wearisome to catalogue all the events in this remarkable movement but one moment of sheer delight must be mentioned. Having for once asserted authority in a display of uncharacteristic virtuosity, the soloist seems to say 'I didn't really mean to bully you' and offers a new theme of child-like innocence based on five descending notes of the scale of C sharp minor. The effect is so beguiling that we sometimes fail to notice how the cellos and basses subtly relate this to the initial repeated-note theme.

Since the concerto began with the piano alone it is quite proper that the Recapitulation should do so as well; yet even here Beethoven has a surprise for us, for whereas the beginning was disarmingly gentle, the reprise shows a heroic aspect quite unlike anything that has come before. Thereafter events proceed more or less according to expectation, the last surprise being the resolution of the cadenza. Since by tradition this was improvised by the performer, some signal had to be pre-arranged to warn the orchestra to stand by. Custom dictated that this should be a trill on the second note of the scale which, having satisfied himself that the players were ready, the soloist would terminate with a positive thump on the key-note, thus bringing in the orchestra for a final playout in which the piano would take no part. In this work Beethoven again confounds expectation by continuing the trill on the second note of the scale *over* the orchestral entry and then dissolving it into an expressive melodic line. A nostalgic reminder of the opening theme disappears in a cloud of scales which, with gradual reinforcement from the orchestra, build to a final climax.

The slow movement presents us with a unique musical drama, the perfect symbol of the soft answer turning away wrath.[4] The orchestra is reduced to strings only, but they begin with a savage intensity; their stark unisons have something of the character of the introduction to a Handel aria. The ensuing passage for piano is not so much a response as a total disregard for the orchestra's aggression. It is like a chorale, enabling the soloist to withdraw into a world of inner contemplation. Again the strings launch their attack; again it fails to disturb the profoundly spiritual calm of the pianist. The string phrases grow more compact but they only cause the piano part to become a shade more expressive. Gradually the strings, though still in unison, find their resolution weakening; at last, all anger spent, they are reduced to a single pizzicato note. Then, and then alone, do we find an openly emotional phrase for the piano, an expression of grief that culminates in a series of trills beneath which the left hand has some extraordinary chromatic passages which are like the anguished wailing of a lost soul. Faintly, as though repenting their earlier harshness, we hear cellos and basses murmur a fragment of the initial theme. Violins have a brief phrase that is like a heavy sigh; it is echoed by the piano, the first and only time that musical material is shared by orchestra and soloist alike. Three chords of E minor, scored so as to emphasise the darkest tones, bring the movement to an end.

With little respect for our emotions Beethoven breaks the spell with a crisp march that seems to come from a great distance. The soloist takes up the tune, all sadness fled. It is as though Puck has flitted into the Capulet's Tomb, and it takes a moment or two to adjust to this lightning change of mood. In this final Rondo the dialogue between piano and orchestra is totally good-humoured, sometimes boisterous, sometimes witty, occasionally smilingly content. At one point the violas have a beautifully lyrical transformation of the opening theme which is taken up with equal affection by the clarinets somewhat later on. The piano writing calls for considerable agility, but appearances of ferocity should not be taken seriously. Towards the end there is a moment of extraordinary calm and beauty — a passage for solo piano in parallel chords; then, as if to say 'Fooled you again!', a series of trills whips up the tempo and there is a headlong rush to finish the work.

[4]Unique that is save for César Franck's almost reprehensible copy in his *Symphonic Variations*.

Piano Concerto No. 5 in E Flat Major (The 'Emperor') Op. 73

The nickname the 'Emperor' by which this work is commonly known would certainly not have gained Beethoven's approval, though it shows the special respect with which it is regarded in musical circles. Here at last it seems as though the piano has come of age and is able to stand up to the orchestra not merely as an equal but as master. Indeed in the opening bars the orchestra is reduced to the level of a lackey opening doors, harmonic doors through which the pianist lets loose a flood of sound. The orchestral chords, three in number, represent the foundation stones on which the tonality of E flat major is built; first the Tonic (E flat), second the Sub-dominant (A flat), and third the Dominant (B flat) with the highest note being the Seventh, thereby ensuring a return to the Tonic. Between each of these majestic chords the piano is given a cadenza of considerable virtuosity, establishing a new relationship quite different from anything Beethoven had employed so far. This dominance established beyond doubt, the soloist is able to relax for a while and allow the orchestra a full-scale Exposition, unusually rich in thematic materials, so much so that I will allocate them letters by way of identification. First comes a march (A) containing two significant features, a swift triplet 'turn' around the key-note, and a martial rhythm (♩. ♪ | ♩   ♪) which is reinforced by horns. A clarinet makes an unsuccessful attempt to treat the march-tune more lyrically but the brass and timpani refuse to accept this emasculation. There follows a striking dialogue between horns and trumpets (in unison) and the first violins (B). The theme is simplicity itself, four descending notes of the common chord; the brass spell out E flat major, the Tonic, the violins A flat major, the Sub-dominant. This very four-square motif is followed by a rhythmically more exciting phrase with strongly accented syncopations and aggressive quaver figuration (C). A sudden *diminuendo* leads to the Second Subject (D), a strange almost ghostly march in the totally unexpected key of E flat *minor*. The rhythm is crisp, even mechanical in effect, and it isn't long before the horns correct this breach of musical protocol by smoothing the phrases out and putting them into the more acceptable key of E flat *major*. The triplet 'turn' from the very first bar of the orchestral tutti makes a fidgety appearance in the violins, evoking a grumbling response from cellos and basses; it is enough to set off not a reprise but an *extension* of the initial theme that builds to a considerable climax. Oboes, clarinets and flutes in turn soothe away the tensions with a sequence made up of descending fragments of scales, (E), each four-note group beginning from a higher point than its predecessor. This placatory gesture is soon rejected by the entire orchestra, timpani thundering and trumpets blaring, while violins and woodwind introduce yet another theme (F) whose majestic descending phrases are rudely disturbed by sharp interpolations of the terse martial rhythm from (A). The mood softens as the violins offer us an expressive though compact melody (G), although this too is interrupted by the martial dotted rhythm. It is repeated several times in the woodwind to a strangely dissonant harmony when, summoned by this macabre little fanfare, the pianist makes a surprisingly undemonstrative reappearance with a quiet ascending chromatic scale culminating in a trill. The orchestra is reduced to silence, allowing the piano to change the character of the initial theme from military to contemplative. We barely have time to absorb this for after four bars the rhythm tautens again and an element of virtuosity makes itself felt. It is enough to rouse the orchestra once again; the dialogue between brass and strings (B) is resumed quite forcefully, only to be checked with a gentle reproof by the soloist who then modulates smoothly to what in effect is B major, though for convenience it is written as C flat major. To a slightly athletic accompaniment from the piano, a solo bassoon reminds us of (C), a suggestion endorsed by other members of the wind family. Suddenly the soloist cuts them off with a fiercely accented octave followed by an angry outburst — both hands in unison — that leads to the truly remote key of B minor. It is in this previously unvisited tonality that the second subject (D) now appears; there is a faintly Oriental flavour, the piano figuration suggesting the tinkling of little bells. As though unable to tolerate this unorthodox behaviour any longer, the orchestra comes crashing in with a severely disciplined version of the Second Subject, now in the 'proper' key of B flat major (the Dominant) for the first time. (We can almost hear the sergeant-major's bark, 'Left-Right! Left-Right!') A few magic passes from the piano bring about a bloodless victory; soon the soloist embarks on a thrilling development of the initial theme (A), now compressed into a single bar, with a positive hail-storm of staccato triplets in the left hand to whip up the excitement. This section is a dramatic interpolation into the original structure of the opening tutti, yet after twenty-one bars Beethoven brings us back on course with a decorated version of (E), now on the piano instead of the wind.

In the centre of the movement there is a substantial section for orchestra alone, bars 227–68 being roughly equivalent to bars 62–112 in the Exposition. Both passages are terminated by a chromatic scale from the keyboard finishing on a sustained trill. It is an easily spotted landmark, leading, on this second occasion, to the Development. This is notable for the complete change of character we find in the initial theme (A). By putting it into various *minor* keys, Beethoven deprives it of its proud military air, making it seem forlorn and curiously disoriented. Some abrasive arpeggios in F minor from the pianist (hands in unison again for maximum volume) drag the orchestra out of the doldrums until at last the full wind, brass and timpani hammer out a martial dotted rhythm derived from a fragment of (A). With a gesture of defiance that was unprecedented at the time, the pianist hurls the chord back at them; they repeat their challenge but again back comes the thunderous reply. After the fourth exchange, the piano part struts arrogantly into a victorious sequence of octaves. (Compare the slow movement of the Fourth Concerto where the orchestra is tamed by infinitely subtler means.) For some twenty bars an intense dialogue is engaged between piano and strings as massive scales rise and fall in contrary motion. It is the one place where Beethoven's nerve seems to have failed him; deaf as he was, he could not be absolutely sure that the piano could hold its own against the strings. He therefore directed that they should play only one beat loud, the rest soft. Modern pianists need no such protection and it is far more effective to let the strings play out until, admitting defeat at last, they genuinely give way. The end of the conflict is signalled by a meltingly beautiful version of (G) in the upper register of the keyboard. This is repeated several times in different keys, its serenity unruffled by occasional mutterings from the lower strings. Nevertheless these signs of discontent do ultimately have an effect, and it is the violas who finally provoke the rest of the orchestra to join them in reiterating the swift triplet from (A). A massive chord of E flat tells us we have reached the Recapitulation. The orchestra lays the same three foundation-stones as before, but the piano cadenzas are much more compact than they were at the beginning of the movement.

After the third of these virtuoso passages the orchestra sets out confidently on what we imagine will be a substantial reprise of the opening tutti, but it is not to be. Clarinets, bassoons and horns interpose a lyrical treatment of the second phrase which the pianist then embellishes with trills. At this point we should remember how a clarinet tried to offer an expressive version of the initial march tune, only to be rudely rebuffed by brass and timpani. It was a seed destined to flower 366 bars later, for now the pianist gratefully accepts the idea, extending it considerably and adding a touch of pathos to the end of each phrase. It is the first significant difference between exposition and recapitulation, though from here onwards every landmark should be clearly recognisable.

Two grand flourishes from the piano and heavily scored martial chords from the orchestra lead us to expect a substantial cadenza. Beethoven expressly forbids the performer to improvise one of his own; instead, he provides one of exemplary but unusual brevity which even dispenses with the formality of a concluding trill. The Coda begins with a beautiful shimmering effect high on the keyboard[5] that gradually descends to less ethereal regions. Some final flourishes in E flat bring this immense movement (582 bars) to an end.

After so elaborate a structure as the first movement it is hardly surprising that Beethoven turns to an altogether simpler conception. This is not to say that

---

[5]It is interesting to compare it with an equivalent near the end of the first movement of Rakhmaninov's Third Concerto.

the slow movement lacks profundity but rather that its material is limited to two main ideas, one notably free from ornamentation of any kind, the other elaborately decorated. The first hymn-like theme is announced by muted strings.[6] It is in B major, a key already visited several times in the first movement wearing the disguise of C flat. The last few bars of the opening tune seem almost to disintegrate, creating a sense of expectancy as we wait for the 'arrival' of the soloist. He brings not only a new theme but a new texture, wide-spaced after the warm dark harmonies of the strings. Two descending passages drift downwards in an almost Chopinesque fashion, leading to an openly expressive melody whose sequences might sound trite were it not for the sheer beauty of each curved phrase. Gentle chords from the strings modulate to D major, whereupon the soloist re-enters with similar material, though tinged with sorrow in the second descent. A brief declamatory passage in parallel thirds and sixths leads to a long sequence of trills, steadily rising as they bring us step by step back to B major. For the first time the pianist is given the initial hymnlike theme, accompanied by quiet pizzicato chords from the strings. The tune ended, the piano part is reduced to a gently rocking figure which serves as accompaniment to the third appearance of the 'hymn', this time in the woodwind. Gradually the music descends into the shadows until nothing is left but an octave B quietly sustained on two bassoons. Mysteriously, the music drops a semitone to B flat — now on horns — the change discreetly underlined by pizzicato strings. As though in a dream the piano presents a barely perceived version of the theme of the Rondo-finale. Then, with the bounding energy of a giant refreshed by sleep, it stamps out the vigorous tune that is destined to dominate the last movement.

The form here is a conventional Rondo. The opening statement is followed by a substantial *tutti* expressing enthusiastic endorsement of the piano theme. An important repeated-note rhythm on trumpets and horns should be marked down for future reference. At the end of the orchestral statement the pianist dashes off a few whirligig scales before introducing a more lyrical episode which a bassoon queries wittily. Several exchanges ensue, some doubting, some exuberantly confident until, dismissing the whole affair with a flourish, the pianist introduces Episode Number Two, a happy little tune in B flat major which soon dissolves into rhythmically ambiguous figuration in the highest register of the keyboard. A torrent of broken octaves leads us back to the Rondo theme in triumphant mood.

An intriguing section follows, with the piano chattering away in a rather frivolous manner while the strings have a quiet but earnest discussion of one fragment of the main theme. In unison they affirm its importance but the pianist soon puts a stop to that with a passage that must surely be a musical

[6]Beethoven, no doubt expecting a shortage of violas and lower strings, only asks for the violins to be muted.

representation of laughter. Without warning the theme re-appears, this time in C major. Scarlatti-like leaps emphasise the mischievous mood of the soloist, who ultimately has to be called to order by a peremptory use of the repeated-note rhythm originally established by the brass. This time it is on violas, then clarinets and bassoons, violas again (more angrily) and, lastly, surprisingly quiet horns. In just as capricious a mood the soloist reintroduces the theme *pianissimo* in A flat major before indulging in a dizzy flight of chromatic scales. A further attempt to establish a firmer discipline proves just as ineffective since it merely tempts the pianist to wander into the extremely remote key of E major, a total contradiction of everything E *flat* stands for.

The martial repeated-note rhythm begins to assume an ever greater importance in the orchestra as the piano-writing grows more aggressive. At last, a lengthy trill calms things down; beneath it the strings gently remind us of the magical way in which the soloist had had the first glimpse of the Rondo theme during the closing bars of the slow movement. It is enough to initiate what is in effect a substantial Recapitulation. The remainder needs no comment save for a remarkable passage near the end during which a solo drum taps out the repeated-note rhythm a number of times beneath a descending sequence of expressive harmonies from the keyboard. Having virtually lost all momentum, the music seems about to come to a complete halt. Then 'Enough of that' says Beethoven and whisks us off to the final chords.

Violin Concerto in D Major
Op. 61

The first performance of this great work was given on 23 December 1806. It was not the most auspicious of occasions since both soloist and orchestra were sight-reading, unrehearsed. Since the work was considered to be unreasonably long it was split in two, the first movement being played in Part I of the concert, the remaining two movements after the interval. By way of diversion the soloist, Franz Clement, played a sonata of his own composition to be performed on one string only with the violin held upside down. This circus trick undoubtedly gave great delight to the audience but little joy to Beethoven. The Vienna press gave a somewhat guarded reaction to the work and despite the efforts of several renowned violinists over the years, the concerto never received its proper due until Joachim played it as a child prodigy with Mendelssohn conducting. Meanwhile several publishers had rejected it and no full score was actually engraved until 1894, eighty-eight years after it had been composed.

It shares with the Fourth Piano Concerto an absence of mere technical display, and just as that work began with an unprecedented gesture, the piano playing alone, so does this, the four quiet drum-taps instantly arresting our attention without recourse to drama. The subsequent chorale-like phrase on the woodwind is the most important theme of the movement, not merely establishing the tonality of D major, but also creating a mood of tranquillity that is a cardinal feature of the work. A balancing phrase, also on the wind, leads to the first string entry, a mysterious D sharp four times repeated that momentarily threatens the tonality by directly contradicting the key-note. Order is quickly and firmly restored, but notice how persistent is the four-beat pattern originally established in bar 1. Some straightforward scales in the wind, climbing up and then dipping only to climb again, give us no warning of the storm ahead — a sudden outburst for full orchestra in B flat major, surprising enough to cause a stunned silence after its first and second phrases. In a moment or two the violins reduce the tension with a brief curling pattern, six times repeated; four tick-tock As, echoing the drum-taps, usher in the Second Subject, a serene pastoral tune no different emotionally from the First. (One might expect to find such a similarity of mood in Schubert but it is extremely rare in Beethoven.) This new theme is also wedded to the repeated-note motif whose importance cannot be over-stressed. Horns, trumpets and timpani continue to repeat the pattern in sombre tones while the violins extend the second subject in the *minor*, modulating into the alien key of F major before returning to D. For a moment they stay poised on a unison A; then, as though saying 'I knew it would fit in somewhere,' Beethoven gives us a beguiling justification for that oddly intrusive D sharp, integrating it into the melody so that it no longer seems out of place. The discovery creates quite an upsurge of excitement which in turn leads to an important new theme sung out by the first violins and answered in near-operatic style by cellos and basses. The tutti ends not with a strong final cadence, as we might expect, but with a gentle descent to the dominant (A) which the soloist proceeds to turn in the opposite direction, climbing to a high G before (reversing the grand old Duke of York's historic tactics) 'marching down to the bottom of the hill then marching up again'.

The soloist's identity having been clearly established, Beethoven now begins his secondary exposition. The first twenty-one bars are repeated virtually note-for-note save for the decorations added by the solo violin. Then the rising scales, originally in the woodwind, take on a more agitated aspect in the strings, causing the soloist to make an excursion into various minor keys and to indulge in a considerably more athletic display. A pro-longed trill gives the cue to clarinets and bassoons to re-introduce the second subject, now in its orthodox key of A major (the Dominant.) As before, the strings give the theme a touch of melancholy by putting it into the minor, accompanied by somewhat angular figuration in the solo part. The relationship to previous events is so clearly established that no commentary is needed for a while. The next event of real significance is again signalled by a sustained trill from the solo violin. Very quietly, the first violins tap out the initial drum-beat rhythm on the note E. (The supposition is that this will prove to be the dominant of A major and lead inevitably to that key.) From the very depths of the orchestra they are answered by a ghostly F natural. This sepulchral voice causes the violins to move upward a semitone to F themselves. Basses and cellos step after them, rising to G, thereby opening the way for a brief visit to C major. Ascending trills on the violin seem to draw the orchestra upwards until the 'proper' destination of A major is reached, an event which the soloist celebrates with an elaborately serpentine scale passage spread over seven bars.

At this point Beethoven launches us with some violence into a substantial tutti that seems to be a more or less exact repetition of the original orchestral exposition, as though from the first *fortissimo* (bar 28). In fact bars 28–101 would appear to correspond exactly with bars 224–98 apart from some variations in orchestration and dynamics. However, there is one profound difference; instead of leading us back to the home key of D major, the music heads for the contradictory tonality of C major; far from being a true recapitulation, this entire section is destined to lead us further afield. At the end of a cadenza easily recognisable as a near duplicate of the one that heralded its first entry, the violin moves subtly into B minor and initiates an important new development. The bassoons lead the way with a variant of the very opening theme; in the background the strings constantly remind us of the four drum-taps while the soloist serves a purely decorative function. By halving the value of the notes (thereby doubling their speed) Beethoven gives the impression that the tempo is quickening; the violinist reacts with slightly more agitated patterns, even building up to quite a dramatic climax. There follows the most sublime episode in the whole movement; beneath a cadential trill from the violin, horns play four repeated Ds as softly as they can. The music settles into G minor. Against a background of quiet string chords and soft reiterations of the four-beat motif the soloist is given a passage that is as expansive as a Chopin nocturne yet as simple as something by Mozart. This is clearly the emotional heart of the movement, yet despite its rhapsodizing, horns, bassoons and trumpets in turn keep an ever-restraining hand on the music, continually relating it to the very first bar of the work. A long chromatic ascent from the soloist brings us back to broad daylight and a massive re-statement of the opening material, now scored for full orchestra. A more or less conventional recapitulation follows with, in due course, a suitable pause for a cadenza. Beethoven left this to the violinist, though one shudders to think what irrelevant fireworks Clement inserted at the first performance. The cadenza that Joachim wrote in his maturity is still a favourite choice, though over thirty have been published. What we do know

is that Beethoven wanted it to end undemonstratively since the entry immediately afterwards consists of a serene contemplation of the second subject,
virtually unaccompanied. It is a moment of unforgettable beauty whose
effect cannot be diminished even by the convention of a final rush to the
conclusion of the movement.

Although much of the slow movement sounds like a spontaneous improvisation on the violinist's part, the actual structure is organised according to a
very strict plan. The opening theme, on strings only, provides the basic
material for a set of variations. Notice the silences in bars 1, 2 and 5, a clear
invitation to the soloist to provide some decoration. The overall plan can be
shown quite simply:

I   Theme on strings only.
II   Theme repeated on horns, clarinets and strings with expres-
     sive interpolations from the soloist (Variation I).
III Theme on bassoon, violas and cellos with still more elaborate
     decorations from the soloist (Variation II).
IV   Theme on orchestra, *forte*, and reinforced by rhythmic com-
     ments from horns and wind (Variation III).

Having led us to assume that we are listening to a strict set of variations,
Beethoven now breaks free from their restrictive implications. An unostentatious cadenza from the soloist leads us to a completely new theme, sublimely
simple yet deeply expressive. It is an interlude that for the first time in the
movement allows the soloist to lead rather than merely to decorate. Its actual
duration is short in terms of bars though it seems almost as if time stands still.
If we add this section to the plan above and then continue we find:

V   Brief accompanied cadenza leading to
VI   New tune on solo violin (Interlude I).
VII   Variation IV, pizzicato strings with soloist shadowing the
      theme in high register.
VIII Interlude II. (Note quiet repeated notes on horns ♪♪♪.).
IX   Elaboration of VI.
X   Return to VIII.

This last section seems about to dissolve into nothingness as muted
horns and then violins give us the faintest possible reminder of the opening
bars of the original theme. Suddenly, and even Beethoven hardly ever gave us
a ruder shock than this, *fortissimo* chords shatter the mood irrevocably,
modulating somewhat obliquely to the dominant of D. A brief cadenza is
demanded of the violinist, though it seems extraordinary that after a move-

ment of such supreme beauty Beethoven should leave this critical moment to the dubious inspiration of the performer. Without more ado, the soloist leads us into the final Rondo.

With only the most rudimentary accompaniment the violin presents us with a theme whose hunting-horn characteristics place the music firmly out-of-doors. After a momentary pause in which the horns do indeed join, the tune is repeated in a higher register, this time accompanied by violins, still so delicately as to seem almost timid. Then, as though they had been in hiding waiting to surprise us, the whole orchestra comes bouncing in with the theme, cheerfully extending it in a boisterously rustic mood. After some twenty bars the music quietens down with no less than eight repetitions of a hop from tonic to dominant, a hop which the soloist copies before initiating Episode I in which the horns establish beyond doubt that 'A-hunting we will go'. Soon the soloist becomes involved in a passage of considerable technical difficulty, the first display of unabashed virtuosity in the entire work apart from what may have occurred during the cadenza. In case this should cause the soloist to lose all touch with the essential matter in hand, violas, violins and cellos in turn offer increasingly firm reminders of the Rondo theme until at last he is compelled to take the hint. A brief pause for breath on a trill, and then the theme is presented again exactly as it was in the opening bars. As before, it is taken up with acclamation by the full orchestra, but this time Beethoven begins to journey away from D major. Brief visits to B flat, E flat, C and F appear to bring him back to D again. 'Do you really mean D?' says the soloist, repeating the notes half-a-dozen times with some disbelief. Comprehension dawns; it isn't D major but the dominant of G minor — same chord, different function. And so we arrive at Episode II, a slightly forlorn tune in G minor whose pathos need not be taken seriously as we discover when it is taken up by a solo bassoon with a vamped accompaniment in the strings. This is Beethoven in what he called his 'unbuttoned' mood, and although the Concerto is habitually regarded with reverence, this movement's spiritual home is the village inn rather than the concert-hall.

The next return to the Rondo-theme is accompanied by a witty dialogue between the orchestral strings and the soloist, each 'raising' the other like gamblers until the violinist sweeps the board with a display of flashing octaves the rank and file can scarcely match. The game begins anew, the theme being presented exactly as it was at the start. (This is unusual for Beethoven; normally he introduces variants.) In fact we soon discover that we are in for a substantial recapitulation of earlier events. Apart from the necessary adjustments to tonality bars 1–88 find their exact match in bars 174–262. In the latter version an expanded treatment of the horn-call from Episode I leads to the cadenza, whose final trill is prolonged for eleven bars beneath which cellos and basses make a number of attempts to bring back the opening theme, gradually losing confidence as the soloist takes no notice of them. Tentative suggestions from the violins lead to a subtle modulation to the surprising key of A flat major and a mischievous reappearance of the theme. By devious means the soloist finds the way back to the home key, handing over to the woodwind with a gesture of aristocratic condescension. The ensuing coda is full of delights; first a dialogue between oboe and violin in which the soloist insists on turning the tune upside down, then some mercurial displays of agility from the soloist followed by some out-of-temper literally 'cross' accents from the orchestra. In the very final pages it seems as though the music is destined to disappear into the distance, so much so that the solo violin is left completely alone. With the delicacy of a butterfly on the wing, the last phrases climb to a high A only to be cut off in mid-flight by two thumping chords from the full orchestra. It is a truly magical ending to a work that knows no peer in its classical perfection.

ALBAN BERG
1885–1935

Serialism

Even today, three-quarters of a century after serialism was devised as one way out of the post-Wagnerian impasse, works written according to the concepts of serial technique need to be explained to a great proportion of concert-goers. Music at the turn of the century was in a Romantic turmoil; Wagner had unleashed extremes of passion hitherto unknown in musical terms. 'Tristan and Isolde' was to other musicians what the discoveries of Freud were to writers; a whole new world was opened and one can trace a direct line of descent from Wagner to early Schoenberg whose gigantic *Gurrelieder* is the ultimate example of post-Wagnerian extension. But not only was the emotional range of music stretching to new extremes; the confines of tonality were crumbling so that it was often difficult to define precisely in which key any specific bar was meant to be — or was it meant to be in *no* key?

Although Schoenberg was essentially a romantic composer, *Gurrelieder* and *Verklärte Nacht* showed him that it was impossible to go further down that particular road; yet he had no wish to make his music less emotional. What he sought was a more satisfactory framework, an inner discipline that would channel these rivers of emotion into some more contained form. After literally years of intellectual struggle he devised a new order for music, serial composition as it came to be known, in which the composer employed what might be described as a totally new grammar and syntax of music. To explain in a few paragraphs a subject which has occupied many a text-book necessarily involves considerable simplification, but briefly Tonal music (pre-Schoenberg) is based for the most part on two concepts of key, major and minor. Key is the generic term for a particular family of notes of which a scale is a step-by-step exploration.

Now in any key certain notes predominate; in the key of C (white notes on the piano) C and G are like the Father and Mother. E is the eldest son and the remaining white notes are the less important members of the family. The black notes in this case would be distant acquaintances, seldom called on in the purest forms of Tonal music. These 'outsiders', chromatic or literally 'coloured' notes, have habitually been used to intensify emotion from pre-Elizabethan days onwards, the historical tendency being for music to become more chromatic as time went by. It may be helpful at this stage to think of key not as a family of notes or even a sort of musical ladder but rather as a mountain with terraces cut around its perimeter. In the latter part of the nineteenth century the clear distinctions between one key and another were beginning to break down, as though the edges of the terraces had become overgrown and nearly invisible. Schoenberg accepted this as an inescapable fact and simply said, in effect, 'there are no more terraces: let us think of the mountain as a whole.' He therefore abolished the Father–Mother relationship and in an attitude of mind that was akin to a sort of musical communism (which was also being born as a political movement at about the same time) decreed that all twelve notes contained within the chromatic scale of one octave were to be regarded as equal. Mention of one octave may be misleading since Schoenberg's vision extends beyond its confines. To him the note C sharp is *any* C sharp; he thinks not of the terraces but the whole mountain. Now if a piece were to be written entirely in D major we might not classify it as 'Seven-note' music but in fact that would be the case; even so, we would not expect those seven notes to be confined within the compass of a single octave. Naturally enough then, though the theoretical basis on which a piece of 'Twelve-note' music is based may be confined to the range of an octave, in practice it is in no way limited to so inhibiting a constraint.

Serialism, or the art of composition through the use of twelve notes related only to each other, is simply a way of thinking, a way of going about the process of organising music, which composition essentially is. Palestrina or Bach (in his fugues, canons or even most of the preludes) organise music according to a fairly strict set of self-imposed rules, rules which are still taught to students as an intellectual discipline rather similar to learning Latin. Schoenberg's rules are actually much freer than Palestrina's or Bach's since they are designed to cater for an intensely emotional style of composition. For each composition a sequence of notes is devised called a Tone-row. It must contain all twelve notes of the chromatic scale though obviously not in the conventional ladder-like order in which we practise them when we are learning an instrument. This row may be conceived in four basic ways, forwards, backwards, upside-down and backwards-upside-down. (The proper terms are Retrograde, Inversion and Retrograde-Inversion but no matter.) A simple analogy is your hand. Hold out your right hand palm downwards; let that be the Tone-row. Now hold your left hand beside the right; you will see at once that the left is the Retrograde of the right: the thumbs are the common starting-point, the journey to the little finger goes in opposite directions. If you want an exact Inversion of your right hand you must turn the *left* hand palm upwards — both thumbs are on the left; turn the *right* hand palm upwards and you get the Retrograde Inversion.

Now no matter how we contort our hands, contracting some fingers, stretching others, bunching them up, putting them sideways or even interlocking them, the *relative* positions of the fingers remain the same. The same principle applies to strict serial music. Suppose we number the twelve chromatic notes 1–12 and decide for the purposes of this particular composition to create this 'row':

$$9\ 5\ 4\ 8\ 3\ 2\ 1\ 6\ 7\ 11\ 10\ 12^1$$

For the Retrograde version read from right to left; for the Inversion imagine the figures to be upside-down; for the Retrograde-Inversion simply turn the page upside-down and read from left to right in the usual way.

Does this mean that serial music is entirely linear? No, since, as we found with the analogy of the hand, we can put it 'sideways'. In other words 9 5 4 8 could become a chord, 3 2 1 6 a strand of melody, 7–11 and 10–12 could be two consecutive pairs:

```
                    6
        3                7
   9         2          11   10
   5              1          12
   4
   8
```

This sort of fragmentation can be applied to all four versions of the 'row' and furthermore the whole row may be transposed so that every note loses it original identity while still maintaining its relative position to its neighbours. This means that any given row has forty-eight (12 × 4) possible permutations. Add to this all the complexities of rhythm, orchestration, and the fact that different versions of the 'row' may appear simultaneously and it will be seen that the system is far from rigid. One last supremely important point must be made before we turn to the Berg Violin Concerto: serialism is a procedure, a method of composition; *we are not supposed to be able to trace the workings of the 'row' as we listen*. When a car is running we do not need to see the internal workings of the engine, the gear-box, the drive-shaft or the back-axle; but if the designer had not put them there . . . let us turn to the music.

[1]Treating C natural as 1, this is actually the opening theme of Frank Martin's *Petite Symphonie Concertante*, a twelve-note theme for a *non-serial* work.

Violin Concerto
(1935)

This work, written in the last year of Berg's life, has become a twentieth century classic. Berg was a devoted disciple of Schoenberg's and it is not surprising that the concerto employs serial techniques in its composition; however it is by no means strictly serial, as we shall discover, since the 'row' on which it is primarily based contains strong implications of traditional tonality. Although commissioned by a violinist named Louis Krasner, the work has an almost macabre association with death for Berg was only too aware that he had not long to live and felt that the concerto was in a way his own Requiem. Moreover it is dedicated 'To the memory of an angel'; the 'angel' was an eighteen-year old girl named Manon Gropius, daughter of the famous architect, for whom Berg had a deep-seated affection. When she died of infantile paralysis he felt the loss as keenly as if she had been his own child. We should therefore realise that the concerto was inspired by love and grief rather than a desire to demonstrate a newly developed technique of composition forbiddingly known as 'dodecaphonic'. All the same, some analysis is helpful if only to comprehend the way the craft element in music is used to harness its emotional force.

The basic tone-row or 'series' which Berg uses consists of four traditional three-note chords (triads) to which four notes of a whole-tone scale are added as an appendage:

Ex. 1

(Note-values here have no significance.)

A little thought shows Berg's keen awareness of established musical relationships, for the first two groups are Tonic and Dominant harmonies in the key of G minor while the third and fourth groups are Tonic and Dominant in A minor. The significance of the final four notes will become apparent later.

The concerto begins with a ten-bar introduction in which the violin seems to awaken by symbolically stretching itself. The four open strings, G-D-A-E, are played in bar 2, prompted by the harp. In bar 4 the intervals of a fifth are stretched by a semitone, and in bar 8 they are widened still further.

An extended *rallentando* leads to the true beginning of the movement. This has often been quoted as a transparently clear demonstration of serialism, easy to comprehend precisely because of the essentially tonal nature of Berg's 'row':

Ex. 2

The next entry of the violin spells out all twelve notes of the 'row' as a straightforward rising arpeggio, lingering momentarily on the ninth note. Example 2 is then transposed up a fourth and given to muted brass after which the violin inverts the theme, playing it as a descending arpeggio which is a mirror image of its predecessor. The development of this idea and its many derivatives is very much on classical lines and the musical anatomist can rummage through the score for hours tracing inversions here, augmentations there. For instance bars 47–57 of the solo part — the first point at which the violinist moves into a semiquaver figure urging the tempo forward as he does so — are duplicated exactly as a horn solo in bars 63–70, though at half speed. This augmentation coincides with the first time that a still quicker figure of triplet semiquavers appears in the solo part. A back reference to Ex. 2 is easily spotted when it appears with the original violin parts transferred to flutes and clarinet two octaves higher while the soloist plays the minim figure initially given to the solo double bass. The first section of the work is folded quietly away with numerous references to the arch of rising and falling fifths that occurs in the very opening bars.

Clarinets change the mood to a delicately poised scherzo, their lilting phrase instantly copied by the soloist. Such dialogues between wind and solo violin are the mainstay of this second part in which Berg, ever mindful of tradition, even marks a section as Trio I to be followed later by Trio II. Trio I can be spotted by a spurt of energetic writing for two bassoons and a terse fanfare for two trumpets and trombone. Trio II comes after a spell of triple-stopping (three-note chords) from the soloist and a relaxation of the tempo. A duet for two flutes is a clear landmark here. The orchestra is for the most part used rather sparingly although one aggressive version of the little trumpet fanfare does stand out when it is extended through the full brass section, trumpets overlapping horns, trombones overlapping trumpets.

A curious interloper in this movement is a Carinthian folk-song played in turn by solo horn and trumpet. It is a tune of child-like simplicity and when it reappears near the end of the work at half speed it is perhaps a last sad image of the young Manon Gropius still able to dance before polio locked her limbs in its limp and nauseating grasp.

The second main movement is marked Allegro but with a further instruction that it should be flexible and free like a cadenza. The solo part is ferociously difficult, sometimes playfully capricious against strongly rhythmic patterns in the orchestra. The actual cadenza is occasionally accompanied by cello or viola and its conclusion is greeted by an exuberant outburst from brass and wind. Typically Austrian dance-rhythms keep surfacing, but perhaps the most important thing to listen for is the frequent reference to the pattern of four rising notes that first appeared as 9–12 in the initial series. (It is of course destined to appear in many different registers, low and high.) Gradually the tempo slows, leading through this very sequence into the final Adagio. Here Berg quotes directly an old German chorale, *'Es ist genug'*, originally composed by Ahle (1625–73) but subsequently used by Bach in his Cantata No. 60:

Ex. 3

With great skill Berg integrates this seemingly alien theme into the score; it emerges quite logically since it begins with a four-note whole-tone ascent that corresponds with notes 9–12 of the original 'row'. As the violin plays the first phrase of the chorale a rising coil of notes climbs out of the darkest area of the orchestra, starting on the contra-bassoon. It is a slightly modified version of the original arpeggio with which the violin spelt out the twelve-note 'row'. At this stage it is like a sigh of remembrance as though Berg was metaphorically joining hands with Bach in shared grief and resignation.

> It is enough; my Jesus comes. Now good night O world,
> I go to the halls of Heaven.

Berg himself had only a few months to live after completing the concerto; he never heard it performed. But in the closing pages the music grows in passion and intensity when all the violins join in unison with the soloist as they too share his emotional outburst. Phrases from the chorale keep reappearing, often in strict counterpoint that may be seen as a homage to Bach. But after the passionate outcry of the violins the music gradually disintegrates until there is hardly a whisper left. The last forlorn notes on the violins repeat for a final time the arch-like shape of the open strings we originally heard in bar 2. The open strings are like the bones of the instrument, needing the touch of the human hand to give them life. You cannot use vibrato on open strings; vibrato is vibrance, the vital spark, and with a last sigh from the double basses the spark expires.

BERLIOZ

1803–69

The climate of opinion about the music of Berlioz has changed considerably during the last three decades; once regarded as the eccentric composer of over-ambitious failures, he is now looked on as a man of extraordinary daring who, despite occasional miscalculations, scored some glorious triumphs. The change has partly been brought about by the availability of the music on records; it is hard for us to believe that between the wars a well-known and respected critic could write a book on Berlioz and admit that he had never had the opportunity of hearing the *Grande Messe des Morts*. It used to be said by people who should have known better that Berlioz couldn't orchestrate, that he couldn't write melodies. Even in his own country recognition was slow in forthcoming; listeners found it hard to reconcile the opposing facets of his genius — on the one hand a serene classicism, on the other an intense and explosive romanticism. Stravinsky said that composers are 'inventors'. None was ever more inventive than Berlioz, whose imaginative ear had an uncanny ability to pluck sounds from the air and put them on paper. Not for him the text-book rules of orchestration, the conventional concept of what might be termed orchestral propriety. His anticipation of the twentieth century approach to sound was truly prophetic. Webern once tried an experiment with a Bach fugue, giving each note of its subject to a different instrument so as to disturb all preconceived notions of 'line' and thereby teach us to think of each note as an individual entity. It was a revolutionary approach which caused a furore yet Berlioz had already done it in the 'March to the Scaffold' from the *Symphonie Fantastique*:

Ex. 1

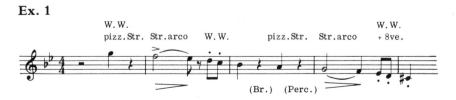

The off-beat interpolations from brass and percussion make the effect even more extraordinary. As to his use of timpani, it was so original that it has no parallel in nineteenth century music, whether in building a melodic line in the March quoted above or in the amazing evocation of thunder at the end of the slow movement where he uses four tuned timpani to produce chords unaided by any other instruments.

In the final movement of this unique work he uses tubular bells in an asymmetrical rhythm seemingly completely independent of the starkly harmonised version of the *Dies Irae* that lies beneath. It is a sound we would not be surprised to find in a Stravinsky score but which is almost incredible in a work written a mere eighteen months after Schubert's death and before Tchaikovsky had even been born.

Symphonie Fantastique
Op. 14 (1830)

The Fantastic Symphony not only uses the orchestra in an unprecedented way but also treats the whole concept of symphonic form from a new and very personal angle. Far from regarding the symphony as an abstract musical form, Berlioz used it as a medium for self-projection, seeing himself as the hero-figure much as Richard Strauss was to do generations later in *Ein Heldenleben*.

There are two main sources of inspiration for the work, De Quincey's *Confessions of an Opium-Eater*, which Berlioz read avidly in a somewhat unreliable translation by Alfred de Musset, and (which is far more important) the composer's own love-life. While still a student he became wildly infatuated with an Irish actress called Harriet Smithson whom he had seen playing in what was probably a rather tatty repertory company doing a Shakespeare season in Paris. Against all the odds he did ultimately marry her, though the outcome was less than happy. However, no emotion in Berlioz's life could ever be simple or straightforward, and even his initial feelings for his Irish lady-love waxed and waned in a characteristically inconsistent manner. In February 1830, while he was actually working on the symphony, he wrote to a friend about his beloved. 'She is still in London, and yet I seem to feel her near me. All my former feelings for her are aroused and combine to tear me to pieces; I hear my heart beat, and its pulsations shake me as though they were the strokes of the pistons of a steam-engine.' Not the most romantic of similies, but at least it was up to date since Stevenson's Rocket had first startled the world the previous year. One finds it hard to take such expressions of passion seriously since at the time he had never even spoken to her. A few months later, and still before he'd had any contact with her, disillusionment with his goddess set in. Rumour had it that her morals were less than perfect, and in the final movement of a symphony which was written to glorify his love for her, he turned her into a witch.

The Symphony has an elaborate programme written by Berlioz himself. This is how he describes its five movements:

A young musician of extraordinary sensibility and abundant imagination, in the depths of despair because of hopeless love, has poisoned himself with opium. The drug is too feeble to kill him but plunges him into a heavy sleep accompanied by weird visions. His sensations, emotions, and memories, as they pass through his affected mind, are transformed into musical images and ideas. The beloved one herself becomes to him a melody, a recurrent theme (*idée fixe*) which haunts him continually.

I   *Reveries. Passions*

First he remembers that weariness of the soul, that indefinable longing, that sombre melancholia and those objectless joys which he experienced before meeting his beloved. Then, the volcanic love with which she at once inspired him, his delirious suffering, his return to tenderness, his religious consolations.

II   *A Ball*

At a ball, in the midst of a noisy, brilliant fête, he finds his beloved again.

III   *In the Country*

On a summer evening in the country, he hears two herders calling each other with their shepherd melodies. The pastoral duet in such surroundings, the gentle rustle of the trees softly swayed by the wind, some reasons for hope which had come to his knowledge recently — all unite to fill his heart with a rare tranquillity and lend brighter colours to his fancies. But his beloved appears anew, spasms contract his heart, and he is filled with dark premonition. What if she proved faithless? Only one of the shepherds resumes his rustic tune. The sun sets. Far away there is rumbling thunder — solitude — silence.

IV   *March to the Scaffold*

He dreams he has killed his loved one, that he is condemned to death and led to his execution. A march, now gloomy and ferocious, now solemn and brilliant, accompanies the procession. Noisy outbursts are followed without pause by the heavy sound of measured footsteps. Finally, like a last thought of love, the *idée fixe* appears for a moment, to be cut off by the fall of the axe.

V   *Dream of a Witches' Sabbath*

He sees himself at a Witches' Sabbath surrounded by a fearful crowd of spectres, sorcerers, and monsters of every kind, united for his burial. Unearthly sounds, groans, shrieks of laughter, distant cries, to which others seem to respond. The melody of his beloved is heard, but it has lost its character of nobility and reserve. Instead, it is now an ignoble dance tune, trivial and grotesque. It is She who comes to the Sabbath! A shout of joy greets her arrival. She joins the diabolical orgy. The funeral knell, burlesque of the Dies Irae. Dance of the Witches. The dance and the Dies Irae combined.

Berlioz sticks to this programme with remarkable fidelity although obviously the time-scale of an entire symphonic movement is very different from a few lines of bald description.

The first two bars, for wind only, create a mood of quiet melancholy. The violins then give us the first suggestion of the *idée fixe* which permeates the entire work; as yet we are only allowed a glimpse of a small portion of the theme but the seed is planted in our minds. After a series of profoundly expressive phrases with some extremely effective comments from pizzicato double-basses, the mood changes abruptly as the violins launch a rapid ascending scale which elicits an excited reaction in the other strings. In a single bar Berlioz checks this exuberance and returns to the opening mood. An expansive melody (flute, clarinet and horn in unison) leads us back to another premonition of the *idée fixe*, this time accompanied by decorative figures on flute and clarinet. After a virtual disintegration of the music an important theme on the horn seems to summon us to some significant occasion. An extraordinary pair of chords, literally shivering with excitement[1] and followed by rapid palpitations tells us that the beloved approaches. Her arrival brings us the *idée fixe* in its first complete version:

Ex. 2.

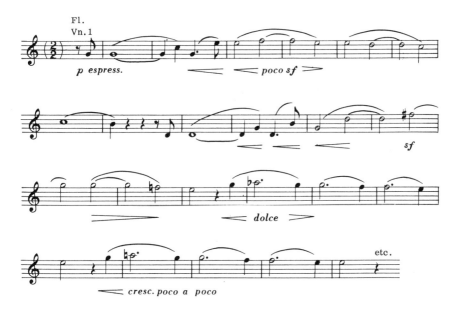

If the tune itself is not amazing, Berlioz's treatment of it is, for instead of under-pinning it with some nice respectable, or even warmly romantic harmony, he gives it a throbbing accompaniment that has the 'pulsations of the steam-engine' of which he wrote. The effect is extraordinary; no living soul could have taught Berlioz to orchestrate or even to harmonise a theme in this way.

Once the theme has been fully stated, the music alternates swiftly between passages of frenzy in the strings and tenderness in the wind; here indeed are the 'delirious sufferings' of which the composer's own introductory note speaks. Even so, he has enough respect for traditional symphonic form to place a double-bar with a 'repeat' sign at the end of the exposition.

[1]The dynamics here are unprecedented in their extreme contrasts: *mf* > *pp* < *ff* — *ppp* in the space of two bars!

The start of the development can be readily identified by a sequential treatment of the first three bars of the *idée fixe* in the lower strings, increasingly distorted as the sequence rises. Soon an extraordinary passage of rising and falling chromatic scales appears, punctuated by loud cries in the woodwind that suggest we are in one of the circles of Dante's Inferno. Three bars of silence (or is it exhaustion?) are broken by a soft note on a solo horn which is greeted with great agitation in the strings. The *idée fixe* returns, this time in the dominant key of G, and given to unison wind covering three octaves. Again the theme provokes an emotional storm which gradually sinks into the darkest regions of the orchestra. At this point an important new theme appears for the first time; it is an expressive oboe solo, the 'return to tenderness' Berlioz mentioned in his introduction. Although the theme itself is new it cannot be separated from the *idée fixe* which persists as a restless counterpoint in violas and cellos. A marvellously sustained crescendo leads to a positively martial version of the beloved's theme, now a veritable Amazon marching in triumph. An *accelerando* with an excitingly striding bass (bassoons and pizzicato double basses) brings us to the ultimate climax of the movement from which there is a gradual disintegration, ending with a sequence of slow sustained chords which are clearly supposed to represent an organ playing. Marked *Religiosamente* they are intended to symbolise 'religious consolation', but after the intense excitements that have gone before, they seem a somewhat perfunctory gesture.

The movement that follows, 'A Ball', is quite properly pure ballet music, beginning with some anticipatory rustlings in the strings and using two harps with notable effect. So far as I know this is the first occasion on which harps were employed in a symphonic score. In due course a deliciously elegant waltz tune appears in the first violins. The orchestration is beautifully economical, the occasional wind chord adding a touch of colour to what is basically a string texture. When the tune is repeated Berlioz shows great ingenuity in handing the 'pom-ching-ching' accompaniment that waltzes demand. With three quavers to dispose of in each bar he gives the first to the strings, the second to the harps, the third to the wind. Only the violins have the tune, but the continually changing colours of the accompaniment give the music a special charm. Three chords from the full wind, horns and strings lead to a sudden change of key (A major – F major) followed by a descending chromatic scale in the cellos. Violins and violas are reduced to a whisper, a tremor of excitement as the *idée fixe* appears on flute and oboe. It is the beloved, waltzing serenely through the assembled company. Clearly she is in the arms of Another since, if we listen to the cellos and basses, we can hear the agitation this vision causes. (The rhythm here is a brilliantly contrived reminder of the throbbing chords which accompanied the *idée fixe* at its first presentation in the opening movement.) As she continues on her way, aloof and unheeding, the waltz theme is divided up between violins and violas, a perfect symbol of the Lover trying to find a path through the weaving pattern of dancers so as to catch a better glimpse of his goddess. A fluttering descent through strings and wind shows his disappointment at not being able to reach her before he is caught up once more in the swirling throng. The waltz continues with continually enriched textures until there is a sudden break, out of which a solo clarinet emerges with a distant version of the *idée fixe*. Does our hero perhaps see his loved one departing in the courtyard below? There is no time for tears as he is swept away in an increasingly animated crowd of dancers.

The third movement is entitled 'Scenes in the Country' and begins with a very evocative duet between oboe and cor anglais, supposedly two shepherds answering each other across the valley. The oboe is required to be played off-stage to give added realism to the scene. To begin with the two instruments are unaccompanied but after several exchanges a barely audible tremor in the violas suggests the threat of rain. There follows a remarkable example of Berlioz' individual approach to orchestration, an extended melody played by flute and first violins in unison without support of harmony. It is a symbol of loneliness, the Lover walking solitary in a deserted landscape. Naturally this extreme economy could not be sustained indefinitely and the texture gradually becomes warmer as the heat of the day makes itself felt. A brief dialogue between the first violins and various individual wind instruments shows our hero listening to the birds. His theme is then taken up by the lower strings while time and again we hear a compact little rhythm (♪♪♪) on the upper woodwind. (Is it a conscious reminder of the quail in the little bird 'cadenza' at the end of the slow movement of Beethoven's Sixth Symphony?)

For some time the music continues in this relaxed outdoor mood when suddenly it is interrupted by a violent shuddering figure on violins and a dramatic outburst from cellos and basses. The woodwind reveal the cause of this emotional disturbance. It is SHE, walking serenely through the fields, as always disregarding the passionate gaze of the onlooker, just as Harriet Smithson on stage playing Ophelia must have disregarded the ardent gaze of Berlioz in the stalls. Indeed the motto of the symphony might well be 'Love unrequited maketh the heart sick'. The Lover's 'reaction' builds to a paroxysm of romantic fervour only to die down in utter dejection as she passes from sight. (Note the extraordinary effectiveness of a single low D flat on cellos expressing a sense of isolation after the impassioned music that preceded it.) Above a gentle pizzicato figure on second violins and violas, a clarinet introduces a new theme which, in time, will prove to be a lyrical counterpoint to the tune originally presented in such simple terms by flute and violins in unison. On this, its second appearance, it has a throbbing accompaniment (the 'pulsating' heart again?) and a sort of *moto perpetuo* in the first violins that is perhaps a symbol of the hero's distraction. The influence of Beethoven is very clear here, though not in the final pages where we hear again the herdsman's pipe (cor anglais only) interspersed with the extraordinary rumbles of thunder already mentioned.

The fourth movement, the 'March to the Scaffold', is an outstanding example of Berlioz' skill as an orchestrator. His demands in this symphony are certainly extravagant — two harps in the second movement only and now extra bassoons, trombones and tubas, cymbals and bass drum. The music of this movement was taken from an early opera of Berlioz, *Les Francs-Juges*. It is possible that the scoring was revised in his maturity, but if not, we should be the more amazed that these extraordinary novel sounds were conceived of in his early twenties when Beethoven was still alive. The opening bars instantly arrest our attention with their menace; two timpani a minor third apart (G–B♭), double basses divided so as to make a four-note chord of G minor, and strange grunts from muted horns low down. A tremendous crescendo from the timpani leads to Theme I, actually a scale of G minor covering two octaves as it descends but so cunningly broken up that we feel it is a genuine melodic line. First stated by cellos and basses in unison, it soon has a descant added by violas (a third higher) and some shrill comments from four bassoons in their upper register. This scale-theme is repeated five times in all with varying counterpoints including, in the fifth version, its own mirror-image.

A rushing scale leads to Theme II, a tremendous march, scored as though for military band. After its first sixteen bars there is a double-bar and an indication that the music should be repeated from the beginning, a gesture towards classical convention that is often disregarded. Shortly after the repeat we find the extraordinary fragmented version of Theme I shown in Ex (1); it is hammered into extinction by the timpani, rising through the four notes G, B flat, D, F and ushering in the return of Theme II. This time the strings are also involved, the violins exchanging a swift and compact little figure which surely represents banners fluttering in the procession. Again Theme I appears in its fragmented version before being transferred to the heavy brass with a flailing motive in the strings that suggests the driver of the tumbril laying about him with a whip to beat off the crowd. Theme I appears in its most massive version yet, punctuated with explosive accents from cymbals and bass drum. An all-pervading dotted rhythm brings increased urgency as the scaffold is sighted. Suddenly, after a series of startling shifts of key (D flat major alternating with G minor), a solo clarinet sings out the first seven notes of the *idée fixe*. The effect is startling, like a sudden close-up in a film, showing the hero's anguished face, his last thought of his beloved before, with a huge crash, the blade of the guillotine falls. Berlioz even depicts the head bouncing across the floor of the scaffold with three pizzicato thuds from the strings. A roar from the crowd (three timpani and side-drum) greets the grisly spectacle, and relentlessly repeated chords bring the movement to an end.

In his original plan for the symphony the finale was intended to be 'a vision of a night of revelry'. In the event it is perhaps fortunate for us that Berlioz turned (temporarily!) against his beloved Harriet on hearing rumours that her behaviour back in London was less than exemplary. (They still had not met.) Deciding to turn her into a witch he composed one of the most astonishing movements in the whole nineteenth-century repertoire, the 'Dream of a Witches' Sabbath'.

It begins with a high shimmering chord in which the upper strings are divided into eight parts while ominous stirrings in the basses suggest the dead moving uneasily in their graves. Unmistakably we hear the flapping of great wings as the witches fly in to the cemetary of a ruined church. There was no precedent for the sounds Berlioz creates in this macabre fantasy; it is, to the nineteenth century, what 'The Rite of Spring' was to the twentieth. Distant fanfares tell us that the leader of the witches is approaching; timpani suggest the sound of a horse's hooves cantering up the path. Grotesquely distorted, we hear the *idée fixe* on a shrill clarinet; it is indeed a nightmare for now the beloved has become a hag, capable of infinite evil. Her arrival is greeted by a great bellowing from the assembled coven. Triumphantly she rides round the graveyard, bassoons cackling their approval and enjoyment. Orchestral bedlam breaks out until there is a sudden hush of expectancy. Cellos and basses take us down into the darkness. Bells ring out from the church tower, eliciting an instant response from one group (violas) which is repressed by a sharp command. Again the bells ring, again the response is checked. It is not yet time to begin the ritual dance; first must come the blasphemy, the perversion of the great Gregorian chant, the *Dies Irae*. First heard on tubas against the irregular clangour of the bells, it is passed on to horns and trombones and then to wind and pizzicato strings, each version seeming more profane than the last. Although the musical content may not be exceptional, the sheer inventiveness of the orchestration is constantly amazing. (It was written thirty-seven years before Moussorgsky's 'Night on a Bare Mountain'.)

At last the Witches' Dance begins, using the theme which had previously been suppressed several times. It is almost disappointing to find it being organised on fugal lines, though violent syncopated interruptions from the brass seem to mock its formality. Academic pretensions are soon forgotten as the music grows increasingly wild. Swift pairs of notes, falling by semitones, suggest cackles of malevolent laughter while, at one point, there is a mysterious descent into the lowest regions of the orchestra and a reappearance of the *Dies Irae*, distant and sinister. A skilfully planned ascent over a long-sustained roll on the bass drum leads to the thematic climax of the movement in which the 'Round Dance' in the strings is combined with the *Dies Irae* in brass and wind.

An extraordinary effect of violins and violas playing *col legno* (bouncing the wood of the bow on the string) leads to the weirdest of all the versions of the 'Round Dance' — woodwind in unison with trills on every principal note.

Once again we hear tubas playing the *Dies Irae* against a series of feverish convulsions in the strings — *pp* to *ff* and back in each bar. The tempo quickens and the movement ends with a touch of banality that is forgivable after the stunning originality that has been evident on nearly every page. Regardless of its subject matter this truly is a Fantastic Symphony, a work of daring that scarcely has a parallel. Had it been written at the end of the century it might seem less astonishing to us now; placed in its historical context it must be regarded as altogether outstanding.

BRAHMS

1833–97

By any standard Brahms had a strange childhood. His father was a double-bass and horn player employed in the Municipal Theatre in Hamburg; his mother, seventeen years older than her husband, was slightly crippled and shrewish of tongue. Money was short with three children to bring up so the young Brahms was expected to earn something towards the family expenses from an early age. One way was to turn out arrangements of popular songs of the day; amazingly, over 150 such potboilers were published while he was still in his 'teens, though he had the good sense to use two pseudonyms, 'G.W. Marks' and 'Karl Würth'. The other way in which he contributed to the family budget was by playing the piano of an evening in a harbour-front brothel. He was an extremely good-looking boy, and the tavern tarts delighted in teasing him. The experience was to have a deep effect upon him psychologically, particularly with regard to his relations to women; indeed, he seems to have been unable to become involved in any deeply emotional (or physical) way with what would have been regarded as a respectable woman, and consorted with prostitutes for all his adult life. It is possible that the disturbing environment of those formative years caused puberty to have been astonishingly delayed in his case. Although we always think of him as heavily bearded, he had no need to shave until he was twenty-four, nor did his voice break until then. In fact it remained unnaturally high-pitched all his life and he schooled himself to adopt an artificially gruff and husky tone so as not to be laughed at.

It does not need a trained psychologist to realise that here we have the perfect recipe for a massive sense of insecurity. However this isn't all, for we have to add the relationship he had with Clara Schumann. As a young man, Brahms idolised Schumann, receiving much needed encouragement and help from the already failing composer. To witness Schumann's gradual deterioration into insanity was intensely painful to him, the more so as he had to share his distress with Clara. There is no real evidence that he and Clara ever had an affair, but he felt a deep affection for her that was to endure for the rest of his life. No doubt he would have regarded the thought of any sexual involvement with her with horror; even the idea would have filled him with guilt.

These aspects of Brahms's life as an adolescent and as a young man are enough to suggest that in his inner self he must have had alarming doubts about his virility — the unbroken voice, the lack of facial hair, the instinctive withdrawal from respectable women, plus the moral barrier that separated him from Clara, the only woman to whom he was drawn. Since she was older than him, he was able to turn her into a surrogate mother, thereby giving added strength to the image of her as untouchable. Their artistic friendship endured for nearly forty years, and it was to her that he would always turn for advice on any newly-completed composition.

His first major works, clearly made to measure for his own style of performance, were three massive piano sonatas — Opp. 1, 2 and 5. Each begins in a grandiose and physically assertive manner, calculated to impress the listener by sheer force. It would appear that precisely because he was afflicted with doubts about his masculinity Brahms felt he must prove, if only through his music, that he was a real man, indeed a superman. It is in the Third Sonata that we first sense his symphonic aspirations. Much of the music sounds more like an orchestral transcription than a piano work, most obviously so in the fourth movement (of five), the so-called Intermezzo. There is hardly a bar that does not suggest orchestral colouring; clearly his thoughts were turning towards the symphony as a medium, and it is no surprise that he soon began to sketch one out. Because he lacked confidence in his ability to handle the full orchestra, he initially arranged it for two pianos so that he could hear its effect. The result was unsatisfactory and he couldn't see how to transfer some of the essentially pianistic sounds into orchestral textures. A compromise was reached; he would turn it into a piano concerto. And so, after much travail, the great D minor Concerto emerged. It could hardly have been more disastrous for a composer whose self-confidence needed every buttress it could acquire for support. When Brahms showed the score to his great friend Joachim, the renowned violinist laughed out loud. 'My dear friend' he said, 'you simply can't orchestrate like that. It won't come off.'

If Joachim's reaction was painful to Brahms, the first performance was even more so. Both in Hanover and Leipzig, the concerto was received with no more than a spatter of applause, accompanied by actual hissing from the audience. Brahms was not even given the credit for being a fine pianist, which one needs to be to play this awkwardly written work. The experience scarred him deeply, and during the ensuing years he turned to chamber-music and songs, as well as taking on such undemanding hack-work as the conductorship of a ladies' choir. If he had felt insecure before, his loss of confidence must now have become a serious handicap. His response was characteristic of the man. The list of piano works subsequent to the First Piano Concerto (which was Op. 15) includes Op. 21 No. 1, Eleven variations on an original theme,

Op. 21 No. 2, Thirteen variations on a Hungarian song, Op. 24, Twenty-five variations and fugue on a theme by Handel, Op. 35, Twenty-eight variations on a theme by Paganini (Books 1 and 2).[1]

It is here that psychological considerations provide a useful clue. I have suggested that the first three sonatas were assertions of virility that Brahms felt he had to make. Then came the concerto whose catastrophic failure must have destroyed what confidence he had managed to build up.

The variations were designed to develop his technique as a composer, the beauty of the form being that it provides a constant prop in the structure of the theme itself, its shape of phrase, its sequence of harmonies, and so on. Even in the variations though, there are still times when one feels he is hankering after an orchestra. The Paganini Variations show a particularly determined effort to cure himself of this tendency, their purpose being to explore every facet of piano technique.

It was with such writing that Brahms banished the orchestra from his keyboard, yet still there were problems of insecurity. Even the Piano Quintet caused him considerable heart-searching. It started life as a string quintet, then became a sonata for two pianos before finally emerging in the form we know it today. No other major composer went through comparable periods of indecision. Beethoven might mull over a work for a long period but at least he knew what it was destined to be. Brahms took more than half a lifetime to gain absolute confidence in his abilities, and even then we find traces of insecurity in the self-deprecating little jokes he would make to Clara Schumann when he sent her a new composition. They give evidence of a longing for reassurance. He didn't even rate himself all that highly as a composer; he once equated himself with Cherubini, and on another occasion was heard to remark that he'd give all his compositions just to have been able to write Mendelssohn's Hebrides Overture.

His First Symphony was kept as a secret preoccupation for many years. When he was twenty-nine he sent a first movement (without the slow introduction) to Clara Schumann. Despite her encouragement progress with the remainder was disturbingly slow; even when three movements had been completed he waited for more than ten years before tackling the finale. 'I shall never write a symphony', he confided to a friend in 1870; 'you don't know what it feels like to be dogged by that giant Beethoven.' Not until he was forty-three was the symphony completed, although even then the composer had reservations, making alterations to the two central movements up to the last minute. However, the psychological block which had caused the birth-pangs of the symphony to be spread over nearly twenty years had been broken down and the Second Symphony followed remarkably soon after the First. Once the barrier had been removed a spate of works followed, four

---

[1]The Sixteen Variations on a theme by Schumann (Op. 9) were written during the period when he was first working on the concerto.

symphonies in all, a second piano concerto, the violin concerto and the Double Concerto for violin, cello and orchestra. Even his relationships with the opposite sex became easier and he derived much pleasure from a warm friendship with a young singer called Hermine Spies who became his favourite interpreter of the Alto Rhapsody. The Third Symphony was written in the year that he met her, 1883, and it seems likely that the happiness she brought him made composition a less daunting task than it had ever been before.

Symphony No. 1 in C Minor
Op. 68

On 1 July 1862, Clara Schumann wrote to Joachim, 'What do you think Johannes sent me recently? The first movement of a Symphony which begins boldly like this . . .' She then jotted down the opening phrase of the Allegro which in the ultimate version emerges from a solemn introduction lasting thirty-seven bars. It is clear then that the introduction was an afterthought, though one in which Brahms skilfully planted materials from which the subsequent allegro seems to grow. The first great arch of sound in this work is tied down to a constantly reiterated C from double-basses and timpani. Violins and cellos climb laboriously upward by narrow intervals while the woodwind and violas move chromatically in the opposite direction; there is a feeling that both lines are striving to escape from the fetters created by the unyielding bass. Release comes through a trill that resolves on to the dominant (bar 9). At once the mood changes with wide-spaced intervals in the wind that are given a little rhythmic pulse by pizzicato quavers in the strings. At the time the phrase seems insecure, as though groping its way, but it is destined to become a gesture of immense power when it reappears in the allegro. A third element in the introduction is easily recognised since it is played by strings in unison, a somewhat bleak version of the notes that comprise the chord of C minor (C–E♭–G) but with the key-note C conspicuously absent. Although it may appear to be of minor importance, it proves to be the seed from which the main theme of the movement grows. The opening arch returns, this time anchored to the dominant (G); cut short after a mere four bars, it is replaced by a brief oboe solo whose wandering path is almost immediately followed by the cellos.

A sudden accent, explosive as a starter's pistol, launches us into the allegro. Although the music is severe in character it has considerable energy, the motive power often being provided by repeated-note triplets that may be a subconscious reference to Beethoven's Fifth Symphony, also in C minor. Strongly accented chords on the secondary beats lead to a fragmentation of the music, its initial ferocity gradually tamed as the strings change from *arco* (bowed) to pizzicato. Two falling fifths — horn solo followed by woodwind — bring us to the second subject group. As if especially aware of the problem of controlling a large-scale symphonic movement, Brahms takes great pains to establish a 'family' relationship between first and second subjects. Thus we find an ascending phrase in the woodwind that is nearly a mirror-image of the *descending* phrase from the very opening bars; beneath it, the cellos offer not the bleak version of a C minor chord we found in the introduction, but a comparable pattern made up from the notes comprising E flat major — though again the critical key-note (E flat) is omitted. The true second subject is an oboe solo which develops into an expressive little dialogue with a clarinet. Against hushed string chords a solo horn suggests an alternative to these caressing phrases which, in due course, is accepted by flute and clarinet; the music comes virtually to a halt.

Violas arrest our attention with a terse phrase of three descending quavers (G♭–F–E♭), quickly taken up by the other strings and developing into a major storm:

Ex. 1

The relevance of this seemingly new idea is shown in the bass, which is an inversion of the main theme. The conflict continues with a reversal of roles as violins and cellos exchange themes. Fierce reiterations of the falling third G♭–E♭ suggest that the exposition is going to end in the unorthodox key of E flat minor but a last minute switch brings us back to C, enabling Brahms to observe the classical convention of a repeat of the allegro section. The second time round the 'switch' takes us to an unexpected B natural and the development begins surprisingly in B major. As before, the common chord theme is notable for its omission of the actual key-note B, the repeated emphasis on D♯–F♯ giving a curious austerity to the music despite its forceful character. This rising third (D♯–F♯) proves to be a significant factor in the development once a solo bassoon (supported by the violas) has slowed it down. A relatively static section follows, only to be interrupted by the ominous three-note pattern in the violas which generates a similar struggle to the one shown in Ex. 1 with the inverted main theme broadened and extended. The forward impetus of the music is checked by a majestic new theme whose expansive phrases are laid out as a dialogue between wind and strings. By giving the illusion of a slower tempo it prepares the way for a number of references to the very opening material of the symphony, a signal that the orthodox recapitulation is within reach. It is a haven that is only attained after a passage of considerable turbulence in the strings.

Conservative as he was by nature, Brahms observes the classic convention of the recapitulation with almost academic punctiliousness and the attentive listener should have no difficulty in following the course of events.

Only in the closing pages are there some surprises when an especially violent outburst leads to a gradual lessening of tension. The final bars are clearly related to the introduction, but the main theme makes its last appearance with the missing key-note (C) now put into place, bringing with it a release into C major and a peaceful cadence.

The second movement, *Andante sostenuto*, shows Brahms at his most lyrical even though the scale is essentially symphonic. The key, E major, follows a famous precedent established in Beethoven's Piano Concerto No. 3 in C minor. Despite the major tonality there is a tinge of melancholy to the music revealed by a tendency to dwell on a flattened third (G natural) at certain points. Such shadows are dispersed by a glorious theme for solo oboe that first appears in bar 17. Once it has run its course the first violins embark on a more floridly decorated melody beneath which second violins and violas weave a contrapuntal imitation. A long sustained note on the oboe introduces yet another idea which is developed further by a clarinet and even commented on by cellos and basses. The relevance of this episode is to be found in the accompaniment, a sequence of gently syncopated chords in the strings whose pattern is derived from the very opening notes of the movement.

Something of a climax is reached when all the strings in unison take up the oboe's second theme beneath a sustained G sharp in the woodwind. A sort of disintegration ensues with four-note fragments passed from wind to strings and back again followed by a sequence of overlapping phrases which succeed in knitting the texture together again. For the first time in the movement we hear the timpani, its quiet rumble heralding the reprise of the opening subject, now in the wind and decorated expressively by unison violins and violas. At last the long-awaited moment arrives, the re-appearance of the sublime oboe melody, supported by the unlikely but effective combination of a solo violin and the first horn. The closing pages of the movement provide an unusual ending that momentarily suggests a sketch for a violin concerto. Did Brahms hope thereby to tempt Joachim to lead the orchestra? The thought is pure speculation but the great violinist did conduct the work in Cambridge a mere four months after the first performance.

A strange feature of the Brahms symphonies is that only in the Fourth is there a true scherzo. In avoiding the conventional display of high-spirited bustle he laid himself open to some criticism and his friend Hermann Levi, a conductor of repute, told Clara that he felt the two central movements of this symphony were more suited to a Serenade. Marked '*Un poco Allegretto e grazioso*', the third movement begins with a gentle tune on the clarinet with little but pizzicato cellos by way of support. The tune is intriguingly constructed from two five-bar phrases, the second of which is an exact inversion of the first. It is followed by a secondary theme scored for a fuller woodwind section featuring descending chains of thirds in a lilting rhythm. The first violins then take over the clarinet's original theme, eliciting a delightful comment from that instrument as they do so.

A modulation to F minor leads to a slight disturbance of the tranquil mood; the strings set up a restless accompanying figure while clarinet and flute in turn introduce a rather more angular melody which is nevertheless shown to be a relative of the initial theme, even if the point is made rather hastily. The disturbance is brief, although it leaves a few ripples beneath the solo clarinet's reprise of the original tune. Suddenly the mood changes completely. A D sharp thrice repeated on unison wind sounds the signal that leads into a Beethoven-like section that is truly symphonic in character. Using only the most concise ideas — repeated notes, fragmented chords — it builds to a considerable climax in which horns and trumpets play a conspicuous part. The whole section is designed to be repeated before the original clarinet tune reappears in the most ingratiating manner. The opening material is reappraised (with some deliciously subtle alterations) before Brahms quietly folds the movement away with a tender reference to the middle section.

The finale is far and away the most substantial movement of the four with an introduction of striking originality. It is an Adagio in Brahms's most sombre mood in which, as in the first movement's opening pages, we catch frustrating glimpses of events to come while as yet remaining unaware of their full significance. For instance, the very first phrase we hear on the violins is a tragically distorted version of the noble tune which ultimately emerges out of the gloom. The broad sweep of the opening bars is interrupted by a strangely breathless figure on pizzicato strings which grows increasingly urgent only to be checked by a return to the darkly brooding opening. Again the pizzicato strings begin their disjointed patterns; this time their flight is more precipitate, leading to a series of swirling figures that flare up to a peak before falling in scattered fragments. With ever-growing intensity the woodwind repeat a three-note phrase E$\flat$–D–C), evoking a thunderous response from the timpani. There is a sudden calm as with great solemnity a solo horn declaims a bell-like theme whose opening three notes are directly derived from the almost hysterical three-note phrases that immediately preceded it. The theme is repeated by a solo flute supported (as was the horn) by tremolando strings. Trombones and bassoons then intone a chorale-like theme which is destined to make an impressive re-appearance towards the very end of the symphony. Again the bell-like tones of the horn theme ring out, their sounds overlapping as bells do. The echoes die away; there is a pause. Then, richly glowing, the great C major tune makes its long-deferred entry, launching the finale on its proper course. Majestic and noble though the tune may be, Brahms does not allow himself to be so carried away by it that he forgets he is writing a symphonic movement, not a rhapsody. The music is tautly constructed according to the precepts of sonata form. Interestingly enough the most fruitful source of development proves to be the second, third and fourth notes of the tune, C–B–C, a concentrated three-note motive whose shape exactly corresponds with the predominant idea of the first movement of the Second Symphony (D–C♯–D).

Once Brahms breaks away from the big C major tune he pitches us into a stormy episode whose semiquaver figuration is derived from the swirling passages that flared up so dramatically in the introduction. As if to confirm this, the flute reintroduces the bell theme, a quotation which is verified by the third horn. The strings now introduce the joyously animated second subject, although its playful mood is soon replaced by a slightly tortuous theme on the oboe that causes considerable perturbation in the strings. A secondary theme on the oboe (dotted crotchets and quavers) can be traced back to the introduction (bar 22), while there may possibly be an allusion to the graceful third movement though it cannot be proved (bars 160–3). Even the ghostly pizzicato passages find a place in the main movement and one can only marvel at Brahms's skill in incorporating all the elements of the introduction into a movement so different in character.

The final Coda is taken at a brisker pace, turning the initially dignified C–B–C of the opening tune into a headlong gallop. Suddenly, and it is surely one of the greatest moments in the symphony, the chorale-like theme from the introduction blazes forth on full brass and strings. Is it perhaps a symbol of victory, a symbol that Brahms had at last conquered the destructive demon of insecurity that for so long had delayed the completion of the work? Perhaps so, for all doubts are certainly banished in the exultant final pages.

Symphony No. 2 in D Major
Op. 73

Brahms began work on this symphony in the summer of 1877; he was staying at one of his favourite resorts, Pörtschach on the Wörthersee, and the idyllic situation seems to be reflected in the relaxed and pastoral mood of this lyrical work. The first movement in particular displays a rare combination of melodic beauty and technical craftsmanship; what seems like spontaneous inspiration straight from the heart is seen on closer examination to be rigorously controlled. The very first page proves to be a rich mine of material; it is shown, reduced to the bare bones, in Ex. 1 on page 132. To the listener this may sound like a continuous melody, discreetly nudged forward by an unassuming bass; to Brahms is is an assembly of fragments each with a potential of its own. The least interesting, 'a' is the most fruitful and in the

Ex. 1

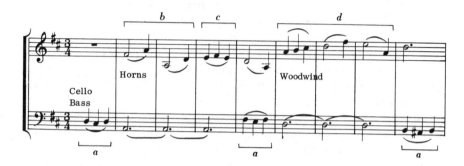

first seventy bars alone this three–note pattern appears more than thirty times in a variety of guises.[2]

The opening phrases suggest an outdoor scene, scored as they are for horns and woodwind alternately. The violins enter almost unnoticed, but once they have risen above the wind they begin a long meandering descent which trails away into silence. A quiet roll on the timpani suggesting distant thunder is followed by three sombre chords on trombones whose potential threat is lifted by gentle reminders of 'a' from the woodwind. The third of these fragments elongates the three–note phrase so that each note is given two beats instead of one (A–G#–A). Then, like a warm ray of sunshine, the violins introduce a free flowing melody whose initial notes are a *compressed* version of 'a'. As the accompanying textures grow richer a solo flute happily copies the violins, extending the tune to new heights. Soon, like buds bursting into flower in the sunlight, fragments based on 'a' crop up in bar after bar until it triumphantly establishes itself again as three crotchets, either in violins or cellos. The climax is short–lived, though it is worth pointing out how changed in character 'a' becomes when it is treated like this:

Ex. 2

This concentrated version of 'a', initially so forbidding, dissolves into a sequence of enchanting musical chuckles on oboes and horns. A richly harmonised string passage modulates smoothly into F sharp minor, the key

[2]It is directly comparable to the three–note pattern C—B—C which plays so important a part in the finale of the First Symphony.

of the second subject. This is beautifully scored for violas and cellos, singing in thirds like a male-voice choir but with the cellos taking the upper part. Meanwhile the violins offer a gracefully drooping accompaniment whose pattern has already appeared a number of times. It is directly derived from the horn theme 'b', again using a compressed version. After some affecting sighs, not to be taken as expressions of true grief, the second subject is taken over by the woodwind and extended in a new direction. With very little warning there is a violent change of mood, a leaping athletic theme in the strings whose jagged dotted rhythm Brahms was to use again to dramatic effect in his violin concerto. The music grows even more turbulent as this taut new rhythm takes hold:

Ex. 3

Each compact three-note unit is based directly on 'a', a truly ingenious example of symphonic development. Soon, as though tumbling over itself, the rhythm becomes syncopated (♫♫♫), creating a curious tension; cellos and violins in canon begin an emphatic dialogue whose seemingly new theme is derived from the first three notes of 'd'. After the biggest climax so far there is a sudden recession of tone as the second subject reappears, this time with violas taking the upper line. A solo flute provides a decorative *obbligato* in a triplet rhythm which is later appropriated by the first violins. It is yet another derivation from 'a'. Leisurely descending scales bring the exposition to a close.

For approximately 180 bars Brahms has confined his interest almost entirely to the potential of 'a' and 'b', apart from the second subject which has the right to be independent. In the development section he devotes greater attention to 'c' and 'd' although, wisely, he reminds us of the opening theme by giving it to a solo horn in the strikingly novel key of F major. At once an oboe seizes on the single bar 'c' and extends it threefold in a descending sequence. It is an idea that spreads with increasing force through the orchestra. Boldly the first violins propose that the neglected phrase 'd' would make an admirable fugue subject, the more so if it is transposed into the minor. The fugue is taken up with some severity until its progress is interrupted by strident trombones bringing an unusually violent reminder of 'a'. Three-note fragment though it may be, it generates a powerful conflict in which brass and wind insist that our proper concern should be 'b' while the strings emphasise with some passion that it should be 'a' — at twice its normal speed. A detailed analysis of the ensuing section would take several pages and a number of musical quotations but it provides an outstanding example of the way in which 'great oaks from little acorns grow'. There is hardly a single bar in which there is not an allusion to 'a', 'b', 'c' or 'd' in some form though the greatest climax of all comes with a massive unison reference to 'b' (strings and trombones) over a thunderous drum roll accompanied by majestic chords on woodwind and horns. A slow descent on flute and clarinet leads us to the recapitulation, newly orchestrated and delicately embroidered by smoothly flowing string passages. Although the music follows a very similar course to that of the exposition it is full of new details that show that Brahms regarded this part of the movement as much more than a mere convention. The first major surprise is the far earlier appearance of the second subject; the second is the wonderful extension of 'c' on a solo horn that leads by an ingeniously devious route to the Coda. This recaptures the relaxed mood of the opening but in even more lyrical terms; the horn-theme ('b' + 'c') is now given to the first violins who expand it considerably until their 'dying fall' suggests that the final cadence is near. It is at this point that Brahms produces the most beguiling surprise as, with a delicately playful touch, the woodwind recall the chuckling phrase that originally preceded the second subject. Even at this late stage we find new treatments of 'a', notably an almost breathless version of off-beat quavers. The movement ends as quietly as it began, 523 bars which, apart from the second subject, have grown almost entirely from four frag-mentary ideas on page one.

At first hearing the slow movement — *Adagio non troppo* — is the hardest to grasp, its form being too episodic to fall into a neat category. The most significant of its four main themes is stated by the cellos at the very beginning and deserves to be quoted at some length:

Ex. 4

Against this expressive theme the bassoons have a somewhat lugubrious counter-theme based on an ascending scale. In the twelfth bar the violins take over the cello theme while the cellos give their greater warmth to the bassoons' rising phrase. Soon a solitary horn begins what seems to be a completely new idea though it is actually derived from the notes marked with a cross in the example above. It appears as if it is going to develop into a short fugue as first the oboes then the cellos take up the idea, but the strings re-establish the latter part of the original cello theme, lifting it to a lyrical climax. Suddenly mood and tone-colour change as the upper woodwind introduce a gently syncopated melody in the dominant key of F sharp major. It is a brief episode, delicately handled. Surprisingly it breaks off in mid-phrase, allowing the strings to intervene with the third main idea, easily recognised by its stepwise movement up the first four notes of the scale. While accepting it in principle, the woodwind change its character completely by putting it into the minor, bringing a restless and disturbed reaction from the violas and cellos. A minor storm develops, ultimately quelled by a return to Theme I. With many variants Brahms continues to explore its possibilities (as well as those of the fugal idea) until trumpets and horns in unison sound an alarm. Reinforced by trombones and timpani, the first violins embark on an energetic figure which proves to be a variation on bar 3 of the original theme. An uneasy peace is restored by recourse to the third theme. Then, after a strange sigh from the strings, the first theme reappears in the woodwind choir, giving it a completely new tone-colour. Sadly the strings fold the tune away and the movement ends with three simple chords of B major.

The third movement is one of the most popular orchestral pieces Brahms ever wrote; indeed an instant repeat was demanded by the audiences at a number of the earliest performances. Although slightly more than half of its 240 bars are marked '*presto ma non assai*' the abiding impression that remains is of the gentle *allegretto* with which it begins and ends. The form is a Brahms invention, an intriguing combination of a rondo, a set of variations and an inversion of the classical Scherzo and Trio. The first impression is that it follows the design the textbooks would call A B A C A; this would make it a rondo with two contrasting episodes. However we do not have to listen too carefully to realise that B and C are both variations on A which puts the movement into the second category. As for the traditional concept of Scherzo and Trio it became (in Beethoven's hands) a pattern of quick-slower-quick-slower-quick. Brahms ingeniously reversed this so that it became slow-quicker-slow-quicker-slow.

The movement begins with an enchanting theme on the oboe accompanied, serenade-style, by cellos posing as guitars. Violins and violas abstain from joining in; but when they do come in they change the mood entirely. Swiftly and delicately they initiate a fairy dance that Mendelssohn himself could not have bettered. It is based on the framework of the oboe theme even though the pulse is a quick two in a bar instead of a leisurely three. A sudden raucous outburst with strongly marked dotted rhythms may seem to be a new idea but Brahms surely regarded it as a free inversion of the original tune. A delightful chromatic descent through second violins and violas guides us

down to the realm of the cellos where, once again, the 'fairy' music reappears.
Themes are tossed swiftly to and fro between strings and wind until four
calming chords from oboes, bassoons and horns check their flight. As though
the whole brief episode had been a fitful dream, the oboe brings back Theme
I, beautifully reharmonised. Unison strings seem to offer a mild rebuke,
establishing a more serious mood. Their frowns have little effect and within
moments there is a quick scatter of notes leading to a delightfully syncopated
theme in the woodwind. It is a subtle refinement of the raucous episode that
occurred earlier. The strings rough it up a little, causing a chattering response
from the clarinets and bassoons; then, to our delight, second violins and
violas once again send the music skipping down to the cellos. Unmistakably
they produce a tiptoe variation on the original theme which clearly has never
been far from Brahms's thoughts. Its reappearance, scored sweetly for strings,
is in the surprisingly 'wrong' key of F sharp major, an error which is
amusingly queried by the woodwind before it is blandly rectified. Once the
tune is reinstated on the oboe doubts creep in and the music shows a fleeting
desire to go into G minor. This allows the violins to produce a meltingly
beautiful phrase which Brahms may unwittingly have lifted from the slow
movement of Mozart's Piano Concerto in A, K 488. The closing bars are the
perfect musical equivalent to Shakespeare's

> '. . . Parting is such sweet sorrow
> That I shall say good-night till it be morrow.'

As if reluctant to break the spell, Brahms begins the finale in a whisper,
the string parts all being marked *sotto voce* (in an undertone). The movement
is a remarkably elaborate version of sonata form in which the themes are
treated with great ingenuity. The first subject is in two sections, the second
being an extension of the first. Note how the falling fourths in bars 5–6
provide a pattern for the start of the second part of the theme:

Ex. 5

p sotto voce

(second part)

The opening phrases die down mysteriously; there is a moment's
silence. Then, with a calculated shock that would have delighted Beethoven,

the full orchestra jubilantly takes up the refrain, extending it with immense energy. Notice how the first bar of the theme is contracted into a concise little group of four quavers (D C♯ D F♯), a usefully flexible pattern which can be made to serve many purposes. After sixty bars a solo clarinet emerges with a calming theme which is taken over by flute and oboe in turn while the strings continue to chatter excitedly about the four-quaver group based on bar 1. A pizzicato arpeggio rising and falling through more than two octaves heralds the arrival of the Second Subject, a broad flowing tune in which violins and violas can revel. Not to be denied, the woodwind choir abscond with it, an action which leads to a rather stormy transformation. Soon a new development makes a strong impression, though it is still a legitimate offspring of bar 1 of the opening tune:

Ex. 5a

The running scales at the end of this example spread like a galloping infection through the woodwind until their exuberance is cut short by some powerful off-beat chords. A brief but exciting episode using a 'Scots snap' rhythm follows. Quite unexpectedly Theme I reappears in its original form, marking the start of the development. (It has been pointed out that the plan of this movement has many points of similarity with the finale of Haydn's 'London' Symphony.)

The first stages of the development are typical of Brahms as he cuts the theme into smaller units which are juggled between the various sections of the orchestra. Turning the theme on its head raises some interesting possibilities, as does a very choppy treatment of the second strand of the theme. Trombones reinforce a substantial climax after which there is a sudden change of mood. A solo flute, accompanied by soft clarinets and a bassoon, introduces what seems to be a new idea. However, a little thought shows us that it is closely related to the opening theme of the movement:

Ex. 6

After this has been exchanged several times between wind and strings, the oboe reminds us of the second part of the opening theme (see p. 136) in the remote key of B flat minor. The forward impulse of the music seems to slacken as we come to a mysterious section in which flute, clarinet and trombone in unison proffer a slow-motion version of the same quotation, causing it to sound not unlike a melancholy rendering of Big Ben's famous chimes. A circling phrase for strings and flute over a quiet drum-roll brings us to the recapitulation. Although all of the material is clearly recognisable, there are a number of subtle changes as well as some shortening of links.

So far, the trombones and tuba have had little of importance to do, but at the start of the Coda they make their presence felt with a richly harmonised variation on the second subject, changing key rapidly from D minor to C major and then to B flat. Three giant chords lead to a sudden recession of tone. A version of the second subject growls away in the bass with Ex. 6 providing an artful counterpoint. The music builds in volume and excitement until a sequence of descending scales in the heavy brass makes us think of a peal of bells. Horns and trumpets make a jubilant fanfare out of the second subject and the movement ends in a blaze of glory. Since the three previous movements each ended quietly this final climax seems all the greater in its effect.

Whenever Brahms felt genuinely pleased with a work he had a habit of making deprecatory remarks about it. On sending the manuscript of this symphony to his publisher he wrote that it was so mournful that it would have to be printed on black-edged paper. To those who knew him such a remark would reveal the special pleasure that comes with the knowledge of a job well done.

Symphony No. 3 in F Major
Op. 90

A gap of five-and-a-half years separates the Third Symphony from the Second, a period of great productivity which saw the birth of a number of important works including the Violin Concerto, the Second Piano Concerto, two orchestral overtures, some chamber works, a dozen songs and two compositions for choir and orchestra. Thirty years before the symphony was completed Brahms had written a scherzo for violin and piano as part of a musical curiosity, a sonata whose other two movements were composed by Schumann and a pupil of his named Dietrich. The sonata was written as a surprise gift for the great violinist Joachim and was inscribed 'F.A.E.', an abbreviation of '*Frei aber einsam*' (free but solitary), a motto which Joachim had adopted as his private philosophy. Brahms at twenty found this unduly misanthropic and adapted it to F.A.F. — '*Frei aber froh*' (free but happy). The relevance of this youthful word-play becomes apparent when we realise that the dominant motif of the Third Symphony is F–A (flat)–F. While the point has often been made, I have yet to read a commentary that admitted that the note A flat in German notation is not A but 'As'. While I accept that the musical motto is significant as a kind of signature, it is my belief that experience had taught Brahms that freedom and happiness did not necessarily go together; the optimistic outlook of the young lion setting out to conquer the world had been replaced by disillusionment and an inner sorrow caused no doubt by his inability to establish an emotionally satisfying relationship with the opposite sex. The F *major* conjunction of the notes F A F was therefore replaced by the F *minor* conjunction F A♭ F. Furthermore, the phrase 'Free *but* happy' carries the implication that happiness is to be achieved *in spite of* rather than *because of* freedom. It is worth pointing out that throughout the first movement the essential major element in the splendidly heroic opening theme (the third of the scale) is 'flatly' contradicted by a determined *minor* third in the bass. Only in the final phrase of the movement is this conflict resolved, a symbol indeed that Brahms had come to terms with life.

> I would know my shadow and my light,
> So shall I at last be whole.
>
> (Tippett: *A Child of our Time.*)

Although the original manuscript was finished in 1883, Brahms was not too proud to make a number of small revisions to the orchestration once he had heard the work played. The symphony is the shortest of the four and it is very possible that the two middle movements were originally planned as incidental music to a dramatised version of Goethe's *Faust*. Woodwind and brass begin the first movement with three massive chords spelling out the F–A♭–F motto theme. The third chord is cut off short and synchronised with what appears to be the start of the first subject, a heroic and passionate tune on violins. Listen, though, to the double-basses, bass trombone and contra-bassoon for it is in their dark regions that you will find the motto; indeed it appears five times in the first twelve bars, ranging through the whole compass of the orchestra. A quiet reiteration of four F naturals in the rhythm ♩ ♩ ♩ ♩ ushers in a more relaxed interlude, but in a moment the motto returns, passing from the lower strings to wind and violins and newly harmonised. More repeated notes bring an extension of the interlude followed by a gradual easing of tension. A solo clarinet presents the second subject in the unorthodox key of A major. It is a wayward little tune whose individuality is emphasised by a change of pulse from two-in-a-bar to three. It has a companion, easily recognised by the two detached notes which precede its supple curves, like a delicately pointed toe beating time to the music. As the music dies down to a hushed pianissimo a solo oboe reintroduces the motto, now transposed to A C A. Violins, pizzicato, dissect this into its component parts while descending arpeggio figures in the wind begin to create quite a commotion. The ear is easily drawn to swift flowing quavers in flute, violins and bassoon but meanwhile clarinet and horns keep their minds firmly on the more serious matter of the motto theme, albeit with a changed rhythm. But even this is blown away in the veritable storm that ends the exposition. (Incidentally Brahms expects the traditional repeat which should certainly be observed in this relatively compact symphony.)

The development, once it is reached, continues the turbulent mood; even the wayward second subject becomes agitated with uneasy syncopations hustling it on its way. As for its dance-like companion, it is not only truncated but also inverted. Suddenly order is restored by a solo horn which emerges out of the ruck, turning the initial motto theme (now C E♭ C) into a theme of some nobility. The tempo slows and for the first time since its original appearance the broad 'heroic' tune with which the violins began the movement reappears. The mood is considerably chastened as Brahms seems to tease us with a number of suggestions that recall the theme without getting it quite right. A timpani roll with a big crescendo pulls things together and F A♭ F duly brings us to the recapitulation. Once again Brahms has accomplished the difficult feat of putting essentially romantic ideas into a classical mould unlike those of his contemporaries who found the constraints of symphonic form too hampering. The only substantial surprise remaining in the movement is the quiet ending in which, as has been said, the 'heroic' theme is untainted by disruptive implications of the minor.

The second movement is deceptively simple, more profound in content than its bland opening would have us believe for at its heart lie some of the most awe-inspiring passages Brahms ever wrote. The beginning is plain sailing with the clarinet leading the woodwind through a long and lyrical melody whose cadences win approving sighs from the strings. A decorated variation follows, only to be cut off abruptly and replaced by a strange oscillation between adjacent notes accompanied by gentle dabs of sound on the weaker beats of the bar. Quietly, clarinet and bassoon in unison intone a chant-like melody whose measured accompaniment gives it the feel of a grave procession. This new theme is briefly taken over by oboe and horn before a return to the original tone-colouring. A charming phrase on the strings gives a gesture of benediction that is echoed by the wind. It is here that we reach the mysterious heart of the movement. The essential material could hardly be simpler — a pair of identical notes repeated, the second longer than the first; it is the placing of the notes that produces so magical an effect, now high and clear on violins, now dark and shadowy in the lower strings, now sombre on clarinet and bassoon. Brahms literally conjures with this tiny musical entity so that we never know where it will next appear.

A reversion to the opening theme, elaborately decorated, brings us back into daylight; indeed the music grows quite restless despite the efforts of several woodwind instruments to re-establish the calm and unhurried demeanour of the opening theme. At last the strings slow down their fussy little comments and, as though apologising for causing a disturbance, introduce a glorious sustained melody that has not been heard before. Again we hear those mysterious harmonies before a quiet reference to the opening theme brings the movement to an end.

There is no scherzo. Instead Brahms gives us an elegiac theme in C minor marked *Poco Allegretto*. The cellos are given the tune, accompanied by whisps of arpeggios from violins and violas. Brahms reduces his orchestra to chamber size and there is a disarming quality of gipsy melancholy in the music, a literal song without words whether sung by cellos, violins or solo horn. A central section is mostly scored for wind though the occasional string phrases lend exceptional tenderness. In due course the initial theme returns, different in detail but similar in conception. The closing bars introduce a novel effect with a rising scale in a dotted rhythm that tries to climb to a high C but just falls short of the mark. It is an evasion of the obvious that is typical of the whole movement.

The start of the final *Allegro* bears a resemblance, on paper, to the finale of the Second Symphony since both movements begin with a quiet but urgent theme scored for unison strings. But where the Second Symphony tells of sunlight, here we find music of the night, with clouds scudding across a fitful moon. The opening theme, wind-blown though it is, finishes with a single pizzicato note on the lower strings. Two notes on trombones announce a solemn chorale which may well be related to the mysterious central section of the slow movement. Having made its effect it is abruptly discarded and a typically choppy rhythm sweeps away the last vestiges of the opening theme. For a time the music hammers away relentlessly in C minor until suddenly a heroic theme in C major emerges on cellos and horn. (It was this theme that made Joachim think of Leander swimming the Hellespont to meet his beloved.) The release of a major key does not last for long and soon we are pitched into a stormy episode in C minor. Attempts by the woodwind to reintroduce the opening theme are swept aside with swift ascending scales and the fabric of the music seems to break apart as brass and strings hack out aggressive pairs of quavers over a magnificent striding bass that rises through two octaves.

At last the first four notes of the movement (C B C D♭) are played sufficiently forcefully (bassoons and horns) to make an arresting impression. The opening subject is then transferred to the wind, punctuated by thoughtful chords from the strings which again emphasise the nocturnal character of the movement. Gradually the chords assume greater importance, reducing the theme to four-note fragments. The solemn chorale that had appeared as early as bar 19 tries to establish itself against a considerable battering from the strings. It takes some time to realise that we are in the midst of a recapitulation of sorts although it is far from being a mere repetition of past events. The emergence of the 'heroic' theme on horns (now in F major) confirms that this is indeed a sonata-form movement, though one of great complexity. A sudden cessation of activity warns us that a new event is imminent. Muted violas introduce an ingeniously smoothed-out version of the initial theme, all urgency removed. Soon a solo oboe slows the theme down still further, reducing it to half speed and giving it the romantic warmth of a major key. Rich harmonies on the brass help to give an impression of added breadth even though the strings continue to fuss. But the stormy winds of night gradually give way to dawn breezes as the solemn chorale reappears for the last time. So subtly that at first we hardly realise it, the motto theme (F A ♭ F) from the first movement returns. It evokes a shimmering reflection of its erstwhile heroic companion which now drifts down like a warm ray of sunshine piercing the morning haze. Thus all four movements have ended quietly, a truly unique feature of a remarkable and perhaps underestimated work.

Symphony No. 4 in E Minor, Op. 98

In 1884, at the age of 51, Brahms turned his thoughts towards a possible third piano concerto, having enjoyed a great success with the epic No. 2 in B flat; but, as he put it, 'I don't know whether the two others are too good or too bad but they're certainly getting in the way.' In the event he started on a fourth symphony, completing it in the following year. In his usual self-deprecatory manner he described it as 'a few Entr'actes' and doubted if it would have much appeal. The initial reaction of Hans von Bülow who was to conduct the first movement was a terse message to his agent: 'Brahms Fourth seems to be difficult, very.' Later, after the first rehearsal he wrote, 'No. 4 stupendous, quite original, quite new, individual and rock-like. Incomparable strength from start to finish.'

Basically the first theme of the symphony is a long expansive melody, but Brahms presents it in a very unusual way, each phrase at first being only two notes (see Ex. 1 opposite). These pairs of notes are shadowed by attendant chords in the woodwind, so that if we were to listen to the wind alone we would get a strangely pointillist impression of the melody, little dabs of sound gently nudging the off-beats. As the tune itself begins to coalesce these accompanying chords become more sustained. Soon, however, Brahms

Ex. 1

p

breaks the theme into fragments again, this time making it into a dialogue between first and second violins. Meanwhile the woodwind provide a counterpoint of flowing scale-passages while cellos and basses play a shadowy version of the theme.

At the point where the opening theme first began to be a sustained line Brahms introduced this small unit:

Ex. 1a

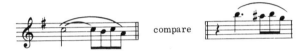

compare

It now begins to assume an identity of its own, whether sustained or in the truncated version also shown in the example above.

A broad sweeping phrase in the strings based on a descending scale leads us to a brief martial fanfare on woodwind and horns. It announces the entry of the second subject, a noble theme for cellos and horns with a somewhat angular accompaniment derived from the preceding fanfare. Violins take over the theme enthusiastically only to find themselves interrupted by the fanfare, emphatically stated in unison wind and horns. A strangely fragmented episode follows, pairs of notes alternating between wind and pizzicato strings that remind us of the opening theme without actually quoting it. In a gloriously lyrical phrase that only Brahms could have written the music rises to an emotional climax; it is short-lived, but a moment to which even the most stony-hearted must respond. It provides part of the material for a new theme in B major, one too many for conventional musical analysis, since its importance merits the label Third Subject. Easily recognised, it first appears in unison on flute, clarinet and horn, accompanied by dancing quavers in the strings. An oboe takes over its second strand which, after a dying sequence, dissolves into a mysterious sustained chord through which the strings rise and fall like a swirl of mist. A rumble of timpani and a distant trumpet-call add a ghostly touch. Tentatively at first but with increasing confidence the fanfare motive begins to dominate the scene until it reigns triumphant. At the very point at which we expect a climax of some finality the music breaks off into two staccato chords. With a complete change of mood flutes and bassoons offer us falling pairs of notes that might irreverently be described as the call of a love-sick cuckoo. It signals the end of the exposition; dispensing with the traditional repeat, Brahms moves on into the development. Before we join him it might be worthwhile to have a brief roll-call of the material so far since the movement is particularly rich in themes of potential importance.

Theme I: Falling thirds and rising sixths, the notes grouped in pairs.
Theme Ia: Its 'attendant' — see page 143.
Theme II: The fanfare, usually on woodwind.
Theme III: Obvious choice for true Second Subject; the big cello tune.
Theme IV: Lyrical tune in B major with dancing accompaniment. Extinguished by 'rising swirl of mist' — also important.

The development begins in bar 145 by pretending to be a normal repeat of the exposition; in other words it is identical to the opening of the symphony. The woodwind soon provide their own variation of Theme I, now in G minor, and accompanied by decorative passages in the strings that all spring from Ia. This variation is shortly taken over very forcibly by the strings (B flat minor) and subjected to some very rough treatment. An explosive accent on timpani and horns acts as a strong enough rebuke to silence these clashes. The 'rising swirl' engulfs us mysteriously again, its coils cleverly adjusted to give a suggestion of the fanfare (Theme II) which then appears in spectral form in the woodwind. Several times the swirling arpeggios rise and fall in their nebulous fashion, interspersed with pleading chords on the woodwind. Just as the music seems in danger of disappearing into a fog there is a sudden outburst of the fanfare motive, now peremptory in its command and leading to a passage of unaccustomed severity. With great skill Brahms transforms the tail-end of the fanfare into a more lyrical phrase (clarinets and bassoons in thirds), and places the shadowy version of Theme I above it, gentle off-beat notes in flutes and pizzicato strings.

We are now almost exactly in the centre of the movement (bar 228 out of 440). In a passage whose solemn and mysterious tones can be compared to the heart of the slow movement of the preceding symphony (see page 140), Brahms creates a wonderful sequence of slow-moving harmonies that suggest a sleeping giant. The only melodic interest lies in sixteen derivations of Ex.1a in as many bars. The effect of stillness is extraordinary, as if becalmed in a miniature Sargasso sea. As though in a lethargic trance, the woodwind play the opening notes of the symphony in expressionless and extended form. Again the misty coil of notes rises and falls through the strings. Another sleep-walking phrase from the wind brings a like response. It is an inspired and totally original way of leading into the recapitulation. This is remarkably true to form until the coda is reached, a landmark one can recognise when some violent clashes on the strings emerge from a particularly aggressive treatment of the fanfare theme. Listen in particular for strident horns in thirds, doubled by shrill woodwind. The 'rising mist' arpeggio assumes the ferocity of a dust-storm. Utterly changed in character, Theme I appears as though beaten out on an anvil. The music drives on with irresistible energy and for once Brahms ends a symphonic first movement with a tremendously powerful cadence.

The slow movement (*Andante moderato*) begins with a severe theme on horns and woodwind. The repetitive rhythm gives it the feeling of a solemn ritual while the actual shape of the melody is a marvellous demonstration of what can be done with three consecutive notes, either rising or falling. Clarinets take up the refrain with a discreet pizzicato accompaniment; after a lyrical and expressive extension of the theme the horns re-enter quietly, though surprisingly just as we expect their phrase to be gently folded away there is a crescendo. Clarinets and bassoons in unison remind us of the severity of the opening theme, adding an important and arresting little three-note fanfare at the end. Brahms makes ingenious use of this before bringing us back to the pizzicato strings who take a rather more pessimistic view of the theme. A brief interlude for woodwind leads to an expressive new development as the strings take up their bows for the first time. The opening phrase is smoothed out and imbued with a warmth that has been missing so far; but the romantic mood is destined to be abruptly terminated by harsh triplets in the woodwind. Though it sounds very different, this new figure proves to be an ingenious variation on the opening theme and the pattern of three notes rising, three notes falling is readily apparent. What one does not expect is the transformation that is to come, for the relentlessly hammered-out triplets give birth to one of Brahms's most memorable tunes. Placed side by side like this the relationship is easy to spot:

Ex. 2

This tune, a cellist's dream to play, is elegantly decorated with arabesques from the first violins. It is followed by a period of seeming indecision as paired semiquavers drift through various sections of the orchestra, finally proving to be an apt counterpoint to the original theme, this time given to violas.

Large-scale movements need contrast, and in the centre of this Andante we find a much more aggressive treatment of the initial horncall. Flurries of rapid figuration give the impression of a quicker tempo even though the beat remains the same. The battering triplets return (see Ex. 2) heavily reinforced by timpani, a display of wrath that serves to make the reappearance of the cello tune all the more beautiful. Now it is the violins' turn to have the melody; yet even this gracious theme is given a more heroic aspect by a variant in which the notes fall just after the beat. Clarinets and bassoons restore a feeling of repose before a soft murmuring in the lower strings, darkened by a timpani roll, casts a shadow over the movement. A poignant phrase on clarinets, derived from the opening theme, brings a tinge of sadness, as though Brahms sees the end of the movement ahead and is reluctant to part from it. Horns repeat the very opening phrase, this time richly scored. Quietly and without fuss the movement ends.

It is followed by an exuberant scherzo, all bluster, like Falstaff describing his heroic part in that famous midnight skirmish. The first two phrases, rough-hewn and abrupt, are greeted with an extraordinary leonine roar, after which the rhythm becomes positively bouncy:

Ex. 3

More blustering follows, and then, as though saying 'I hope I didn't frighten you' Brahms transforms Ex.3 into a bland little tune without an ounce of malice:

Ex. 3a

Within seconds the boisterous mood of the opening returns and Brahms amuses himself — and us! — by turning the theme upside-down. The rat-a-tat rhythm shown in Ex. 3 then becomes mysterious while a curiously shaped theme on unison woodwind seems to be leading towards something sinister. Not a bit of it. Instead of mystery we find comedy, a delightful second subject on violins, with laughing scales on the woodwind as commentary (see Ex. 4). This theme is then reduced to a skeleton which in turn becomes a ghost. A sudden crescendo brings back the opening theme which develops into a piece of slapstick humour, leonine roars alternating with timid squeaks from the woodwind. (The dialogue between fortissimo timpani and tremulous triangle shows that we are not meant to take this conflict seriously.)

For a time Brahms continues to use this now familiar material whose salient features are easily recognised. But when for the first time we hear the woodwind choir playing the opening theme as quietly as they can in the remote key of D flat, it is a warning that a change lies ahead. Sure enough, the tempo eases back and a soft little interlude, a mini-trio, ensues. Where the material for it comes from is soon made clear as the full orchestra reverts noisily to the original tempo. We are now just past the half-way mark, and although much that is to come will prove to be familiar, Brahms still has some surprises in store. For instance the smiling second subject is considerably changed in character by tautening the rhythm:

Ex. 4

nor can we fail to notice a magnificent crescendo that builds up over a reiterated drum-beat that continues the same crisp rhythm ($\sqcap$ $\sqcap$) for twenty-six bars. The humour of the movement is certainly not subtle, but it is of a kind that Beethoven would have enjoyed when he was in what he called his 'unbuttoned' mood.

The final movement is a magnificent demonstration of the craft of composition. Beginning with an impressive eight-bar theme borrowed from Bach's Cantata no. 150, it then offers thirty strict variations followed by an extensive coda. We have seen how in his formative years Brahms wrote a number of sets of variations as a sort of self-imposed apprenticeship. This movement shows the culmination of those hard-earned skills. While it was probably the most taxing to write, it is the easiest to comprehend since the essential framework remains unaltered time after time.

Now this movement has been described both as a chaconne and as a passacaglia. These are old dance forms involving variations on a strictly observed framework. The difference can best be described by thinking of a chaconne as a set of variations on a sequence of *chords* while a passacaglia is an elaborate superstructure built over a repeated sequence of *notes*. A ground-bass is a passacaglia in which the note sequence remains in the bass line all the time. This movement has elements of both forms.

Once the theme has been announced Brahms sets out to prove the basic simplicity of his framework by relating it all to two notes. Six times the horns reiterate the keynote of E before grudgingly admitting the fifth or dominant note of B into the scheme. Meanwhile the opening sequence of harmonies has been repeated by plucked strings, a curiously threatening sound after the blare of brass and wind.

Next the woodwind provide the first of the many lyrical decorations which are destined to flower above this stark frame. From here onwards a catalogue of events is all that is needed.

Variation 3	consists of heavily accented chords employing the full orchestra.
Variation 4	brings an impassioned tune on the violins, the prevailing theme clearly marked in the bass.
Variation 5	A variation on the above with additional wood-wind decorations.
Variation 6	Further elaboration in violins over sustained bass line.
Variation 7	A new rhythmic pattern, dotted quavers and semi-quavers, disrupts the bass line.
Variation 8	Bach-like semiquaver figuration in violins.
Variation 9	Intensified version of above with increasingly important woodwind.
Variation 10	'Breathing' effect of harmonies exchanged between wind and strings.
Variation 11	Variation of above with delicately poised triplets.
Variation 12	Change of time to 3/2, thus extending the length of each bar. A flute solo of ethereal beauty.
Variation 13	Shift to E major; brief expressive phrases exchanged between solo woodwind.
Variation 14	Solemn trombones establish a feeling of almost religious stillness.
Variation 15	An elaboration of above.
Variation 16	Repetition of original theme on woodwind topped by a soaring entry from strings.
Variation 17	Gusting tremolandi with theme on cellos.
Variation 18	'Bending' version of theme, especially in wind and brass.
Variation 19	Bright staccato quavers in dialogue between strings and wind.
Variation 20	Variation on above with triplet quavers.
Variation 21	Full orchestra with rushing scales in strings.
Variation 22	'*Reculer pour mieux sauter*'; a sudden recession of tone with floating off-beat chords in wind.
Variation 23	Theme in brass surrounded by energetic triplet figures.
Variation 24	Ferocious climax with timpani marking each bar.
Variation 25	Variation of above with violins playing counterpoint from Variation 2.
Variation 26	Soft contrast: theme on horns, slightly modified.

Variation 27	'Breathing' chords on woodwind: flowing quavers in strings.
Variation 28	Variant of above with new descant in wind.
Variation 29	Cross-rhythms in wind: off-beat pizzicato in strings.
Variation 30	Final build up to the *Più Allegro*.
Coda	Theme very strong against tumultuous arpeggio figuration in strings. Dramatic rising scale-motif in trombones taken up and developed by strings. The framework of the theme is continued by implication but no longer strictly observed.

Brahms lived for another twelve years after completing this symphony but wisely he never attempted to write another one. It would hardly have been possible to produce a work that could cap this magnificent finale.

Piano Concerto No. 1 in D Minor
Op. 15

In June 1854 Brahms wrote to Joachim, 'I wish I could leave my D minor sonata alone for a long time. I have often played the first three movements over with Frau Schumann, but I find that I need even more than two pianos.' In his search for the 'even more' he then set about orchestrating this Sonata for Two Pianos, only to find that the essentially pianistic nature of the material created an insuperable problem. There was nothing for it but to recast the work yet again, this time as a Piano Concerto. Nothing except the First Symphony gave Brahms as much trouble, and three years after we first learn of its existence through his correspondence we hear of it again in tones of disgust. 'You can't imagine what trouble it has given me; it is one botch-up from start to finish and bears all the hall-marks of amateurishness. I am trying to get rid of this and finish it for good.' The trauma of the first performance has already been described (see page 124) and to add to his humiliation Brahms's usual publisher refused to accept the work. It is hard to believe that the score, together with the necessary rehearsal arrangement for two pianos was not published until 1873, fourteen years after the first performance. Yet when we hear the work now we wonder how anyone can have failed to appreciate its intensely dramatic opening, truly music for heroes. Its greatest novelty lay in its starkness, its lack of harmonic padding. At the time the general tendency was for scores to contain ever more notes, more lush harmony, more richness of colour. Had Brahms used the opening material in a Tragic Overture it might have been better appreciated; but it is a concerto, and the essence of the nineteenth-century concerto was athletic display, popularly of a somewhat facile kind.

The opening pages have been described by Tovey as 'one of the mightiest utterances since Beethoven's Ninth Symphony'. Over a volcanic rumble from timpani and double basses the explosive first theme erupts in unison violins and cellos; with its jagged leaps and fiery trills it suggests Mount Etna at its most awe-inspiring, spewing trails of molten lava down its scarred flanks. If the image seems far-fetched it is undeniable that the shattering opening is followed by a phrase so bleak and grief-stricken that it seems to symbolise the aftermath of some great catastrophe (II). It is not hard to imagine it being used to accompany cinematic images of bewildered humans searching the wreckage of homes devastated by the overwhelming forces of Nature. But Brahms was not a Berlioz or a Wagner and, extreme though the emotional contrast may seem at this point, the violins' lament is underpinned by constant (though subtly modified) references to the blazing opening phrase — now reduced to ashes in the cellos. The gulf between violins and cellos grows ever wider until the upper strings seem to disappear in the prevailing cloud. Ushered in by a brief ascent by cellos and basses, a new theme appears (III), the sombre hue of clarinets and bassoons silvered by *tremolando* violins. The key is B flat minor, the darkest corner of the tonal world. The music seems to freeze into immobility before, with a brutal shock, Brahms produces six giant hammer-blows that burst open the door to D minor once again. The first theme reappears; this time violins and cellos are in conflict, goaded on by horns. Out of an angry torrent of descending quavers a rugged four-note phrase emerges (IV). It may seem to be only of passing interest but the Beethoven-like persistence with which Brahms hammers away at it should tell us that it is of some importance, as indeed it proves to be. A fanfare of sorts in strings and wind brings a hint of glory in a brief excursion into D major but it is an unconvincing triumph as the bassoons tell us when they persist in dwelling on such essentially *minor* elements as C natural and B flat. For the second time in this remarkable opening tutti the music seems to be coming to a halt. One feels something must happen to break the deadlock. It does.

Without a trace of virtuosity the piano begins a meditation on the previously aggressive four-note phrase (IV). The left hand plays a passive role, simply taking over a three-note pattern the cellos have just played no less than twelve times. The right hand has a series of gently flowing phrases which have the serenity one might find in the accompaniment to a Bach aria. For fifteen spacious bars there is no sign of storms ahead, but once the left hand begins to duplicate the right the music gathers strength like a tidal wave. Within seconds the tremendous trills of the opening theme become the subject of a titanic conflict between soloist and orchestra, only resolved as the orchestra takes the opening theme and forcibly wrenches it into a new shape.

Over a left hand accompaniment whose angularity precludes any suggestion of tenderness, the piano now has its own version of II. Theoretic-ally in the dominant key of A major, the music is strangely ambivalent, drawn constantly towards the desolation of A *minor*, a desolation which becomes only too clear in the ensuing version in virtually unrelieved E minor. Again the music seems to disappear into the clouds, again the lower strings usher in Theme III. This time the pianist clothes its sad strains in shadowy triplet figurations which are devoid of any hint of brilliance. It is a world of such greyness that we can hardly believe it when a trill starts hesitantly and then begins to blossom as caressing phrases in the orchestra tell us that F major (the true 'relative' major of D minor) has at last been reached. Exerting the true prerogative of a soloist, the pianist now introduces a new theme of great nobility. In time its majestic chords give way to a rippling figure above which we find an increasingly passionate extension of the fanfare that had appeared as a short-lived moment of triumph in the opening tutti. As the piano part dies down a solo flute followed by an oboe echoes the fanfare motif. (At this stage it is pared down to a mere two notes but one should store them in one's mind since they are destined to assume a far greater importance.)

When in due course the strings take over the theme so eloquently presented by the pianist, they quickly build it to a climax. It is here that two horns in unison declaim the fanfare motif in truly heraldic colours — inciden-tally revealing to the observant listener that its first two notes were actually the seed from which the noble second subject flowered. Against swift runn-ing passages in thirds from the piano, quite an exchange of fanfares develops, although in the strings rather than the brass. However, the horns' proprietary rights to such material are not to be denied and after some rhapsodising from the pianist we hear the fanfare in full from a solo horn. It seems to be sounding a curfew of sorts since a beautiful nocturnal episode follows based on an expressive *major* version of III.

If night it is, we are in for a rude awakening for, with a sudden and unwonted display of virtuosity, the pianist launches into a powerful cascade of octaves, derived from the initial two notes of the fanfare. It makes a dramatic start to the development which not surprisingly re-introduces the opening theme, this time surrounded by swirling octave figures from the soloist and subjected to many transformations. Theme II reappears in even darker hue, the tune now in the lower strings, but it is Theme III that undergoes the most striking change. The transformation from introspective melancholy to ferocious energy is accomplished by a dramatic compression. To make the comparison simpler to appreciate I will put the two examples in the same key (see p. 152). Each time that this theme has appeared it has been preceded by an ascending phrase of five chrotchets, a simple example of musical 'joinery' that we assume to be of little importance; but it too now

undergoes a transformation:

(2b becomes the bass of 1b)

These two insignificant little phrases, 1b and 2b, dominate the remainder of the development. 1b is even made into an enchanting dance, the only light-hearted moment in the whole movement. It is marked by quicksilver arpeggios in the piano part alternating with nimble octaves which no longer have an air of menace. But menace lies ahead as piano and orchestra exchange massive blows centred on the dominant (A). With a thunderous roar the timpani celebrate the return to the tonic key of D minor. Here Brahms has a magnificent surprise; above a continuously sustained D the pianist begins the main theme in a completely contradictory key, a tone above.[3]

The ensuing recapitulation is full of invention such as the orchestra's ferocious treatment of the gently meditative theme with which the soloist made his first entry. Nevertheless, even in new guises, the themes used are all clearly recognisable. A thrilling ascent in violins and woodwind coupled with a striding *descent* in the lower strings leads to more hammer-blows which the pianist parries with dramatic octave passages. These lead logically to an extensive use of the four-note pattern (IV) in the final pages; the movement ends with unrelenting energy and a Beethoven-like insistence that the 'home' key must be established without compromise.

If the tragic character of this first movement was a direct reflection of Brahms's horror at Schumann's abortive attempt at suicide, the slow movement may be regarded as a requiem for Schumann, for over its quiet yet undemonstrative opening theme Brahms wrote the words '*Benedictus qui venit in nomine Domini*'. The scoring, for muted strings with serenely gliding thirds in the bassoons, suggests the tones of an organ, and the music is notable for its restraint and repose. When, after thirteen bars, the piano enters it does so with the two hands doubling up, again suggesting an organ in its density of texture. Quiet exchanges between soloist and orchestra remind one of the

---

[3]It sounds like E major though in actuality it is the dominant of A minor.

sung responses in a church service. After an especially hushed phrase for strings the piano introduces new material, a spread octave in the right hand initiating a somewhat tortuous and chromatic descent over an increasingly widely spaced left hand part. This, together with certain elements of the preceding passage, convinces me that Brahms is alluding to Schumann's great masterpiece, the Phantasie in C major, Op. 17. A second and extended descent leads to a strange improvisatory passage in which the piano writing is extraordinarily austere, denying any inclination towards sentimentality. Sentiment is briefly suggested by a tender phrase given to a pair of clarinets but is instantly denied by the full orchestra. Again the pianist resumes the bleak and angular style of the previous episode, utterly unlike anything else in the romantic piano repertoire. This time oboes and clarinets in turn are allowed a touch more sentiment before the woodwind choir brings back the 'Benedictus'. This is turned in new directions by the orchestra before the soloist enters as before; but now restraint is cast aside, and the music builds to an impassioned climax.[4] Harp-like arpeggios and timpani-like trills from the piano disturb the tranquillity of the woodwind chorale before the strings exert a calming influence. A brief and wholly unostentatious cadenza (whose quietly ascending trills may conceivably symbolise Schumann's soul ascending to heaven) leads to a last benediction from the orchestra.

The final Rondo puts such private thoughts aside. Out of the same stable as the finale of Beethoven's Third Concerto, it begins with a robust statement of the rondo theme from the soloist. This is taken up with some enthusiasm by the orchestra before a solo bassoon leads the soloist astray into the 'wrong' key of C sharp minor. This deviation causes a moment's hesitation before a possible route 'home' is spotted. A downward plunging scale through four octaves brings the music back on course, allowing the orchestra to reaffirm their belief in the rondo theme. A quiet interlude ensues in which the violins seem to be searching for a tune while the pianist follows after them in a curiously hesitant way. All is well as the elusive second subject at last materialises. It is worth waiting for, a glorious tune in F major whose smooth *cantabile* line offers a marked contrast to the choppy rondo theme.

The strings then have an episode more or less to themselves. Its gentle syncopations die away to nothing. Suddenly an arresting horn-call (shades of *The Flying Dutchman*!) issues a summons not to be denied, and the soloist makes a dramatic return to the scene. The rondo theme duly reappears in full orchestral dress, to be supplanted by a graceful new theme in the violins whose initial rising arpeggio establishes the key of B flat. The pianist shows a certain reluctance to become involved in this, preferring to embark on a long sequence of trills that might well be called 'The Lark Ascending'. However, after a few bars of indecision, an elegantly decorated variation of the violins'

[4]Cf. Schumann Phantasie Op. 17, first movement.

theme does appear. And now comes a truly unexpected episode, a miniature fugue based in the violins' theme though transposed into the minor. Its tip-toe stealth may have been inspired by the ghostly *fugato* in the slow movement of Beethoven's Seventh Symphony. As though aware that this academic excursion might be taken too seriously by his listeners, Brahms doubles the speed of the fugue subject, causing it to sound like a snatch from a Mendelssohn scherzo.

In carefree mood the pianist enters, cleverly combining the horn's summons, the violins' grace, and the rondo's basic shape. A sudden outburst of virtuosity leads back to the rondo theme on the orchestra, the pianist reinforcing the bass with some ferocity. After a fair amount of *sturm*, not to mention *drang*, a soloist offers a modified version of the second subject, now in D minor instead of F major. A dramatic timpani roll and the horn 'summons' tells us that the cadenza, notably absent from the first movement, is now imminent. Marked '*quasi Fantasia*' it has some of the characteristics of a Bach toccata and is far removed from the flashy fireworks offered by contemporary pianist–composers. Even avoiding the convention of a closing trill, it ends with a dying fall that leads into a beautiful extension of the theme originally initiated by the violins. Now in D major, a key unvisited so far in this movement, it allows Brahms to embark on one of those nostalgic twilight codas that were to become one of his specialities. The music becomes even slower as oboes and then horns reveal the pastoral possibilities inherent in a small segment of the rondo theme. Descending trills float dreamily through the piano part before some sweeping scales tell us that Brahms is not going to end quietly after all. As though the players have suddenly glimpsed the time and have no wish to miss their final drink, the music sets off at a much brisker pace heading for the final cadence with an irresistible momentum. It is a fitting ending to a work of quite outstanding originality, so far ahead of its time that it is small wonder that audiences were baffled. There are quite persuasive arguments for claiming it to be the greatest piano concerto ever written, even though the Second is larger in scale and more lavishly endowed with melody, as we shall soon discover.

Piano Concerto No. 2 in B Flat
Op. 83

The considerable gulf between the two piano concertos is evident from their opus numbers, 15 and 83. The second concerto was initially sketched in 1878 but three years passed before the composer put the final touches to the score.

Unusually, there are four movements. Brahms was once asked why he had included the stormy and passionate movement that convention calls a scherzo though it is far from being a jest. His reply was characteristic: 'Well, you see, the first movement is so harmless . . .' Ask any pianist who has wrestled with the extreme technical demands of this most challenging concerto whether he regards it as harmless and see what reply you get. Brahms was much given to such misleading remarks and in one letter described the work as 'quite a little Piano Concerto containing quite a nice little Scherzo'.

The opening bars give little idea of the immense scale of the music that lies ahead. A solo horn plays a theme that has all the romance of a distant view of Camelot:

Ex. 1

(Notice that the first bar consists of three rising notes and, on the fourth beat, three falling notes. Both elements are important and may be treated separately.)

The pianist gathers up an accumulation of chords of B flat major before quietly echoing the last five notes of the horn solo. A second phrase comes from the horn, eliciting a similar response. Woodwind and then strings propose a lyrical extension which turns surprisingly towards the minor. Without a hint of preparation the pianist launches into a cadenza of almost brutal ferocity, the paired right hand octaves seeming like the snapping jaws of a cornered dragon. The cadenza, though brief, covers a huge span, the final bars hammering insistently at the dominant (F) at the opposite extremes of the keyboard. With this giant gesture Brahms establishes the absolute authority of the soloist, just as Beethoven did with the opening flourishes of the 'Emperor' concerto. Yet those who describe this work as a symphony for orchestra with piano have some justification since the orchestra rarely plays a supporting role. Certainly the tutti that now follows is conceived on the grandest symphonic scale. The romantic opening horn–call is transformed into a grandiose march in which the descending triplet soon begins to establish its independence. A 'stretching' phrase on the violins (up a semitone, down an octave) leads to a soaring climax after which there is a gradual lessening of tension. Violins present the graceful second subject over a pizzicato accompaniment from cellos and violas, but after a mere eight bars there is a momentary silence. A swift rising scale pitches us into a violent theme whose jerky rhythms are soon combined with flashing scales. They lead to a stark and forbidding derivative of the initial horn theme, now in D minor and seeming set to stay there. Two convulsive trills force the music back to F, at which point the soloist makes an awe-inspiring entry, enough to command immediate silence. After a brief flourish he begins a free extension of the opening horn-call which increasingly converts the first three rising crotchets into a triplet of rising quavers. An argument ensues, the full orchestra insisting on the 'correct' crotchet figure, the pianist preferring the more athletic triplets. Their differences are settled with a less contentious dialogue which is momentarily obscured by a swirling cloud of notes that range right across the keyboard. Reminders of the second limb of the opening theme are offered by the first flute, but the soloist treats them rather waywardly.

Soon a new theme appears, easily recognised by the initial rhythm, like someone knocking at the door:

Ex. 2

The tiny fragment created by abstracting the second and third notes proves to be enormously important. It is amazing what a great composer can do with so small a unit as a rising semitone, as we are soon to discover. The flute makes the point most graphically while the pianist is given a hair-raising sequence of skips in contrary motion. The rising semitone is then turned into a falling one and treated in a more leisurely fashion (paired crotchets). A more capricious treatment, dancing triplets, is then ironed out by the strings, establishing a relationship to past events that we are unlikely to have realised.

But what of the second subject? Has it been forgotten? 'Certainly not!' says the pianist throwing any pretence at caution aside and introducing a rough-hewn version very different from the elegant phrases the violins had offered in the tutti. An explosive arpeggio brings back the violent jagged theme from the exposition which, having generated a brief conflict with the lower strings, gives way to an obstreperous newcomer. Its stamping rhythms and dynamic energy are immensely exciting and they build to a huge climax in which elements of the opening horn-call can be clearly recognised, whether as chunky chords in the bass, or repeated patterns of descending triplets that leap across the keys.

At last the pianist is given a brief respite as a major storm develops in the orchestra. Referring to both first and second subjects, its relevance is easy to comprehend. A long chromatic descent brings release from the orchestral fury; as though from a distance we hear a solo horn reminding us of the opening theme, now darkened by transposition into the key of F minor. As before, its final notes are echoed by the piano.

At this point Brahms introduces a daring innovation. Cadenzas are normally the exclusive preserve of the soloist and the arresting cadenza that occurs so near the beginning of this concerto would seem to be purely pianistic. We are the more surprised then when its first six bars reappear in a version for piano *and* orchestra. It is a striking effect which leads to an extension incorporating the 'stretching' phrase from the initial tutti. Brief allusions to the compact rhythm that begins Ex. 2 are disregarded by the soloist who introduces a completely new episode in B minor, easily recognised by the fact that the two hands duplicate each other and by the persistence of its dotted rhythm. Soon the woodwind try to establish some tonal stability with strong sustained chords around which piano and strings indulge in a strenuous argument. The crisis is resolved by a *fortissimo* statement of the first three notes of Ex. 1 powerful enough to create a sort of dust-cloud of notes from the piano. Twice more in succession the three ascending notes are stated with the utmost emphasis, settling on the dominant of B flat (F major) and evoking an even more nebulous response. A magically shimmering figure high on the piano finds a subtle route back to B flat; as from a distance we hear the initial horn-call and, almost before we are aware of it, the classic recapitulation arrives.

Although considerably condensed, the material is all familiar until the advent of the coda which is heralded by some extraordinary trills combined with off-beat chords. Suddenly they are reduced to a low grumble in the bass, an effect almost as sinister as the drums at the start of Berlioz' 'March to the Scaffold'. I cannot do better than quote Tovey's description of this wonderful moment: 'Out of subdued mutterings the first theme again arises and hovers, while the air seems full of whisperings and the beating of mighty wings.'[5] After an amazingly prolonged chromatic descent through four octaves of the keyboard the clouds are dispersed by three mighty chords based on the familiar opening theme. The cue is seized on by the pianist who, for the first and only time in the movement, actually plays the initial horn-call, albeit on a heroic scale. A considerable extension of the triplet at the end of bar 1 follows, with piano and orchestra vying with each other in a contest of strength. A long diminuendo suggests the possibility of a quiet ending but it is not to be; a brilliant ascending scale and a clattering trill signal that the end of this truly heroic movement is in sight. The three majestic chords which conclude it were clearly designed to elicit storms of applause and it is a pity that the concert manners of today demand that the movement should be greeted by a silence broken only by a few restrained coughs and a brief murmur of approval.

The material of the ensuing scherzo was originally conceived as a sketch for a violin concerto but Brahms quickly realised that it demanded the greater

---

[5]D.F. Tovey, *Essays in Musical Analysis*, Vol. III, (O.U.P., 1935).

dominance the piano could give. The movement begins in grim earnest with angrily repeated chords in the orchestra above which the piano part seems to writhe, fighting to get free. After a struggle lasting for 42 bars there is a sudden change of mood as unison strings offer a truce in the shape of a phrase that harps insistently on the note E. As though given its freedom, the piano accepts the offer; an inspired improvisation follows, lyrical and expansive. Even the tiger-like spring with which the movement began is tamed until it is reduced to a gentle rocking figure in the strings. The music dies away to nothing so that the obligatory repeat catches us unawares with the renewal of the conflict.

After the repeat there is an extensive development of the initial phrases, the excitement being heightened by some splendid striding octaves whose majestic chromatic ascent seems to lift the music bodily. The innocent string phrase that once eased the tension is now transformed into something savage with horns baying like some barbaric war-cry. Four full-blooded repetitions of the initial five notes of the movement lead to a sudden transformation as the music shifts into D major. At a slightly steadier tempo the strings proclaim a fanfare-like theme that is type-cast for horns and trumpets. (Their turn will come!) A majestic sequel follows, coming to a cadence of Handelian splendour. The soloist's response is totally unexpected, a variation on the fanfare theme that is fiendishly difficult. The tumultuous octaves we find in Liszt or Tchaikovsky are child's play compared to these, partly because they must be played *pianissimo*, partly because of the angularity of the phrases. (The variation is in D minor, the second limb being in three-part counter-point.) The orchestra say 'Amen to that' with their solemn sequel, now hushed. It prompts a free, almost Chopinesque rhapsody which is called to order by a grave reminder of the fanfare theme from unison strings. A thrilling crescendo brings back the fanfare in its full glory with horns and trumpets joyfully claiming their just rights.

After some quietly pensive chords from the woodwind the pianist reintroduces the initial theme of the movement. It is a curious false start which the orchestra refuses at first to accept. The reason for this becomes apparent after a strangely static passage; it is because the roles are to be reversed. Thus in the true reprise the strings play what was once the pianist's, the piano plays what was once the orchestral part. It is a brilliant way of observing a classic convention while giving it an entirely new tone-colour. Thereafter the movement proceeds on more or less predictable lines, ending with a powerful coda that leaves soloist and audience gasping.

On hearing this concerto for the first time, nobody is likely to forget the impression made by the hauntingly beautiful cello solo which begins the slow movement. It is a literal song without words which the violins, after supplying an ethereal descant, cannot refrain from taking over for themselves. Oboe and solo cello then join in an exquisitely tender duet that would not be out of place in *Bohème*. It is an idyllic scene into which the piano enters with an air of reverence, as though anxious not to break the spell. The pianist is then given an improvisatory solo which seems to be divorced from all that has gone before. In fact it is closely related, as the example below reveals. The first two bars show the start of the cello tune (transposed up an octave), while the final bar shows the beginning of the piano 'improvisation'. Transfer the rhythm of the first to the melodic contour of the second as suggested and the relationship becomes clear.

Ex. 3

The next orchestral entry casts a shadow by changing to the minor; this produces a disturbed reaction in the piano part. The trills and swooping arpeggios disguise the closeness to the theme which Brahms still maintains by simply converting dotted crotchets and quavers into notes of half the value. All the skills he had acquired in the numerous sets of variations written in his twenties are brought to bear here, for though the movement is in no way a set of 'variations on a theme' the techniques employed are similar. All the listener need keep in mind is the extraordinary adaptability of this pattern:

It appears most frequently as chords in the right hand, fractionally after the beat.

The central section of the movement is like a nocturne in which a pair of clarinets have a tune of such infinite calm that it seems as though suspended in the air. The pianist's left hand supplies the accompaniment while the right hand follows the outline of the clarinet theme with isolated notes that are like individual stars picked out against the velvety night sky. In twelve bars Brahms says as much as many composers do in an entire slow movement.

Were it not for the sheer beauty of the solo cello tune, its reappearance would seem almost irreverent after this truly profound interlude. The key, F sharp major, might present a problem to a less skilled composer, but a beautifully subtle modulation brings us back to the tonic (B flat major) and a more or less exact reprise of the opening stanzas, elegantly decorated by the soloist. A long ascending trill, richly harmonised, brings this sublime movement to an end.

The final Rondo is one of the most tuneful movements in the entire repertoire with such a prodigal outpouring of melody that it is like an album of musical snapshots, each one more delightful than its predecessor. The first tune dances on air, the sole accompaniment in the orchestra consisting of little sighs of pleasure from the violas. The violins soon take it over to a skipping figure from the piano. The pianist then produces tune number two by toying playfully with the final notes of tune number one. A swift ascending scale in thirds in the unlikely key of D major brings back tune number one which proceeds to show unexpected muscle. An abrupt jerky rhythm from the piano heralds the entrance of the next 'character', clearly a Hungarian gipsy, and a voluptuous one at that. Yet another tune appears, its opening notes a caress followed by a gurgle of delight in rippling thirds. The clarinets show their approval of this one with pizzicato cellos supplying a light-footed accompaniment. We have now had four distinct themes, each one enchanting in its own right. As though this were still not enough Brahms now produces a deliciously silly melody whose rhythm (♩ ♫♫) is the same in every bar. Once it is taken over by flutes and oboes the pianist is given nimble little comments that suggest peals of laughter.

For more than 180 bars Brahms plays with these tunes, juggling with them so that we are never sure which one will appear next. He then decides that it is time to introduce a rather tougher element, but even that is merely an extension of one fragment of the opening theme. The moment of severity is short-lived and soon the pianist is back with an even more playful version of tune number two. From here on the listener needs little guidance since despite the inventiveness with which they are treated the tunes are always clearly recognisable.

Towards the end of the movement the pianist whips up the tempo with harp-like chords in the left hand and agile octaves (in triplets) in the right. Even this proves to be an ingenious variation on the opening theme, but it serves admirably to lead the final gallop home. If I had to choose one movement from the entire classical repertoire to convince a philistine that a concerto movement could be utterly delightful from start to finish I think I would select this. Small wonder that he felt that to write a Third would prove impossibly difficult.

Violin Concerto in D Major
Op. 77

Like other great composer-pianists before and after him, from Mozart to
Bartók, Brahms wrote his two piano concertos with his own style of playing
very much in mind. A violin concerto was a different proposition and it is
interesting that the greatest composers have rarely ventured on more than
one unless, like Mozart, they were skilled enough to be concert-performers
on the instrument. Fortunately for Brahms he enjoyed a close friendship
with Joachim, one of the greatest violinists of the day, and it was to Joachim
that he turned for advice when it came to writing the solo part of this
concerto. Advice given was not necessarily advice taken and although he left
the composition of the cadenza entirely to Joachim he often preferred his own
original ideas to Joachim's more violinistic 'improvements'. This was not the
case with the two central movements of what was originally intended to be a
four-movement work. 'The middle movements are failures,' wrote Brahms
in the winter of 1878; 'I have written a feeble Adagio instead.' Surprisingly
the concerto was not particularly well received even with Joachim's advocacy
and it took some time for it to be absorbed into the repertoire. In 1894, three
years before his death, Brahms had the pleasure of hearing the concerto
played by a twelve-year old prodigy, Bronislav Hubermann; it was a sign
that the work was no longer regarded as beyond the powers of all but the very
greatest of masters.

Like the Second Symphony, with which it has more in common than a
shared tonality, it was mostly written in Pörtschach where, to this day, one
can see a lakeside café with the proud inscription that 'within these walls the
great composer Johannes Brahms composed his immortal violin concerto'.
The tranquil atmosphere of the beautiful Carinthian lake resort seems to have
brought out the most lyrical aspect of Brahms's genius, and the opening bars
of the concerto breathe contentment. Three significant themes appear
immediately in sequence; the first (I), on unison violas, cellos, bassoons and
horns, spells out the essential notes of D major; the second (II), on oboes with
a gently rocking string accompaniment that suggests the waters of the
Wörthersee, shifts through C major and G major to the dominant of D *minor*;
it is in this darker key that idea number three (III) makes a dramatic appearance with striding octaves in unison strings and wind. With the advent of the
full orchestra, I reappears in the grandest manner, first overlapping itself and
then 'diminished' to notes of half the original value. An impressive descending scale, like a peal of bells, brings us to the second subject group, which like
the first, consists of three distinct themes. The first (A), initiated by oboe and
horn in unison is then extended by the strings, which, having led us to expect
a crescendo, suddenly recede into a remote *pianissimo*. Four unison notes on

woodwind bring a touch of solemnity which a gracious curve fails to dispel. A strangely bleak theme (B) creates a stark change of mood with its plaintive suggestion of G minor. With sudden ferocity the strings produce an explosive theme with an aggressive dotted rhythm (C) which has as its sequel a repeated pattern of four descending semiquavers against which the lower strings and then the wind have a strong marching ascent. This rich choice of material, seven themes of potential importance, is spread over a magnificent opening tutti of ninety bars. Which theme will the soloist choose to make the most effective entry?

At first hearing it sounds almost as if it is a new idea entirely, but the rocket-like arpeggio which shoots upwards through two octaves to the forceful octaves in the second bar is simply a disguise; in fact Brahms has taken the serene opening theme (I), put it into the minor, and changed its character from gentleness to a highly-charged intensity. Fragments of the dotted rhythm (C) seem to goad the soloist to even more strenuous effort until a climactic chord from the orchestra breaks the tension, allowing the violin a long descent through a sequence of arpeggios as oboe and clarinet in turn play a minor and extended version of I. As the violin continues its athletic progress the woodwind make several references to this new development until at last the music is allowed to return to the major key, bringing back the opening theme in something like its original mood. This whole opening paragraph for the soloist could properly be described as an accompanied cadenza and it lasts almost exactly half the length of the initial tutti, forty-six bars as opposed to ninety. A sustained trill tells us that the rhetoric is over and, with masterly placing, the violin is given the original version of Theme I for˙the first time. Beneath it the violas have an unostentatious accompanying figure which is destined to become gloriously triumphant at a much later stage.

As might be expected from so classically-minded a composer as Brahms, the secondary exposition follows very similar lines to the original tutti although the violin's decorative additions allow the occasional extension of an idea. Theme II duly appears (now in cellos and violas), while the dramatic octave leaps of III provoke a strong reaction from the soloist, whether three-note chords of surprising power or brilliant arpeggios circling round the open E string. A change from busy semiquaver figuration to more leisurely triplets brings us to the second subject group (A) which follows its original course as far as the four solemn unison notes in the woodwind. It is here that Brahms produces a lovely surprise. The brief curving phrase in the woodwind that originally led into the gloom of G minor (B) is now taken over by the soloist and turned into a beguiling new theme (E) of which not even a hint was given in the exposition. One is tempted to call it the true second subject since it is developed at some length by both soloist and orchestra. After thirty bars of enchantment the bleak theme (B) does appear, cold and comfortless. Just as the music seems in danger of coming to a complete halt the soloist launches a vigorous attack with theme (C). For some time battle is joined until a torrent of notes from the violin over a held chord in the wind brings the secondary exposition to a dramatic close.

With an inspired break from tradition Brahms begins the development by giving the full orchestra the version of I which had initially been the soloist's prerogative. Naturally it is shorn of some of the trimmings but is none the less effective for that since now the brass can make striking inter-polations which would have seemed overweighty when pitted against a solo violin. Our surmise that E may well be the true second subject is confirmed when violins and cellos enjoy it to the full, even bringing a touch of sunlight into the gloom of B. This theme, up to now an occasional brief patch of shadow, is now taken up by the soloist and developed in a richly expressive manner. Transferred to the orchestra it then gives an opportunity for a delightful new decoration to be exploited, one tiny rhythmic unit (♫♫) sufficing for no less than twenty bars without creating the slightest feeling of monotony. It is so delicate and graceful that it comes as a real shock when the orchestra, prompted by sudden angry trills from the violin, turn grace into aggression. A short but violent storm breaks out, only to be quelled by a strident chord on full brass and wind. It is the signal for III to reappear, its giant steps marching purposefully through the orchestral bass while the soloist has an extraordinary powerful figure shaped from falling or rising minor ninths. (A—G♯ descending of A—B♭ ascending.) A timpani roll underlines a series of tense allusions to C and I, now thrown into unaccust-omed proximity, until the long-postponed but inevitable climax arrives with a triumphant reprise of the opening theme, now clad in martial glory. A calming entry from the violin re-establishes the original pastoral mood and leads us to a classic recapitulation in which every landmark should be easily identified. A short passage for full orchestra based on I allows the soloist a few seconds' respite before the cadenza.

The coda which follows allows the soloist a sublime meditation on the opening theme before whipping up the tempo with a series of fanfare-like flourishes which are based on the unassuming figure originally allotted to the violas as mere accompaniment some 420 bars previously.

The *Adagio*, in the event the last movement to be written, begins with a miniature wind serenade, a clever device calculated to give the listener's ear a rest from string tone. The melody is given to a solo oboe; it is as well that it is so memorable since the ensuing violin solo is entrusted with an elaborate and ingeniously expanded variation, easy to follow if one bears the original tune in mind. At the halfway point there is a seemingly final cadence emphasised by a trill, but just as we expect the music to come to rest there is a sudden rise of a semi-tone and a shift to the alien key of G flat major. For a moment the music seems uncertain of its direction until the soloist takes the initiative and leads the way into a central rhapsody. Despite the increasingly florid decoration in the solo part the music is built on a very simple frame, mostly derived from a single bar of the initial theme. The pattern is easily recognised, a four-note chromatic descent which, by the process known as diminution, doubles its speed.

This is further simplified to three descending notes (C♯ B A), a version which encourages a brief but passionate exchange between solo violin and orchestral cellos. After a considerable emotional climax has been generated the oboe gives a gentle reminder of the opening theme. The soloist's contribution at the time is simply a descending scale in 'broken' octaves; on paper it looks boringly pedantic but in performance it is one of the most beautiful moments in a notably expressive movement. Having gracefully acknowledged the oboe tune, the violin part continues its descent with similar figuration. A brief interchange between strings and wind brings us to the coda in which the soloist takes the first three notes of the main theme and extends them in a new direction. The oboe bids a touching farewell to its melody and the movement ends in the twilight mood that is one of Brahms's most personal characteristics.

The finale is a joyous Rondo that pays tribute to the Hungarian folk-music that both Brahms and Joachim loved. The rondo theme is announced by the soloist and then taken up enthusiastically by the full orchestra. A sweeping downward scale introduces a rather less ebullient secondary phrase which turns into a ferociously difficult display of double-stopping (two notes at once) beneath which the lower strings can be heard grumbling that they have been deprived of their fun too soon. Their complaint has some effect for back comes the theme in full orchestral dress, seeming to tumble over itself as the rhythms are cleverly contracted.

It is time for a display of virtuosity and the soloist obliges with flashing bow and flying fingers. A flurry of increasingly rapid scales leads into a bold subject that is basically an ascending scale in octaves, the taut rhythm giving it a military swagger. It is answered by a similar pattern travelling in the opposite direction. These two opposing elements create quite a stir in the orchestra until an apparent deadlock is reached with a number of repetitions of the rising third F♯—A. The soloist resolves the problem by bringing back the rondo theme whose first few notes then become a subject for continued discussion in the orchestra while the soloist shows that practising arpeggios when a student did have some musical value after all. Suddenly bored with memories of past drudgery he introduces a delightful new tune in graceful 3/4 time. At first the orchestra show no interest in this, continuing with their previous preoccupation; but soon an oboe and then a flute accept the lure. The lyrical interlude that follows is suddenly broken up by harshly accented chords which, after a few frenzied scales, lead to the ascending octave theme once more. As before, this provokes quite a storm in the orchestra which is diplomatically resolved by a return to the rondo theme, or rather its less bouncy subsidiary. Again grumbles of discontent in the bass lead to a full-blooded statement of the rondo which is interrupted by a brief cadenza for the soloist.

The music becomes more capricious as delicate trills and flighty arpeggios keep us in a state of suspense. Egged on by the horns, the soloist tries a number of experiments with the opening phrase, finally, in exasperation, cutting loose with a rapid sequence of descending arpeggios. The tempo quickens to a brisk march, causing a change of rhythm in the rondo theme; there is a distinct feeling of heading for home as even the rising octave theme turns into a helter-skelter. But then, just as it seems that we are on the brink of a final cadence Brahms introduces a last poetic touch — a quiet chromatic descent in the woodwind, some brief fluttering phrases from the violin and every indication that there is going to be a surprise ending. In fact the ending is the conventionally loud affirmation of the 'proper' key of D, but the orthodox gesture is made to seem a surprise by the imaginative *diminuendo* which precedes it.

BENJAMIN
BRITTEN
1913–76

Variations on a Theme of Frank Bridge
Op. 10

Britten's talents as a composer surfaced remarkably early, a fact that has been increasingly realised with the publication and performance of boyhood works that had not been publicly available during his lifetime. In the fostering and development of this talent he was extremely fortunate to have studied with a first-class teacher, Frank Bridge, who was himself a composer of substance. Bridge obviously realised that his young pupil had exceptional qualities because he would sometimes give the best part of an entire day to a single lesson. He demanded the highest standards of work; in Britten's own words:

> This strictness was the product of nothing but professionalism. Bridge insisted on the absolutely clear relationship of what was in my mind to what was on the paper. I used to get sent to the other side of the room; Bridge would play what I'd written and demand if it was what I'd really meant. He taught me to think and feel through the instruments I was writing for; he was most naturally an instrumental composer, and as a superb viola player he thought instrumentally.[1]

Britten wanted to show his appreciation of the help Frank Bridge had been to him in a way that would really mean something to the older man. When, therefore, in 1937 Boyd Neel commissioned the twenty-three year old composer to write a work for the Salzburg Festival, Britten decided to write a set of variations for string orchestra on a theme by Bridge. The score is inscribed 'To F.B. A tribute with affection and admiration'. The actual composition took no more than ten days, showing not only that Bridge had taught his brilliant young pupil well, but that now he was fully fledged, and able to tackle the problems of composing at the most advanced level without any help from teacher. The theme Britten chose is a nostalgic little tune in waltz time, with a tender falling phrase like a sigh (see Ex.1 opposite). It can be seen at once that bars 4–6 are themselves a variation on bars 1–3. The next part of the theme is simply a transposition of Ex.1, beginning on C sharp instead of E. There follows a slight elaboration, with poignant F naturals put in as a prefix; but the only significantly new element consists of paired quavers rising to the merest suggestion of a climax (Ex.2).

---

[1]From 'Music All Around Me' by Antony Hopkins, pp. 42–3. It is an extract from an article that first appeared in the *Sunday Telegraph* in 1964 and was then translated into a broadcast talk and recorded in this form by Benjamin Britten for BBC 'Music Magazine' of 9 January, 1966.

Ex. 1

p con tenerezza

Ex. 2

The work begins with a stirring introduction which focusses almost entirely on the conflict between C naturals in the bass and a perfectly conventional E major chord above. (The reason for choosing this particular mixture is clear enough since it anticipates exactly the way that Bridge harmonises the very first note of the theme.) Over a sustained C in the bass, violins, violas and cellos in turn exchange brilliant fanfares based on E major arpeggios with occasional alien notes thrown in to give added spice. Out of this exciting tumult emerges a ghostly chord on four solo strings. (The Bridge theme is taken from a string quartet.) With tender simplicity the theme begins, its harmonies lightly etched by the guitar-like chords plucked softly by the other players.

The first variation is almost entirely concerned with the passionate phrase shown as Ex. 2 above. Over the rich dark chords of the lower strings the violins muse uneasily on that segment of the theme alone. The supporting harmonies are for the most part fairly orthodox, but presented in that fresh and intriguing way which Britten particularly exploited in his earlier years. In a mere twenty bars this expressive Adagio contains a wide range of emotion.

Variation 2 is entitled 'March', though for the most part it is curiously spectral in feeling, a 'Marche Macabre'. Its material is drawn from the first two phrases of the theme which are compressed so that the falling fifth becomes a fourth (D–A) while the B is flattened. Violas, cellos and basses set off with crisp precision but far from military tread. In the seventh bar, just before a quiet sustained trill in the violins, this derivation of the theme is inverted. Pizzicato interpolations from the second violins make a striking effect as do the piccolo-like trills above. An exciting crescendo brings the march theme to the violins but before long the ghostly patrol disappears into the distance.

Variation 3, 'Romance', is an extended aria for all the violins in unison over a softly vamped accompaniment with a subtle rhythm. The melody is derived from bars 7–8 of the theme. Once again Britten modifies the first interval, this time stretching it to a fourth. A change of rhythm is all that is necessary to complete the disguise.

Ex. 3

(The second part is transposed to simplify comparison.)

The tune is so easy to listen to that we may fail to realise that during the first four bars the pizzicato bass follows the exact pattern of Bridge's theme (bars 1–6).

Variation 4 is called 'Aria Italiana', a title that suggests an operatic love-song of the more sentimental kind. But Britten's parody is more blistering than that: he visualises one of those frantically busy operatic arias where the heroine, surrounded by countermarching troops, exhorts her loved one to deeds of derring-do, phrased with all the virtuosity at her command. The theme is forgotten except for the initial impulse provided by the falling fifth. Such genuine musical wit is a rarity and this variation caused huge delight at the first performance in Salzburg.

Variation 5, 'Bourrée Classique', is also based largely on the falling fifth that begins Bridge's theme. Here it is flogged mercilessly on the two open strings A–D. There is more than a touch of Prokofiev in this and it may be that the parody is intentional if a mite malicious.[2]

Variation 6 provides a Viennese Waltz as a compliment to the Austrian audience to whom the work was first to be performed. Neither '*Rosenkavalier*' nor '*The Merry Widow*', the music moves swiftly with a violin part that suggests the empty gossip of society ladies in a smart café. In the first bar we hear the ubiquitous falling fifth. Thereafter the material is mostly derived from bars 7–8 of Bridge's theme. First it is fashioned into a chromatic loop of notes which is extended in various ways. It then appears as a langourous melody in the middle strings, the initial rising third being repeated several times before being allowed to flick down to the end of the phrase. It is one of the longest of the variations and is technically one of the most challenging.

Variation 7 is an extraordinary 'Moto Perpetuo' which bears little relationship to the theme. It is basically a single strand of notes, unharmonised, as though we were suddenly able to hear one giant string instrument of infinite

[2]Donald Mitchell proposes Stravinsky as the target though I feel the young Britten would have respected him too much to satirise him.

range — music for a superhuman Paganini striding across a dozen strings.

The eighth variation, 'Funeral March', is the most profound in content. A drum-like rhythm in the bass harps persistently on Bridge's falling fifth; but the melody above is also based on a falling fifth, though now the intermediate steps are filled in to make a partial scale. Scooping *glissandi* suggest cries of lamentation and the influence of Mahler (whom Britten greatly admired) can be felt in almost every phrase.

Variation 9, 'Chant', is a strange interlude with eerie harmonics casting a chill that seems to inhibit movement save for some restless fidgeting in the violas. It is like a winter landscape in which we see a starving animal scratching in the snow in its search for food.

Variation 10 is called 'Fugue and Finale'. The fugue subject is an urgent and breathless transformation of bars 1–6 of Bridge's theme, but it is the treatment of the material that makes this fugue truly unique. It is the very essence of fugal composition that the music should accumulate part by part so that in a fugue for quartet we hear first one, then two, then three, then four lines with a texture that consequently grows in density as each part is added. Britten's fugue *looks* like a fugue on paper; one can see how violins, violas and cellos enter in turn. But the *sound*, as in the 'Moto Perpetuo' is like a single strand, even though the fabric is made up from many overlapping fragments divided between the various instruments. With the entry of the double basses the fugue subject is put aside and replaced by suggestions of a grotesque march. The falling fifth becomes more and more insistent until rushing scale passages seem to sweep the sound away. Double basses descend to their lowest E, setting up a throbbing pulse. As though in a whisper the fragments of the fugue begin to assemble, this time in several different keys. With a stroke of sheer magic the original theme appears as if in a dream, surrounded by the continuous rustle and murmur of the elfin fugue. At last the players all converge on one note which grows in intensity until it is like a searchlight beam, only to fade away again into near darkness. With great tenderness Britten begins a long farewell to the theme, an extended coda whose final bars lead us to expect a quiet ending; but a sudden gust of wind seems to scatter the pages away leaving the orchestra no option but to converge on a final impressive unison.

The Variations were an instant success and proved to be the foundation of Britten's international reputation. Within two years they received fifty performances in Europe and America. They remain one of the truly out-standing works in the string orchestral repertoire.

CHOPIN

1810–49

Piano Concerto No. 2 in F minor
Op. 21

Although this work is still habitually referred to as the Second Concerto it was actually the first that Chopin wrote. He was only nineteen at the time and undoubtedly regarded such an ambitious project as a necessary passport to the fame he hoped to attain in more cosmopolitan capitals than Warsaw. He had already shown outstanding qualities as a teenager and his teacher, Elsner, wrote in his diary that his young pupil had opened 'a new era in piano music through his astonishing playing as well as with his compositions'. A trip to Vienna in July 1829 made him realise the relative poverty of musical life in Poland but all the same he greatly impressed a number of distinguished musicians who heard him. 'All these Germans (sic) are amazed by me', he wrote to his family, 'and I am amazed at them being so amazed by me.'

The concerto cost him immense labour, partly because, despite his youth, he was forging a completely individual style of writing for the keyboard. The first book of studies (Op. 10) was occupying him at the same time and while each study is concerned with one particular aspect of technique the whole set show an astonishing originality in their pianistic layout. The concerto was first performed on 17 March 1830 and although he had an inadequate instrument which was sometimes swamped by the orchestra he scored a huge success with the audience. A second performance on a better piano was at once arranged for 22 March. One of the critics wrote, 'Chopin does not play like others; he gives the impression that every note passes through the eyes[1] to the soul, and that the soul pours it into the fingers.'

The concertos have both been criticised for the lack of interest in the orchestral parts, but it should be realised that Chopin was not trying to emulate Beethoven. He was writing at a time when the piano was becoming the dominant instrument. Great pianists enjoyed the adulation given to pop-stars today and the public was eager to be dazzled by feats of virtuosity. Chopin was known to play his concertos as solo works, dispensing with the orchestra. He was passing through a period of indecision; was he to be a pianist who composed or a composer who performed? It is an intriguing comment on musical fashion that when in the following year he arrived in Paris, he received a letter from his revered teacher advising him that playing the piano was only the beginning of a career; he would be wise to turn his talents to opera since the piano concertos of Mozart and Beethoven were already forgotten! We may consider ourselves fortunate that the advice was disregarded.

[1]The custom of playing from memory in public had not been established.

The F minor concerto actually begins with a substantial orchestral exposition, considerably longer incidentally than anything to be found in the concertos of Schumann, Liszt, Tchaikovsky, Grieg or other less admired composers of the mid-nineteenth century. The opening bars may be quiet, but their softness is misleading; it is not weak but rather an expression of aristocratic melancholy, soon dispelled by defiant chords for full orchestra. The first eight bars will in due course be accepted and elaborately decorated by the pianist, but quite a substantial portion of the opening tutti belongs to the orchestra alone. Admittedly we are given a taste of the second subject, but it assumes a somewhat martial manner which gives a very false impression of its romantic potential. After a rousing sequence built from a more athletic phrase the music dies down, creating a sense of expectancy. With a wonderfully commanding phrase covering almost the entire span of the keyboard the soloist makes a dramatic entrance. A brief fill-in from the left hand allows us to recover from the shock and then, in the most lyrical style, we hear the piano version of the opening orchestral phrase. A cynic might dismiss it as little more than an act of courtesy since once the gesture has been made the soloist introduces a completely new theme, soon to be decorated in characteristic fashion with exquisite roulades.

A passage of pure development follows, based essentially on alternations of dominant and tonic harmony. But where a classical composer would have been content to use conventional scales or arpeggios as decoration over an orchestral foundation, Chopin shows his extraordinary flair for inventing new ways of presenting such basic materials. Each group of notes has some subtle twist, a change of shape here, an unexpected chromaticism there; and although to the heedless ear the piano part may seem like aimless chatter, there is hardly a phrase that does not contain implications of melody. The beautiful arabesque of single notes that leads into the second subject is a perfect example, an extended arpeggio-like figure that skilfully avoids any obvious pattern. (Pedants may identify it as a 'dominant ninth' but that gives little hint of its magic.)

The second subject is greatly extended in the piano part, ending with a feather-like run and a sad cadence in C minor that Chopin marks '*con duolo*'. Within two bars 'grief' is replaced by 'resolution' — *risoluto*. It marks the beginning of perhaps the most memorable episode in the movement which, after modulating through several keys, leads to a captivating tune that has a suggestion of fairy bells chiming in a summer breeze. A surging left hand marks a change of mood and the music builds to a heroic climax.

A substantial orchestral interlude follows, enabling the soloist to mop his brow; its relationship to the original exposition is curious, as though Chopin vaguely remembered how it went but couldn't be bothered to check it. The next solo entry produces a beautifully simple variation on the opening theme, the two hands in unison. However, the air of simplicity is misleading, and within moments the pianist becomes involved in a passage of extreme agitation. The technical demands are formidable without the more blatant exhibitionism we find in the Liszt concertos. A brilliant descent in chromatic thirds reinforced by the left hand leads to a short orchestral interlude which is the cue for a recapitulation of sorts, much shorter proportionately than what we would find in a Beethoven concerto. Surprisingly the movement ends with orchestra alone as though the youthful composer was determined to show that this was music to be taken seriously.

There is little that needs to be said about the slow movement except that it is one of the most beautiful Nocturnes that Chopin ever wrote, a literal Nocturne for piano and orchestra which, like several of the similar works for solo piano, has a dramatic central section by way of contrast. Five bars of orchestral introduction suffice to set the scene before the pianist embarks on the most ravishing melody. One feels that here is a permanent record of what Chopin's improvisations must have been like; however elaborate the decorations may be there is a sense of spontaneous invention so that at moments one can almost see a smile on Chopin's face as he causes his listeners to gasp at the fluency with which he embroiders an otherwise conventional cadence. In the centre of the movement the strings begin an agitated *tremolando* on the chord of A flat minor; above, there is an impassioned recitative for piano, the two hands in unison. It is a remarkable piece of writing in the grand manner of heroic Romanticism. With modern pianos there is no need for the strings to stay as quiet as is indicated in the score; the drama should be shared. At last, all passion spent, an enchanting bell-like chime from the piano leads us back to the opening theme, even more elaborated. The movement ends as quietly as it began, a totally remarkable achievement for a nineteen-year old composer.

The finale is a rondo in the style of a mazurka. The piano leads off with the main theme which the orchestra comments on without saying much of consequence. A second version of the theme follows with some skips that Scarlatti would have appreciated; the formal close on the orchestra merely confirms the key of F minor.

The first episode follows, beginning with a downward rush that has a slight similarity to the pianist's initial entry in the first movement. A delightful variation on the rondo ensues, now in A flat major, with a continuous flow of triplets that cover a wide range of the keyboard. Once again the orchestra rounds off, this time with a rustic rhythm that effectively takes the music out-of-doors. The pianist now presents the second episode which is a theme with a suggestion of a horn-call about it. Chopin had already become very interested in Polish folk-music, and the second limb of this tune must be modelled on a folk-dance. It too becomes the subject for brilliant variations before reappearing in the rather unexpected key of C major. The music loses impetus for a moment before a long chromatic descent from the upper reaches of the keyboard leads neatly back to a reprise of the rondo theme.

A solo horn-call seems briefly to anticipate Richard Strauss, a sort of 'Till Ready-spiegl'. It is the signal for the coda in which the horn-call is taken over by the pianist's left hand while the right dazzles us with glittering figurations that seem to be the musical equivalent of laughter. The entire concerto bears out Elsner's opinion that Chopin had opened a new era in piano music; to have done so when he was still virtually a student underlines the remarkable individuality of his genius.

DEBUSSY
1862–1918

Although Debussy was in no way exploited as a child prodigy he certainly had enough innate talent to be one. In July 1874, shortly before his twelfth birthday he played the formidably difficult F minor concerto of Chopin in the advanced piano class of the Paris Conservatoire. It was the compulsory set-piece for the top prize that year and despite his extreme youth Debussy gained an honourable mention. Two years later he won the Second Prize for piano and it was confidently predicted that he would win the First Prize the following year. It was not to be, for despite his natural gift the idea of being a concert-pianist had no great appeal for him; besides, as he grew older his style became increasingly eccentric. A fellow-student, Gabriel Pierné, described Debussy's playing while he was still in his teens:

> He used to astonish us with his weird playing. I don't know whether it was due to native awkwardness or timidity, but he used literally to throw himself at the keyboard and exaggerate every effect. He seemed to be in a violent rage with the instrument — to treat it with impulsive gestures, breathing noisily as he performed difficult passages. He had a habit of emphasising the strong beats with a sort of panting or raucous breathing. These faults became gradually less noticable and at times he produced marvellously soft and delicate effects. These qualities, good and bad, gave his playing a very individual character.

Debussy won many distinctions at the Conservatoire but he was a far from model student, failing his harmony exams year after year owing to his refusal to obey the academic rules. He exasperated his teachers yet they could not deny his talent; some regarded him as a dangerous influence who might corrupt his fellow-students by the unorthodoxy of his ideas.

A curious musical link was established when, at the age of seventeen, he became resident pianist to a wealthy Russian widow, Nadezhda von Meck, who for years had been Tchaikovsky's patroness. She kept a trio of musicians on her staff to entertain her, and night after night the young Frenchman would play chamber-music or piano solos to while away her lonely evenings.

She took him with her to Florence, Venice, Vienna and then north to Moscow. It must have been a dream-like experience for the still adolescent youth, coming as he did from a semi-working-class background where the prospects of foreign travel must have seemed remote. No doubt it helped to cultivate his love of the exotic, not to mention his contempt for conventional behaviour.

By modifying his highly individual style to suit the conservative taste of the jury he managed to win the coveted Prix de Rome in 1884, entitling him to a two-year sojourn in Rome to further his studies. He found the enforced stay abroad irksome and failed to meet all the conditions that the prize imposed. Soon after his return to Paris he became involved with a pretty young blonde called Gabrielle Dupont; they shared a penurious existence together for nine years though Debussy, ever susceptible, was a less than faithful lover. In 1897 his philanderings caused Gabrielle to attempt suicide. Debussy was contrite but the damage was done and two years later he married one of Gabrielle's friends, Rosalie Texier, having given a piano lesson in the morning to be able to pay for the wedding breakfast. Over the previous few years he had been persevering with his major project, the opera 'Pelléas et Mélisande', but other works, notably 'Prélude à l'après-midi d'un faune' and the 'Nocturnes' for orchestra, had been completed and established his growing reputation.

The preliminaries to the first performance of 'Pelléas' were marred by a violent quarrel between the composer and the author, Maeterlinck, whose wife had been considered for the title-role. Characteristically Debussy had started to rehearse with another singer without saying anything, so enraging Maeterlinck that the two men were nearly involved in a duel. Meanwhile Debussy's marriage showed signs of losing its initial bloom since Rosalie had little comprehension of his music. In 1903 he began a liaison with a banker's wife named Emma Bardac which was soon to cause a scandal that shocked even his Bohemian friends. In the summer of 1904 Debussy left his wife and joined Mme Bardac in an apartment she had bought for them. A few months later Rosalie tried to shoot herself and was taken to hospital with severe chest injuries. That Debussy could continue to compose in the midst of such melodrama demonstrates the supreme egotism of genius; but even he was not insensitive to the antagonism his actions had aroused. Faced with a damaging divorce suit he and Mme Bardac fled to Eastbourne to escape from what he described as 'this tedious fuss'. It was there, within the sound of the sea, that he completed his orchestral masterpiece *La Mer*.

The first performance took place on 15 October 1905, exciting more controversy than enthusiasm. Many of the audience were openly hostile to Debussy since the scandal was still in the forefront of people's minds. Even so, some of the Parisians' disappointment may well have stemmed from the fact that the title led them to suppose that the music would be more openly descriptive than it is. The critic of '*Le Temps*' said, 'I neither hear, see nor feel the sea;' but for all its evocative qualities '*La Mer*' is not a descriptive tone-poem such as Richard Strauss might have written. It is no accident that Debussy called the work 'Three symphonic sketches', sharing the attitude Beethoven had shown in the 'Pastoral' symphony when he said it was 'more an impression of the countryside than an actual painting'. The titles of the three movements, 'From dawn to mid-day on the sea', 'Play of the Waves' and 'Dialogue of the wind and the sea' are sufficiently vague to allow one to fill in images for oneself. (Erik Satie made a classic joke at the first rehearsal when, referring to the period 'from dawn to mid-day' in the first movement, he said he particularly liked the bit around half-past ten.) It was not until the London première in 1908 that *La Mer* was fully appreciated; Debussy himself conducted and, despite considerable nervousness caused by his lack of experience with the baton, he steered the orchestra through the intricate score with notable success. Nevertheless *The Times* critic seemed to have reservations:

> For perfect enjoyment of this music there is no attitude of mind more to be recommended than the passive, unintelligent rumination of the typical amateur of the mid-Victorian era. As long as actual sleep can be avoided, the hearer can derive great pleasure from the strange sounds that enter his ears if he will only put away all idea of definite construction or logical development.[1]

Just how misleading this suggestion is we shall now discover.

[1] E. Lockspeiser, *Debussy* (Dent, 1936).

'La Mer'

1. 'De l'aube à midi sur la mer'

The movement begins as quietly as possible; harps set up a gentle alternation of adjacent notes (F♯—G♯) which are then given a little rhythmic flick by muted cellos. It scarcely seems important enough to be called a theme but its rhythm is like a signature which appears a number of times whether the paired notes are rising or falling. Violas have a slow ascent based on rising fourths which prompts a high shimmer on violins like the first tentative streak of sunlight in the grey dawn-mist. The 'rhythmic flick' appears several times in various woodwind instruments; muted trumpet and cor anglais in unison offer a longer phrase, easily recognised by the five repeated notes with which it begins. It is worth remembering since it spans the whole work. A long descent through the strings leads to a slightly more animated section in which the 'rising fourths' phrase gathers momentum. Daylight breaks through as second violins and violas begin a rippling figure which certainly depicts the surface of the water stirred into motion by a gentle breeze. Cellos have a continuously reiterated pattern not unlike the one that Mendelssohn uses so effectively in the 'Hebrides' overture. Above these repeated wavelets four muted horns have a long melancholy theme whose modal scale gives it a hint of plainsong. Debussy has the habit of throwing fragmentary themes into the score so that as we listen we may find it difficult to gauge their ultimate importance — a plaintive tune for oboe and solo cello in unison, a swift rise and fall on a flute that suggests the flight of a bird skimming over the waves. But as the strength of the breeze clearly increases, the 'plainsong' theme in the horns becomes more prominent while glittering figures in the woodwind suggest the white crests of the waves sparkling in the sun.

There is a momentary lull before a remarkable passage for cellos, divided into four parts — Debussy specifies sixteen players. Their energetic new theme, starting with the 'rhythmic flick' from the introduction, soon spreads to other sections of the orchestra, first the woodwind and then, more powerfully, woodwind and horns. Meanwhile the waves gather force unmistakably as the strings pound out an exciting repetitive rhythm. A gradual *diminuendo* tells us that the wind is losing its edge though the water remains choppy. Cor anglais and trumpet recall the theme from the introduction, the one with five repeated notes to begin with; skilfully Debussy reintroduces other fragments from the opening pages, clearly recognisable to us now, even if not to *The Times* critic of 1908. A patch of haze (cor anglais and cello in unison against sustained string harmonies) leads us to suppose that the movement will end quietly, but suddenly the mist is dispersed by a glorious blaze of sunlight as the full brass lend their weight to the orchestral mass.

2. 'Jeux de vagues'

This movement serves the same function as a scherzo in a symphony. It is less substantial than the outer movements and a little more openly pictorial. The orchestration is both scintillating and translucent, a textbook of delicate effects that have often been copied but never surpassed. Nobody can have taught Debussy how to put these sounds on paper, how to imagine them with such assurance. By putting it into its historical context we can better judge the individuality of Debussy's style. Stravinsky's *Firebird* has something of the same inventiveness, but in 1905 Stravinsky was still a student. If Debussy had a rival it would have been Richard Strauss who had produced most of his large-scale tone-poems by 1900. *Don Juan*, *Tod und Verklärung*, *Zarathustra*, *Till Eulenspiegl* and even *Don Quixote* are all late nineteenth-century works. Without disrespect to Strauss, for all his brilliance he was extending a Wagnerian style, adapting it to his own purposes. Debussy had struck out in a much more individual way, consciously shaking off all traces of Wagnerian influence. His harmony is much more elusive than that of Strauss, who tends to glory in the common chord, even though his rapid and frequent shifts of key disguise the fact. When Debussy uses common chords he tends to move them in parallel motion as blocks of sound; elsewhere his use of the whole-tone scale (six consecutive intervals of a tone) gives an enigmatic 'off-centre' quality to every harmony.

Thematic analysis is hardly worth while in this movement. After a brief shimmering introduction a cor anglais produces the most important fragment, an upward flick of four notes which then flowers into a nimble, vaguely oriental theme. First cousin to this is an idea that is easily spotted since it begins with two trills on unison violins. A tortuous phrase for horns leads to a swiftly pattering rhythm on flutes and clarinets. Almost everything thereafter is derived from one or other of these initial materials. The beauty of the music lies not in the themes but in the kaleidoscopic colour, constantly shifting as indeed the reflections of light on water do. Surprisingly the movement ends with a whisper.

3. 'Dialogue du vent et de la mer'

It is in this movement that Debussy fully justifies his use of the word 'symphonic' in the subtitle, 'Three Symphonic Sketches'. Much of the material is culled from the slow introduction to the opening movement, yet it also has some strongly defined themes of its own. After some menacing rumbles that tell us a storm is building up over the horizon, the woodwind introduce the first of these; it is instantly repeated at a higher pitch with the added strength of horns. Growling bassoons and chattering cellos should not distract us from listening to cor anglais and clarinets who recall the 'rhythmic flick' from the very opening of the work. The memory once awakened, a solo trumpet confirms our recollection with a very positive version of the theme from the second page that originally began with five repeated notes. These are now dispensed with as unsuitably hesitant. A swift succession of urgently rising scale fragments in the strings gives a vivid suggestion of waves rushing towards the shore.

Suddenly, above the angry tug of the swell, the woodwind begin a hauntingly beautiful phrase whose first two notes, a falling semitone, are derived from the 'rhythmic flick' in the introduction. The tune is long drawn-out by Debussy's standards, but in the background one senses the racing tide. Soon the strings begin a wildly tossing figure against which we hear Neptune's horn-call summoning the winds to whip up the seas. Bassoons and pizzicato cellos build up the excitement by reiterating the theme from the introduction which has now shed its initial repeated notes for good. Repeated several times, this theme builds to a huge climax. Debussy seldom uses the full orchestra so that when he does the impact is that much greater.

A chromatic descent through trumpets, horns and trombones in turn leads to a lull in the storm. (Notice the high solo cornet's reference to the 'rhythmic flick' theme from the opening). There is a soft mysterious trill on low clarinet and bassoon before softly but majestically the horns introduce a solemn new theme, richly harmonised. It is destined to play a crucial part in the final climax although at this stage we only hear it twice. Soon it is time for the other great theme of this third movement to return, the long haunting tune beginning with the falling semitone. Now it is on flute and oboe with an altogether less agitated accompaniment — a murmur on harps and a high sustained note on violins. A glockenspiel produces a playful variant which is copied by horns and woodwind in turn. At last the strings are allowed to bring their full expressive power to the 'falling' theme. It is an emotional high-spot not to be missed.

For a while Debussy throws his various themes into disorder, as though different currents were converging in a rocky cove; but by this stage they should all be easily recognised. The strings whip up the excitement with increasingly urgent figures until a majestic climax is reached as the solemn brass theme reappears like the God of the Seas arising with his trident from the waters. A short swift coda, again derived from the introduction, brings this truly symphonic movement to an end. It marked a new stage in Debussy's development, showing that not only could he handle the largest orchestral forms with complete authority, but that he had new light to shed on traditional concepts of musical structures.

'Nocturnes'

In 1892, at the age of thirty, Debussy began to compose '*Trois scènes au crepescule*' (Three twilight scenes). The first movement was intended to be called 'A study in grey' but the inclusion of a solo violin part, surely unsuitable for such a role, showed that Debussy lacked a clear vision of the work. With the fastidious self-criticism that he applied to his music, if not to his morality, he scrapped the project, retaining only the best of the ideas for possible future use. They emerged some five years later in *Nocturnes*, a set of three wonderfully descriptive pieces which, though they lack the symphonic strengths of *La Mer*, yield nothing to it in terms of the imaginative use of tone-colour. The composer himself provided an introductory note which freely acknowledges the frankly descriptive nature of the music.

> The title *Nocturnes* is to be interpreted here in a general and, more particularly, in a decorative sense. Therefore it is not meant to designate the usual form of the nocturne, but rather all the various impressions and the special effects of light that the word suggests. *Nuages* renders the immutable aspect of the sky and the slow, solemn motion of the clouds, fading away in grey tones lightly tinged with white. *Fêtes* gives us the vibrating atmosphere with sudden flashes of light. There is also the episode of the procession (a dazzling fantastic vision) which passes through the festive scene and becomes merged in it. But the background remains persistently the same: the festival, with its blending of music and luminous dust, participating in the cosmic rhythm. *Sirènes* depicts the sea and its countless rhythms and presently, amongst the waves silvered by the moonlight, is heard the mysterious song of the Sirens as they laugh and pass on.[2]

Although the full score was published in 1900 a subsequent edition printed twelve years after the composer's death shows a number of important modifications he made in the light of experience. A detailed study of the two scores might prove a fruitful subject for a thesis but need not concern us here since the original version is no longer played.

1. 'Nuages' (Clouds)

If there is any truth in the maxim 'Great minds think alike' supporting evidence is to be found here since the opening harmonic sequences, bleakly scored for clarinets and bassoons, are remarkably akin to Stravinsky both in timbre and idiom. (In fact, whether Debussy consciously realised it or not, the melodic curve of the initial phrase was lifted note for note from a

[2]Ibid., p. 189.

Mussorgsky song called 'Sunless', an act of petty larceny that was also committed by Stravinsky in '*Le Rossignol*'.) After two static chords on divided violins beneath which there is a far distant rumble of thunder from the timpani, the opening phrases are resumed by muted strings, richly divided into eight or more parts. There is a passage in Joyce's *A portrait of the artist as a young man* which provides a wonderfully exact parallel to this music: '. . . the slow-drifting clouds, dappled and sea-borne, . . . voyaging across the deserts of the sky, a host of nomads on the march . . .'

Gradually the texture increases in density as though the clouds are forming into sky-mountains, their peaks tipped with an illusion of snow. A plangent little theme on the cor anglais appears from time to time, an expression of loneliness; a recurring pair of notes on unison horns depicts the siren of a small tug as it chugs its way down river.[3] On the whole the woodwind have a relatively small contribution to make until a solo flute introduces a more openly lyrical melody in F sharp major; doubled by harp it brings a ray of sunshine into the grey sky. It is echoed by a solo string trio but is soon lost in the prevailing mist. There are few pieces in the entire orchestral repertoire in which less appears to happen and yet there is a magic about the sheer sound which casts its own especial spell.

2. 'Fêtes' (Festival days)

The second movement is far from Nocturnal in the usual romantic sense; it may be a night scene, but it is a scene of noisy revelry at one of those fairgrounds which to this day the French so enjoy. An exhilarating tarantella-like rhythm sets the mood while whirling runs in the woodwind suggest helter-skelters and merry-go-rounds. The pace is hectic as crowds swirl round the numerous side-shows, only arrested for a moment by a strident brass fanfare and a roll of drums — perhaps the stentorian voice of the ringmaster in the circus-tent. Woodwind suggest the excited chatter of the spectators in brilliant repeated triplets (note the 15/8 time signature, five beats to the bar) as the music continues its headlong rush. At one point a long swaying theme in unison wind may represent a group of drunken revellers walking with arms linked through the heedless crowd. Suddenly, as a considerable climax is reached, there is an abrupt change of mood and tempo. As from a great distance we hear the thump of drums and the tread of marching feet. It is the band of the Garde Républicaine approaching in ceremonial dress.

[3]Other commentators maintain that the chromatic melody on the cor anglais represents the ship's hooter, an insult to Debussy's ear when the horns provide so much more accurate a description. The mistake presumably arises through a reported conversation between Debussy and a friend, Paul Poujaud; Poujaud doubtless confused cor anglais with '*cors*' – horns.

The gradual crescendo as they come nearer is marvellously graded by systematic augmentation of the orchestral resources. With the addition of trombones, tuba and a martial side-drum, Debussy skilfully reintroduces the whirling scales from the start of the movement, as though hordes of children are rushing alongside the band to get a better view. Arrived at their destination, the bandsmen halt and put down their instruments. The opening music resumes, not quite so noisily as before since presumably the band has attracted too much attention and the stalls are relatively deserted. Soon the carnival is in full swing again with one important newcomer in the shape of a striking theme given to the violins. It is related to the triplet quavers that dance attendance on it, though not an exact augmentation. Gradually the crowds depart; tender farewells are exchanged between oboe, flute and bassoon; a drummer from the band beats a brief tattoo as he disappears into the distance; lights flicker and die as the streets finally empty.

3. 'Sirènes' (Mermaids)

As though in preparation for *La Mer*, 'Sirènes' describes a moonlit seascape in which the voices of mermaids cast a supernatural spell. To achieve this effect Debussy employs a small choir of sixteen female voices, an additional expense which concert promoters tend to resent. The voices sing a wordless chant for which the composer does not even suggest specific vowel-sounds. The most important theme appears first on a solo cor anglais, a favourite instrument in Debussy scores; it is easily recognised by the triplet embellishment on the second note and by its sad chromatic fall. It appears a number of times in diminished form before becoming a hypnotically repeated pattern in the violins.

A gently undulating melody appears in the voice-parts; notice especially a version for mezzo-sopranos alone with an extraordinary depiction in the strings of the glitter of moonlight on water. A sweeping scale rising through two octaves leads to a brief climax in which the horns have an important two-note figure suggesting the sound of conch-shells blowing. Debussy's use of pairs of adjacent notes is extraordinarily inventive, and here we do find an apt comparison with *La Mer*. As befits a moonlit scene the colouring is mostly subdued, *piano* or *pianissimo* being the most frequently used dynamic. The absence of significant themes would seem to be a severe handicap but it is in the nature of Debussy's genius that he can engage our interest by the constant play of colours rather than by memorable tunes. We may not find ourselves singing as we leave the concert-hall, but we will find that we have been put into a trance of sorts and that our minds are filled with such sounds as were heard on Prospero's island.

Images
(1910–13)

There is something inherently respectable about writing a symphony or a concerto, and if a composer writes exactly the same amount of music in the guise of a symphonic poem, we tend to assume that in some way it is a work of lesser stature. To deny a composer the highest rank because he never wrote a symphony is about as silly as to say that a man could never be a first-class citizen unless he owned a frock-coat. The symphony was the great monumental form of the late eighteenth and early nineteenth centuries. By 1880 it had largely been replaced by other forms, and what symphonies there were were frequently graced with explanatory titles so that the composers could get the best of both worlds by gaining the prestige attached to the word symphony while not actually adhering too closely to the form. Debussy is a perfect example of a composer who was clear-sighted enough to realise that the classical forms, based as they were on conflicts of tonality, were of little use to him. But the sheer work involved both spiritually and physically in the creation of works like *La Mer* or the orchestral *Images* was just as great — greater in fact, for there was no ready-made mould into which he could pour his ideas.

The full score of *Images* runs to 205 pages of exquisitely conceived orchestral colour. Debussy had in mind a somewhat vague scheme of associating these pieces with three countries, England, Spain and France. The Spanish part, which is longer than the other two combined, is itself divided into three sections. The first movement seems to have been the one that gave him the greatest difficulty in that he ultimately left it uncompleted. (The orchestration was finished by André Caplet.) It is called '*Gigues*', a title to which he originally added the word 'Tristes'. 'Sad Jigs' seem to be a contradiction, but then contradictions would appeal to a mind as subtle and elusive as Debussy's. It starts in utter stillness, and anything less jig-like it would be hard to imagine — nor less English for that matter.

An oboe d'amore, its tones rather more individual than the ordinary orchestral oboe, plays a sad little tune which hardly disturbs the vague misty background. There's still little sign of a jig, even a sad one.

Even when Debussy shows his hand more openly the only thematic shape to appear is a falling third. But just as skilfully as any symphonist, Debussy takes this shape and converts it into a more sharply defined rhythm. If the ensuing melody vaguely reminds you of a folk-tune called the Keelrow you're entirely justified — it's meant to. It is indeed the only element of 'English-ness' in this very French score, but it's there for a purpose, just as there are Spanish rhythms and melodic shapes in the movements that are associated with Spain.

The jig begins to fall into shape, the rhythm becoming firmer and more clearly marked. But the music seems to be of two minds and part of the fascination of this very under-estimated piece lies in the way Debussy preserves two conflicting and apparently irreconcilable moods simultaneously. The sad piper's tune reappears, but the dance-rhythm fidgets along underneath it.

To examine the scoring in detail would be the work of hours; we take Debussy's orchestral virtuosity for granted nowadays but one only has to look at any one of its pages to be struck by the extraordinary delicacy of calculation which went into them. Here a chord is scored for four desks of violins only, another for three; there a single note on the harp is marked *piano* but stressed; a solo viola is matched with a high bassoon; every sound is imagined with such exactitude and such finesse, and this applies all through *Images*.

Part Two, the so-called 'Iberia', is the most popular. It is divided into three distinct sections, but despite the very large orchestra Debussy uses, the sound is never coarse or ostentatious. The rhythms too, though they obviously have a markedly Spanish flavour, are wayward and unpredictable, the melodic lines being deliberately stretched across the accompanying figures in such a way as to prevent the shapes from ever being trite.

The first section of 'Iberia', *Par les rues et par les chemins*, conjures up a picture of Spanish villages. Now, descriptive works are liable to be episodic, whereas symphonic works demand repetition and development. Debussy's 'Iberia' is infinitely more symphonic in its approach than, say, Rimsky-Korsakov's *Capriccio Espagnole*. The actual material in this movement is treated with a remarkable economy and discipline. Of course the outlines are not defined in the old manner of first and second subjects, bridge passages and the like, but there is the sort of continuous drive that one expects from a symphonic movement, and the themes are inter-related; these are not impressionistic sketches dashed off in an impromptu fashion, but beautifully controlled compositions, full of conscious craftsmanship, and an avoidance of cliché that is quite remarkable. Debussy even denies himself the easy satisfaction of a grand slam finish to the movement, the final chord being allotted to just two clarinets.

The second section, *Les parfums de la nuit*, is an evocation of the sounds and perfumes of a Spanish evening. It is the quintessence of Debussy, with little in the way of a climax in the whole of its span; *piano* or *pianissimo* appear in nearly every bar, a constant demand for restraint from conductor and players alike. It is music of suggestion rather than statement, of distance rather than proximity. There is not a single *forte* until the fourteenth page and even that is short-lived.

Melodies, such as they are, tend to be fragmentary, and are usually made from three or four adjacent notes. A brief climax near the end leads us to suppose that there might be a positive ending but the music dies away, leaving the final phrase to a solo violin and flute in unison, merging without a break into the third section. This, 'the morning of a public holiday' according to the title, skilfully blends the sound of church bells into the score, a touch of realism that could scarcely be avoided. The movement serves the function of a scherzo but, colourful and gorgeous though it is, it is still music of suggestion and under-statement. To start with, the spell of the langourous evening lingers on and one can imagine the composer being disturbed from sleep by the distant throb of drums, the sound of voices and footsteps in the street below. Soon the violinists and viola-players in the orchestra are instructed to hold their instruments sideways like guitars, and the combined strings produce a wonderful thrumming rhythm in this *'marche joyeuse et alerte'*. Shrill clarinets suggest the amateur efforts of a village band, though a solo fiddler shows surprising accomplishment. Once again, though, the avoidance of any real vulgarity is extraordinary and within moments the sound is sharply suppressed as if the disturbed sleeper had slammed his window shut to keep out the unwelcome sounds. The gesture is in vain for soon we join the throng in the village square; for once Debussy allows himself the indulgence of a grandstand finish.

The final *Image*, 'Rondes de printemps', appeared long after the others. It is headed by the inscription 'Vive le mai! Bienvenu soit le mai avec son gonfalon sauvage'. (Hail May! Welcome May with its wild banner.) Perhaps because Debussy was ravaged by cancer it presents a less than idyllic view of Spring and a critic of the time castigated him for writing such 'wintry dances'. As if to emphasise his disassociation from the conventional view of springtime, Debussy makes extensive use of a popular song 'Nous n'irons plus au bois', subjecting it to distortions that sometimes disguise it effectively from an inattentive ear. There is also an early allusion to a nursery song 'Do, do l'enfant do'. They are tunes that must have had a special appeal for Debussy since both appear in one of his most famous piano pieces, *Jardins sous la pluie*. Although the orchestration is as brilliantly individual as ever, there is a feeling that inspiration was flagging and the composer admitted that he had had to struggle to finish the work. The constant pain he suffered from the malignant disease that was to destroy him must have made composition an ever more arduous labour; if 'Rondes' is less than a total success, it is still a notable monument to human courage.

DVOŘÀK

1841–1904

Few composers better illustrate the American belief in the 'rags-to-riches' fairy story than Dvořák; how suitable, then, that towards the end of his life he should have been invited to America to become director of the recently founded National Conservatory of Music in New York. Did the governors of that august-sounding institution realise that they were appointing the son of a village butcher who had been brought up in the depths of the Bohemian countryside more than forty miles from the nearest city? Butcher and inn-keeper though he was, Dvořák's father was clearly a remarkable man who had taught himself to play both violin and zither. He gave young Antonín every encouragement to learn music from the village schoolmaster who, by good fortune, was enough of a musical Jack-of-all-trades to be able to give the boy a solid foundation on violin, viola and organ. When the child was still only twelve years old he was sent to live with an uncle some distance away, partly to learn German (an essential asset if ambitions were to be realised) but also to study music more intensively. Although he had already set his heart on becoming a musician there was a time when any such prospect hung in the balance. His father had become virtually bankrupt and insisted that his son should return and learn the proper trade of butchering; there was surely more money and security in meat than in music. Fortunately the uncle had seen the boy's dedication at first hand and offered some financial help towards his training; thus it was that one autumn day in 1857, the sixteen-year old boy and his father set off in a farm-cart to travel the forty-five miles to Prague where he was to enrol in the organ school. He made no great mark as a student — his report said he was 'weak in theory' — but became a good enough viola player to join an orchestra which played popular music in the city's smartest restaurants. In time it formed the nucleus of the Czech National Opera orchestra and it was in the somewhat claustrophobic en-vironment of the opera-pit that Dvořák really learnt the art of orchestration in the most practical manner. The salary may have been pitiful but the experience was beyond price. Every spare penny from his meagre wage was spent on manuscript paper and for eleven years he ploughed a hard furrow for himself, composing quantities of music, most of which he would burn to save money on fuel.

The conductor of the opera-orchestra was Smetana and it was from him that Dvořák acquired a belief that the folk-music of his native country could be a proper source for a composer to draw on, even in concert works. The influence of Wagner had threatened to engulf Dvořák's natural musical inheritance and no doubt he felt for a time that childhood memories of music he had enjoyed with his father had little relevance for a serious composer. After fruitless years the first work to establish him as a composer of potential interest was a fervently patriotic *Hymnus* (Op. 30) for chorus and orchestra. Its enthusiastic reception gave him much-needed encouragement and his first published composition, Six Songs, was issued in the same year (1873). Despite these propitious omens he continued to consign even quite substantial works to the flames, exercising ruthless self-criticism towards everything he wrote. One early opera, *King and Collier* was not merely destroyed, but entirely re-written with not so much as a single aria carried over into the new version. The première was highly successful but the opera subsequently foundered owing to its feeble libretto. However, Dvořák's name was becoming known and in 1875 he was given a small government grant in recognition of his talent.

It was at this crucial time that his work first came to the notice of Brahms who was to prove to be an important influence in more ways than one. Mutual admiration of each other's music was gratifying, but more to the point was the older composer's standing in Vienna, the musical capital of Europe. It was Brahms who persuaded Simrock, his publishers, to take an active interest in Dvořák's music, thereby putting him on the road to international fame. By 1877 he was able to devote his energies entirely to composition though it was perhaps unfortunate for posterity that the opera theatre held such a fascination for him that much fine music was squandered on ill-chosen libretti. With growing recognition came greater confidence though four symphonies were held back for later revision; this led to considerable confusion since the sixth symphony to come from his pen was published as No. 1, the seventh as No. 2 and the fifth as No. 3. Only symphonies 5–9 were published during his lifetime.

In 1892 Dvořák was invited to become director of the newly founded National Conservatory of New York for the enormous salary of $15,000 a year. He spent three years[1] in America during which he wrote some of his finest music including the ninth symphony 'From the New World' and the cello concerto which many regard as his greatest masterpiece. In spite of the acclamation he received he became desperately homesick and was only too glad to return to the less demanding pace of life in Prague. Although world-

[1] He took five months' 'home leave' in 1894.

famous he preserved a peasant simplicity, one of his pleasures being to wander round the railway marshalling-yards looking at steam engines. (Amateur psychologists may like to ponder the difference between Brahms, who had a large collection of toy soldiers, and Dvořák with his passion for trains.) Honours were showered on him in the closing years of his life[2] but he was not one to sit back and rest. The search for a satisfactory libretto continued and the last three major works he wrote were all operas, of which only *Rusalka* has acquired a place in the operatic repertoire outside Czechoslovakia. Orchestral music and chamber music were his true domain, his feeling for orchestration being so felicitous that orchestral players have a special affection for his music, so gratefully is it written.

[2]He was the first musician to be made a member of the Austrian House of Lords!

Symphony No. 8 in G Major
Op. 88

In August 1889 Dvořák was hard at work on a piano quartet, destined to be his Op. 87. 'Three movements are finished already', he wrote to a friend, 'and the finale will be in a few days. It's going unexpectedly easily and the melodies simply pour out of me.' The quartet was actually completed on 19th August. Barely a week later he began to jot down ideas for a new symphony; clearly the days of burning manuscripts were over. On 6 September he began the first draft of the opening movement, finishing it by the 13th. Three days later he had composed the second movement; the third was completed on the following day and the fourth by the 23rd. The entire symphony was fully scored by 8 November, a striking feat of creativity from a composer who had failed to achieve any recognition until he was thirty-two.

Although Dvořák clearly specifies G *major* as the key, the symphony actually begins in G minor, a surprise that must have set the critics' pencils scribbling at the first performance. When we consider the speed at which the symphony was composed it may even be that when the splendid opening theme came into his mind Dvořák was not entirely sure whether the music might stay in the minor or not. Certainly part of the charm of this work lies in the way that ideas seem to pop out one after the other, a broad singing tune for cellos, a little bird-call on the solo flute, an introductory fanfare for the strings and so on, all done with the facility one might bring to writing a letter rather than a major work of art. In fact the first six pages of the score can justifiably be classified as an introduction in which the most important element turns out to be not the long cello tune but the frail little flute solo which immediately follows it. This is duly confirmed by the horns who take over the flute's theme with considerable vigour while the strings are still busy playing 'curtain up' music. The introduction is terminated with a sharp rap on the timpani and an explosive unison D from the full orchestra. Cellos and violas set out boldly on a theme that could serve as a model for a national anthem, (see Ex. 1) though its seriousness of purpose is somewhat deflated by the frivolous little bird-call on the flute. A few bars of good-natured knock-about lead to a powerfully reinforced statement of the flute tune, now far from frail. Dvořák spins out its last three notes by several repetitions passing from clarinets to bassoons, from violas to horn solo; then, after a momentary pause, the strings introduce a beguiling new theme that rocks to and fro from F♯ to G♯, nudged forward by a capricious little curve from the cellos. It has such instant appeal that one is tempted to identify it as the true Second Subject at once, but the slick labels of conventional analysis are hard to apply in this most *un*-conventional movement and we soon find an even more likely candidate in the woodwind. It is easily recognised, drawing attention to itself with a dotted rhythm on the up-beat followed by an upward leap of an octave. The strings proceed to explore its possibilities in quite a serious way with striding octaves in the basses and trombone enforcing some interesting modulations by their relentless rise. An impasse is reached on the dominant of B major, at which point the woodwind produce a ravishing new melody. (Had he not recently written 'the melodies simply pour out of me'?) Since this is the sixth clearly identifiable theme to appear in sixteen pages of score it seems absurd even to contemplate calling it a Second Subject, but it is greeted with such obvious enthusiasm by the full orchestra that we cannot discount its importance. Only time will tell us if it has a major role to play. However, there can be no doubt that the little flute tune is a principal character since the brass now give us a forcible reminder of it, even though it is shorn of its rather flippant tail. Muted trumpets, timpani and horns take turns at reducing it to a mere rhythmic pattern as the music grows ever quieter.

Anyone fortunate enough to be following a score will notice that Dvořák has ruled a double bar-line down the page at this point. It is a small gesture of acknowledgment that if he were writing a classical symphony this is where the repeat of the exposition would come. 'But don't let's bother with that' he seems to say and pushes on into the development with what sounds remarkably *like* a repeat. Back comes the broad cello tune in G minor; back comes the frail flute bird-call. Just as we are gulled into thinking that he has observed the classic convention of a repeat the music begins to venture into new territories. The flute theme is smoothed out and turns into a dialogue with an oboe during which there are some disagreements about the proper tonality. Meanwhile the cellos assume the role of an ageing cuckoo. This avian episode is rudely interrupted by a tremendous blast from the full orchestra followed by a phrase that sounds uncommonly like a call to arms. The once frail flute theme is conscripted into the military by bassoons and lower strings and there is a general feeling of urgency if not emergency. Clarinets and violas hum their way through the tune I described as a potential national anthem (to which the flute adds a brisk fife-like counterpoint) before Dvořák seems to decide that it's all getting a bit too frivolous. The bassoons begin a study in strict counterpoint, taking the preceding theme at double speed and initiating a remarkable passage of a fugal nature in which the subject-matter goes through a series of ingenious transformations as shown in Ex.1 on p. 196. Swift descending scales in triplets add to the excitement and the fugal exercise culminates in a huge climax in which horns and trombones make dramatic use of the first three notes of the minor/crotchet version (the third line of Ex.1).

There follows the most truly symphonic section of the movement in which bassoons, horns, cellos and basses hammer out the third transformation of the theme shown above while the violins have an intense version of the original flute bird-call, now in E minor and with its flippant ending converted

Ex. 1

into energetic rising arpeggios. A sudden restoration of G minor, reinforced by trombones and timpani, brings back the opening theme of the symphony, now resplendent on trumpets despite being battered by a Force Nine gale in the strings. Although it is the sort of climax that seems to have been lifted straight from Tchaikovsky, Dvořák emerges unscathed as it dies down, allowing a solo cor anglais to restore the original flute tune to its former shape. Clarinet and flute in turn voice their approval though the flute still tends to treat the theme with some caprice. The recapitulation which has arrived in this unorthodox manner dispenses entirely with the 'national anthem' tune and pushes on impatiently into the second subject group. Familiar friends reappear and the movement is rounded off with an exciting coda which makes enterprising use of the dotted rhythm that stems from the innocent-sounding bird-call that seemed so insubstantial when it made its first shy appearance.

It is worth saying that the truly symphonic part of this movement does not really materialise until the second half. There was a real danger that with such an abundance of themes the work would just ramble on with no cohesion, but Dvořák's laboriously acquired skills came to the rescue, enabling him to exert the more intellectual disciplines which symphonic movements need.

The slow movement appears to be based on a piano solo written earlier in the same year called 'At the old castle'. It is like a miniature tone-poem and clearly reflects Dvořák's love of the country with its frequent suggestions of bird-song. The opening phrases have a touch of pathos, a nostalgia perhaps for childhood days in the little village where he had been brought up. A falling two-note pattern persists in the flutes until it is unexpectedly transformed into a strong gesture in the strings as though the persistence of the figure had become irritating. In a moment the frown disappears, dispelled by one of the most enchanting episodes even Dvořák ever wrote. The strings have a series of little descending scales in C major like a minute chime of bells while the wind instruments extend a long line of melody that soars lazily as a kite in a summer sky. A violin solo confirms the outdoor feeling of the music as fluttering *tremolandi* in the second violins suggest the rustle of leaves. Then, as though Dvořák had said 'This is a symphony, not a divertimento,' the idea is extended by the full orchestra with a thrilling ascent in horns and trumpets leading to a majestic climax.[3]

The opening music returns with the order of events somewhat changed, but the falling two-note pattern in the flutes and the rather doleful clarinet phrases are familiar enough by now. What is new is a more impassioned development of the initial theme, now treated in quasi-operatic fashion with a duet between cellos and violins of the kind that usually sees the hero tearing himself from his lover's embrace to go to a certain but honourable death. Reiterated trumpet calls heighten the drama and for a moment it seems as though we may be heading towards a dramatic finale. In a trice the crisis is resolved and to everyone's relief the lovely C major tune returns, now on strings instead of woodwind. As the movement unwinds towards a peaceful cadence there is one more brief eruption of violence, but it is soon soothed away by the ubiquitous two-note motif.

The ensuing movement can hardly be called a scherzo as the tempo, *Allegretto grazioso*, makes clear. It is rather a charming Intermezzo, a dreamy waltz to be danced on a terrace in the moonlight. The rippling accompaniment in the woodwind suggests the splash of water in a nearby fountain while occasional dancing staccato notes in the strings rival Mendelssohn in their fairy-like delicacy. As if these delights were not enough, Dvořák introduces a central section in G major in which flute and oboe offer a tune which is unashamed of its simple peasant stock. While the tune itself is disarmingly unsophisticated the accompaniment is extremely subtle rhythmically with approving little taps on the drum falling in unexpected places. The tune is enjoyed to the full by the rest of the orchestra before a reprise of the first section. As for the final coda, it presents a nimble variation on the central section, a technique Dvořák

[3]I have not seen the piano pieces Op. 85 but presumably this passage relates to 'the Old Castle'.

may have copied from the comparable movement in Brahms's Second Symphony. All set for a boisterous finish, Dvořák surprises us with a sudden hush and a final chord that is like a sigh of sheer contentment.

The trumpet fanfare that opens the finale was added as an afterthought but it certainly arrests our attention. The form of the last movement is essentially a theme with variations, with a slight inclination towards a rondo. The cellos spell out the theme in two clear-cut eight-bar phrases, each of which is repeated. The first variation follows immediately, still led by the cellos while variation two proves to be a somewhat rowdy version for full orchestra. Variation three allows the flute an opportunity for a more graceful approach but such subtleties are soon displaced by another outburst from the full band. A rough-edged unison passage for strings leads to the episode that would more properly belong in a rondo since it is in C minor and has only the most tenuous connection to the theme. It degenerates into the one passage where Dvořák's inspiration seems to have flagged, a sequence built on notes a third apart that sounds like a children's counting game. It is more reassuring when trumpets and horns reintroduce the opening fanfare in a harmonised version; it is then put through some strange distortions over a striking sequence of harmonies before the strings treat it with furtive disrespect.

The return of the theme in more lyrical guise gives us a recognisable landmark and some tranquil variations provide a welcome contrast of considerable beauty. A gradual *ritardando* leads us to expect that the movement may end in a Brahmsian twilight, but having given the impression that sleep is imminent Dvořák rudely arouses us with a lively blast from the full orchestra and sweeps us off to a boisterous if abrupt finish. The very last bar is silent, a musical joke which it takes a subtle ear to appreciate; in fact one more note is required to complete the rhythmic pattern. By depriving us of it Dvořák makes the ending seem a trifle more precipitate.

Symphony No. 9 in E Minor From the New World Op. 95

Once Dvořák had arrived in New York in September 1892 he quickly settled down to his duties as director of the new National Conservatory. Although his surroundings must indeed have seemed like a New World to him he was determined not to neglect composition; first he had to put the finishing touches to a cantata 'The American Flag', a work composed more out of a sense of duty towards his hosts than from genuine inspiration.[4] He had brought with him his most recent composition, a most original setting of the Te Deum, conceived as a miniature symphony with sections corresponding to slow movement and scherzo in addition to the two outer movements. His patroness, Mrs Thurber, tried hard to persuade him to write an operatic version of *Hiawatha*, a poem which he already knew and admired in a Czech translation, although his many visits to England had compelled him to become quite fluent in the language. He was quite taken with the idea and filled several notebooks with sketches, one of which was to bear fruit in the middle section of the slow movement of the symphony.

Four months after his arrival he began serious work on the symphony, finishing the first three movements in short score in less than three weeks. Orchestrating them occupied him off and on through the spring of 1893; the finale was written and scored in May. The following month his family joined him and together they set out for Spillville in Iowa where there was a Bohemian settlement. It was quiet and peaceful and the presence of so many of his countrymen made him feel at home. Yet even though it was supposed to be a holiday the urge to compose was irresistible and he was soon at work on the F major string quartet. The entire quartet was written between 8–10 June. The autumn brought a reluctant return to the city where, in December, the new symphony had its world première in Carnegie Hall.

'The papers say that no composer ever had such a triumph', wrote Dvořák to his publisher. 'Carnegie Hall was crowded with the cream of New York society and the audience applauded so much that, like visiting royalty, I had to take my bows repeatedly from the box where I was sitting.'

The symphony begins with a slow *pianissimo* introduction, the tune being given to the cellos. In the fourth bar there is a sudden explosively accented note on two horns in unison, a seemingly inexplicable interruption of which more anon. The cello phrase is repeated at a higher octave by a solo flute. The stillness is again shattered, this time by a violent abrupt phrase on all the strings, five times repeated, and punctuated by *fortissimo* timpani and shrill woodwind chords. Peace is restored. Flutes and oboes have a cheerful snatch of syncopated melody which is followed by a significant phrase for horns and lower strings which heaves its way out of the deep and sinks back again. (It is the seed from which the main subject of the symphony is to grow, but we are not to know that at the time.) The pattern is repeated, building to a climax swiftly reached and swiftly repressed. The first movement proper is about to begin.

In all honesty I must admit that the explanation of this introduction I am about to offer has no documentation of any kind to support it, nor have I ever

[4]It was not performed until after he had left America.

heard it suggested by anyone else; yet I am convinced that these opening
pages are a description of Dvořák's first arrival in New York harbour. The
first quiet cello phrase shows him awaking, aware that the ship is still at last
after the long Atlantic crossing. The ship's siren sounds a peremptory blast —
the horns in bar 4. Dvořák draws the curtain from his porthole, letting in the
daylight — the flute tune — and hears the tremendous clatter of the anchor-
chain being lowered — the violent string and timpani passage. The ship
settles in the calm water as a passing cabin-boy whistles a cheerful little tune
— the woodwind phrase; a lazy swell lifts the ship momentarily, perhaps in
the wash of a passing steamer — the rise and fall in horns and strings — ropes
are thrown to the quayside (a comparable phrase to the 'anchor-chain' but at a
higher pitch) and with the final crescendo the ship is slotted into her berth.
Seasoned traveller though he had become, the arrival in New York must have
made a deep impression on Dvořák, and I see no reason why he should not
have recalled the experience in musical terms. The hypothesis fits so neatly
and I can see no real *musical* justification for the sundry violent interruptions
that occur to disturb the peaceful atmosphere of the opening phrases.

A famous horn-call provides the first subject of the ensuing *Allegro molto.*
Dancing attendance on it is a little subsidiary theme in thirds on clarinets and
bassoon. The two ideas are repeated with a changed ending. Four brass
chords lend their massive support to the strings as they extend the horn theme
further, turning its last four notes into a sequential pattern that builds to a
notable climax. The initial theme is confirmed in its importance by trombones and horns, *fortissimo*, after which the strings make a long and joyful
sequence out of the subsidiary fragment. After some swift byplay between
the violins and their deeper-voiced brethren the music gradually calms down
to prepare the way for a new idea. Given to flute and oboe in unison, it is in the
unexpected key of G minor. It certainly has a folkish flavour but Dvořák
vehemently denied that any of the themes were actually based on Negro or
Red Indian folk-music. The second bar, oscillating between A and C, should
be particularly noted as it is to be used extensively in the near future. The tune
itself is duly taken over by second violins over a rustic drone bass before being
transferred to the cellos and basses. It is at this point that the little oscillating
phrase from the second bar assumes such importance, providing the basis for
a continuing pattern which extends over some eighteen bars before taking on
an altogether happier mien in G major. Meanwhile flutes and clarinets are
clearly supposed to be imitating the chirruping of birds while an expressive
phrase in the bass seems to give a sigh of present content tinged with past
sorrow. Sweet as a cradle-song, the strings have a gentle rockabye to introduce the true second subject. It is an enchantingly unpretentious little tune for
solo flute which wishful thinkers have somehow persuaded themselves to
have been influenced by 'Swing low sweet chariot'. It seems unlikely that if
Dvořák meant it to be a quotation he would begin it with the fourth word.
(One might as well claim that Brahms's Fourth Symphony was inspired by

'Pop goes the weasel' since its first two notes are identical to those allotted to 'weasel' in that equally famous tune.) Violins are quick to seize the chance of playing the flute melody against gentle syncopations from clarinets and bassoons. A short climax is generated in which even the trombones lend their added weight to the second subject, perhaps making us realise for the first time that both the first and second subjects begin with the same rhythm ♩ ♪ | ♪ ♩ | .

After the obligatory repeat the development begins with a slight distortion of the second phrase of the flute's tune — the dominant (D) is sharpened, a point which Dvořák makes four times to get us accustomed to it. Since D sharp is the so-called 'leading-note' of E major, it enables him to make an easy transition to that key. The second subject now becomes the topic of discussion between various contrasted instruments, horn, piccolo, trumpet and, in a quickened agitated version of its first four notes, in the cellos. Meantime the oboes remind us of the almost forgotten subsidiary to the first subject. The cellos' abbreviation of the second subject assumes greater importance with a four-fold repetition in the violins leading to a dramatic reappearance of what I described as the 'lazy swell' in the introduction, now as vigorous as the initial horn theme (trombones and lower strings). Horns have a notable distortion of the second subject as the mood of agitation mounts. Soon we are caught up in an orchestral storm, possibly a memory of the Atlantic crossing, in which trombones convert the opening theme into a giant wave while shrill strings describe the gale-force winds. One can scarcely miss the trumpets' insistent repetition of the abbreviated fragment from the second subject which, as the storm subsides, turns out to be a convenient little pattern to fit against some more expressive treatments of the first subject. These make a useful bridge to lead into a formal recapitulation. It follows predictable lines until a sudden blast for full orchestra in which trumpets and trombones present a battle of wills between second and first subjects; the violins have an exciting new version of the first subject, compressed to half its normal length and piled up in an ascending sequence which then descends in a fierce chromatic scale. Four trumpet-calls seem to sound an alarm as the movement hastens forward to a dramatic finish.

The second movement is one of the best-known in the entire repertoire with its touchingly simple cor anglais solo and its dramatic references to the opening allegro in its central section. (The fine progression of harmonies at the start may well have served as a model for Rakhmaninov in the slow movement of his Second Piano Concerto, so similar in conception are the two introductory phrases.) Muted strings take over from the final impressive brass chord preparing a soft bed of harmony on which the cor anglais tune can lie in comfort. In its original version this tune was significantly different in detail, and much the poorer for it.

Ex. 1

The change from pairs of equal quavers to the dotted rhythm we now know made a world of difference. In the second limb of the tune the addition of a clarinet moving in parallel a tenth below is a masterly idea, giving a dark shadow to the cor anglais' expressive tones. Note too the way in which a quartet of clarinets and bassoons fold the tune away, tenderly repeating the last five notes, first as an exact copy and then twice as slowly as if reluctant to leave it alone. The opening sequence of harmonies is repeated in the woodwind and then the strings embark on a variant of the melody which seems to lose its way before the cor anglais puts it back on course. Muted horns hold us in suspense for a moment, leading to a change of mood and content. In his sketches for this constrasting section Dvořák originally suggested the title 'Legend', perhaps thinking to put it to some different purpose. Flute and oboe present the tune together, circling round the first three notes of the scale of C sharp minor. (The cor anglais theme is in D flat major; this central section could be said to be in D flat *minor* but such a theoretical key would present awkward problems of notation.) The accompanying strings suggest the rustle of leaves in the forest and, as is so often the case in Dvořák's music, we have the feeling that the music belongs out of doors rather than in the formal surroundings of the concert-hall.

A third theme makes its appearance, a veritable funeral procession in character with its sombre theme on clarinets and the measured tread of double-basses. It may have been suggested by a forest burial in *Hiawatha* but there is no need to try to relate it to a specific incident. Themes two and three are both presented again in different orchestral colours before the woodwind, led by a solo flute, break in with a series of cheerful bird-songs. They may at first seem both irreverent and irrelevant but a moment's thought shows that they are directly related to the cor anglais tune, quickened in tempo and somewhat compressed.

Ex. 2

Innocent bird-song is swiftly transformed into a minor volcanic eruption as trombones break in with a powerful version of the main theme from
the first movement while the violins forcibly remind us of the opening notes
of the second subject from that movement and the woodwind offer a shrill
condensed version of the second phrase which rightfully should follow. Thus
we find four thematic fragments combined, three from the first movement
and one from the second — since the trumpets insist that the cor anglais tune
should be our proper concern. The combination is ingenious enough to
justify showing it in simplified score:

Ex. 3

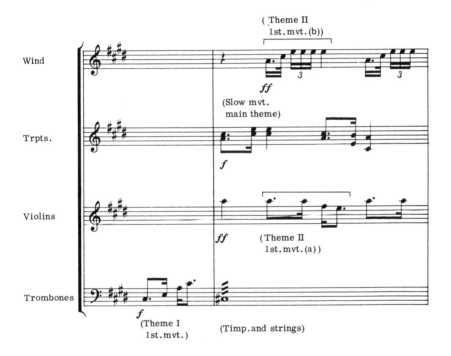

This fusion of the two movements soon resolves into a reprise of the cor
anglais theme; peace is restored. Once again the violins seem to lose their way
during the second part of the tune. Their momentary lapse is more than
compensated for by a gloriously expressive phrase that they have on their
own before the return of the solemn opening chords brings the movement to
a deeply satisfying close.

    The scherzo is popularly supposed to have been inspired by an American-
Indian warrior's dance although it is doubtful whether Dvořák actually saw
one. Certainly we can imagine the timpani to be tom-toms, and the dissonant
chord which the strings repeat over thirty times between bars 8–19 is clearly

designed to represent the thudding of feet on the bare earth. (It is an intriguing precursor of the famous repeated chords near the start of Stravinsky's *Rite of Spring* though the primitive Russian tribe is considerably more savage and ill-tempered.) The actual theme is made up from fragments, at first in the woodwind with the clarinets following a bar behind their shriller brethren, secondly in the first violins with the seconds providing a swirling counterpoint. The full orchestral version that soon follows is immensely exhilarating with the theme in the bass and an interesting new countermelody in the form of a syncopated chromatic descent.

With the central 'Trio' we return to Dvořák's native land as flute and oboe introduce a tune that has all the hallmarks of a Czech folk-song. (Note the interesting rhythm in the string accompaniment.) After the cellos have been given a tantalising taste of this eminently singable tune Dvořák works his way back to the opening material which duly comes to what sounds like a very rousing finish. Whispered references to the opening pattern tell us that there is more to come — or is this a surprise coda? The surprise comes from the cellos who unexpectedly remind us of the horn-call from the first movement. The quotation ends with a slight distortion which is queried by several instruments in turn. The violas then offer the same reminder and again the distorted ending is questioned by flute and oboe. However, the violins realise the potential of this novel ending and, smoothing it out a little, turn it into a delightful accompaniment to 'Trio II'. This proves to be another folk-dance with a skipping rhythm. 'Leave out that nonsense about my having made use of original American melodies' wrote Dvořák to a former pupil who was going to conduct the work; and here is a tune that confirms the point for it is pure Czech. It has a second part whose nimble grace tells us that it is for the girls to dance rather than the men. There follows a delicious alternation of trills between strings and woodwind which may be interpreted as cooing turtle-doves or giggling dancers according to personal preference. The 'Trio II' tune then returns rather more elaborately orchestrated.

According to classical precedent the main part of the scherzo is then repeated. The Coda gives the horns the opportunity to introduce another variant on their original theme from the first movement, causing the woodwind to remind them that they're still in the scherzo; but the quotations from the first movement gather strength with a solo trumpet even producing an elongated version of the original second subject. Then, like a toy engine running down, the movement appears to lose its momentum. There is a moment's silence after which Dvořák slams the lid with an abrupt *fortissimo* chord.

The finale is marked '*Allegro con fuoco*' ('with fire'). The introduction prepares for the entry of the main theme in a manner reminiscent of a circus with its rather too obvious widening of intervals; but once the theme arrives on horns and trumpets it proves to have genuine grandeur. The strings, left on their own, are hard put to it to match the splendour of the brass and welcome the added reinforcement from the wind. But soon the full orchestra becomes involved in some frankly rustic music which shows Dvořák's peasant up-bringing rather too obviously. Redemption comes in the form of a lovely clarinet solo which creates an atmosphere of absolute peace only occasionally disturbed by impatient cellos.

The next episode for full orchestra in this loosely constructed movement does have a hint of 'Black and White Minstrel' about it with its thumping 'clap hands' rhythm in the timpani part and its 'ragtime' quavers in the violins and flutes. It is the only real concession to Americana and lacks the quality the fine opening theme has led us to expect. A brisk episode follows, mainly led by the strings, during which we become increasingly aware of a phrase which may irreverently be referred to as 'Three blind mice'. (They don't run very far but they crop up all over the place.) After tiptoeing their way through the strings, *pizzicato*, they appear in delightfully elegant dress in the woodwind, the third note handsomely decorated with a trill. As though this is all becoming too frivolous, horns remind us of the splendid initial theme but fail to impose a more serious approach on the rest of the orchestra. In fact the cellos and basses take all the dignity out of the theme by playing it double speed, though not loudly enough to draw attention to their lack of respect.

This leads to another ingenious combination of ideas: the violas play around with the disrespectful version of the theme from the last movement: flutes and clarinets summon a memory of the slow movement's theme, grafting on to it part of the *last* movement's theme at its proper speed: violins and then cellos remind us of a fragment from the Scherzo. Three movements are thus related to each other, a fusion which Dvořák enjoys sufficiently to extend for several pages. The only significant theme to be missing is the initial horn-call from the first movement; sure enough, after a suitably impressive build-up it makes a stirring reappearance, only to be displaced by a long delayed return of the true theme of this rather too episodic finale. In a climax that Tchaikovsky could not have bettered, trumpets and then trombones proclaim its dominance. Once the point has been hammered home Dvořák can afford to relax; quieter versions ensue until the violins can bring their warmest tone to the second subject, the one that had originally appeared as a clarinet solo. Gradually the music eases back in tempo as a far more expressive form of the 'Black and White Minstrel' tune appears in the woodwind. (Don't miss a delicately humorous transformation of the initial horn-call which bubbles up in the bassoon parts.) A solo horn ascends to a perilous top E in another reminder of the 'motto' theme — as the initial horn-call from the first movement has now proved itself to be. (It appears in all four movements.) An exciting fanfare on horns heralds a more massive extension of the 'motto' after which the main theme of the last movement reappears in its full glory on trombones and horns, surrounded by the peasant dance which, when it first appeared, had seemed a little too rustic for its context. As the excitement mounts Dvořák produces a master-stroke of invention, the opening harmonies of the slow movement utterly transformed. This huge climax gradually subsides as little fragments of the preceding movements drift past like leaves blown in the autumn wind. Against soft pulsating beats from the timpani a solo horn has a lengthened version of the main theme which is then copied by the full orchestra. At a slightly slower tempo the trumpets have a strangely distorted ending to the comparable phrase while trombones remind us of the initial horn-call from the first movement for the last time. In a final sprint for home the tempo quickens; a triumphant conclusion is certain — or so it seems. Yet the very last chord contains a surprise since, though it is cut short in the strings, wind and brass hold it for a long chord that fades away to the quietest possible sound. If, as I believe, the opening of the symphony symbolises his arrival, was this gradually diminishing chord a sub-conscious expression of Dvořák's wish to see New York recede on the horizon as he made his homeward journey?

Violoncello Concerto in B Minor
Op. 104

Although Dvořák wrote the cello concerto during the latter part of his stay in New York he altered the finale substantially after he had returned home. Rather as Brahms had turned to Joachim for advice when writing his violin concerto, Dvořák sought help from a renowned fellow-countryman called Hanuš Wihan to whom the work is dedicated. Wihan certainly helped over some of the finer points of cello technique but composer and performer fell out when it came to the matter of cadenzas. Wihan wanted to insert a cadenza in the last movement to show off his undoubted virtuosity; Dvořák couldn't stand the idea and even wrote to his publisher forbidding any alterations without his express permission in case Wihan went behind his back. In the end the first performance was given in London on 19 March 1896 by Leo Stern.

Since the cello is much larger than the violin, and since there are fewer cellists than violinists in an orchestra, one might be forgiven for assuming that a cello would be louder and more penetrating than a violin. Therefore it should in theory be easier to write a cello concerto than a violin concerto, if only because it should surely be able to dominate the orchestra more easily. In fact, noble though its lower register undoubtedly is, when matching a solo cello *against* an orchestra a composer will tend to use its middle and upper range practically all the time. Problems of balance are far more acute in a cello concerto than in a violin concerto, which may be one reason why there are fewer of them. Considering what a wonderful instrument it is, the cello is surprisingly short of repertoire; there was never a golden age for cellists, as there was for violinists in the seventeenth and eighteenth centuries, or pianists in the nineteenth. There is a notable lack of concertos by the really great masters, Beethoven, Mozart and Brahms or in our own day Bartók or Stravinsky. Casals and, more recently, Rostropovich have inspired a number of works, but one wonders how many will take a permanent place in the repertoire. There is little doubt, though, which is the greatest nineteenth-century cello concerto; it must surely be Dvořák's. He had actually written one thirty years previously, but he never orchestrated it, and clearly regarded it as an apprentice work. Maybe it bore no immediate fruit, but down in the subconscious, it must have planted not so much a seed as a veritable acorn, for there is no questioning the splendour of the work that ultimately appeared in his maturity.

The start is unassuming enough, rather similar to the beginning of Tchaikovsky's Fifth Symphony in its colouring, with sombre clarinets spelling out a theme, accompanied by the lower strings. It's as though Dvořák was preparing our ears to start listening in a lower register than usual.

(Notice that the third bar, which is to prove especially significant, is itself a variation on bar 1.)

Violins and violas now take over, largely concentrating on the shape and rhythm of bar 3; within moments a substantial crescendo has built up and we are confronted with the opening theme in majestic splendour. It is also turned into a dialogue of sorts so that strings and wind alternate, one echoing the other. Gradually things quieten down, although the cellos try to start an insurrection with a rising scale which is duly copied by the woodwind. This theme sounds more important than it is since Dvořák makes no further use of it. It is merely a way of delaying a little further the entrance of the second subject, surely one of the most beautiful horn solos in the concerto repertory. The second part of this 'song without words' is taken over by a clarinet and then extended further by other woodwind instruments. After so lyrical a passage the outcome is a little surprising, a burst of rustic revelry which one feels belongs more to a set of Slavonic Dances than a cello concerto. It's almost too naive, as though Dvořák was saying 'Well, I'm only a simple country chap at heart you know'. And so he was of course, which is one reason why his music is so delightfully accessible. However, it's worth pointing out that this particular rustic dance doesn't appear anywhere else in the movement, as though even he may have thought 'Perhaps I shouldn't have . . .' The bucolic outburst soon dies down, resolving onto a quiet chord of B *major*, darkened by low trombones and a soft timpani roll. In a passionate and resolute style the soloist enters with the opening theme, subtly suggesting B major but actually on the dominant of E minor. The strong three–note chords give an epic quality to the music while the dotted rhythm of the third bar is soon made more impetuous by an ingenious transformation, here transposed for ease of comparison:

The increase in excitement finds release in a brief cadenza for the soloist into which Dvořák inserts fanfare-like figures which, for the sake of balance, are given to the woodwind in preference to the brass. A rising sequence of trills, against which flute and clarinet continue to remind us of the opening theme, leads us to a delightful variation. To the careless ear it may sound like a new theme but, as is shown in (b) in the above example, it is clearly derived from Theme I. Carried away by the sheer pleasure of this discovery, Dvořák develops it into a little episode on its own until, after a high trill on the dominant (F♯) the soloist returns to the proper matter on the agenda by recalling the opening phrase *fortissimo*. A graceful and ornamental descent leads to the second subject which the soloist understandably appropriates to himself. After this noble theme has run its full course a newcomer appears in the shape of a new theme for woodwind; it rocks gently between two adjacent notes while the soloist has a delicately fluttering accompaniment that demands great agility of bow and finger.

Yet another tune emerges from Dvořák's fertile mind as the fluttering triplets cease; it is a derivative of the 'rocking' theme but is very different in effect. It seems so spontaneous a development that it is hard to believe that Dvořák rejected three alternatives before arriving at this, the most satisfactory solution. Clarinet and flute give the tune their blessing with a beautiful counter-melody. As if aware that he has been dabbling with irrelevancies for long enough, the soloist begins a dramatic climb whose ultimate aim is a return to the opening material. This is achieved by a number of references to a compressed version of the opening four notes (♩. ♫ ♩), ending with a plunge to a low D.

The full orchestra responds with a grandiose treatment of the opening theme over a reiterated 'pedal'[5] D in the bass. There is a gradual *diminuendo* enhanced by a remarkable solo for the third horn-player whose descending

[5]A 'pedal-point' in the bass is a note that is sustained regardless of the harmonies above.

arpeggio covers a span of two-and-a-half octaves. Though it is nerve-racking for the player, it is intended to tranquillise the audience, preparing us for a considerable change of mood. Cellos and basses seem to pull the opening phrase down into the shadows. Another ingenious variant of the opening phrase has a momentarily disturbing effect, first in the cellos and then the violins, but the ultimate purpose of this section is to bring us to the true heart of the movement, a deeply felt contemplation of Theme I in the remote key of A flat minor. Above a barely audible accompaniment from the strings the soloist extends the tune by doubling the length of the notes and, in conjunction with a solo flute, turns it into a miniature elegy.

As though awakening from a dream, the cello plays a gently oscillating figure which provides a persistent accompaniment to a new theme in the woodwind. Its first three notes establish a relationship to Theme I but it is a cousin several times removed. A sudden timpani roll provokes a more energetic reaction from the soloist until, with a great wash of sound, the orchestra overwhelms the soloist just as he makes a sensational glissando climb (in octaves) to a high B. It is here that Dvořák shows his willingness to defy convention if he so chooses; a normal recapitulation would have to begin with at the very least an acknowledgment of the first subject's importance. Dvořák bypasses this completely and begins his recapitulation with a full orchestral version of the lyrical second subject. It is of course accepted gratefully by the soloist who thereafter follows a fairly predictable course. The final coda re-establishes the importance of the first subject which, in the closing bars is turned into a triumphant fanfare by the brass.

The slow movement is unusually rich in material, so much so that it seems unnecessarily pedantic to label themes that flow so naturally one from the other. First to appear is a folk-like melody on the clarinet, soon to be echoed by the soloist. Notice how a dangerously static moment in the clarinet tune is filled with a graceful arpeggio from the cello — a perfect example of the way the composer of a concerto will leave a 'pocket' in the orchestral part for the soloist to fill. After the third of these arpeggios the mood changes from simple song to heartbreak as the cellist has a descending sequence that anticipates the moving lament in the finale of the Elgar cello concerto. It leads to a tearful sequence of paired notes in which the music seems to sob in unrestrained grief. As if in consolation the clarinet brings back the opening theme, only to be forcibly interrupted by a ferocious outburst on the full orchestra in G minor. The interruption may last for only four bars but it effects a total change. The cello begins a passionate song whose opening phrase descends through five notes of the scale (D—G). It is a quotation from one of Dvořák's 'Four Songs' Op. 82. The composer had just heard that his sister-in-law, a charming young actress called Josefina Kounicová, was seriously ill; the quotation seems to express his longing to be back in his homeland so that he could be with her. (There is a further quotation from the

Op. 82 songs in the finale, inserted into the coda as a memorial to her after Dvořák had learned of her death.) The 'sobbing' motif returns, as does the violent G minor phrase on the orchestra; indeed, the movement alternates between the lyrical and the passionate.

The stroke of true genius is the cadenza which appears just after the horns have given us a solemn reminder of the opening theme. (Note the 'muffled drum' effect in cellos and basses.) The cadenza begins with the solo cello meditating freely on the opening theme; but after a few bars it is joined by several wind instruments which unmistakably imitate the sounds of the countryside. A flute warbles like the nightingale; bassoons croak like bullfrogs; a pair of flutes coo like doves. This sudden evocation of the country shows Dvořák's dissatisfaction with the urban environment and his intense longing for the rural peace of his homeland. As such it is strangely comparable to the second movement of Bartók's Third Piano Concerto (see page 56) which, like this work, was written far from home.

In the final pages of the movement there is a return to the opening material and even a feeling of some consolation. Six bars from the end there is a sudden pang of sorrow, followed by an ethereal descent in harmonics and a lingering farewell on the clarinet.

The finale begins as a march very much in the manner of Tchaikovsky. Over the distant left-right tread of cellos and basses the horns offer a sketch of the main theme, leaving the finer details to be filled in by the soloist. An exciting if somewhat conventional build-up leads to the solo entry, a sturdy tune in B minor which Dvořák clearly intended to be the basis for a rondo. The orchestra endorse it with enthusiasm and the first episode duly follows — somewhat skittishly, it must be said, after the resolute character of the theme. Within less than thirty bars the rondo theme is back, first on flute and oboe over skirling trills from the cello and then on strings and brass. It is at this point that the rondo framework begins to weaken since Dvořák embarks on a series of episodes which delay the return of the theme for nearly 190 bars. The first intervention is a 'marche militaire', unrelated to anything that has preceded it. The soloist's attempt to match the power of the orchestra is not all that convincing so, with positively feminine guile, the 'march' is converted into a tender caress calculated to melt the heart of any soldier. One of Dvořák's typical 'rocking' tunes appears on a solo clarinet, enchantingly teased by the cello. This delightful flirtation is prolonged for some time until the cellist tires of the game and launches into some agile triplet arpeggios which, after considerable cavorting, lead back to a reprise of the 'marche militaire' — now in D major instead of B minor. By a slightly devious route the cellist finds the way back to the rondo theme, sneaking it in so that we hardly notice; the orchestra does, though, and gives it a rowdy reception.

The exuberant tag the violins attach to its tail is repeated several times and then cleverly ironed out to introduce yet another episode at a more moderate tempo. Here again we find the composer drawing on the resources of the folk idiom. As the tempo quickens once again the flute has a particularly naive tune which the cellist disregards entirely, preferring for once to show off the fluency of his technique. The orchestra continues to concentrate on the folk material but the cellist becomes increasingly capricious. At last the rondo theme reappears, but this time the soloist toys with it, arousing the ire of the violas as he does so.

A solemn fanfare on the brass puts a stop to the frivolity and leads to the truly inspired coda which has the lilting tenderness of a lullaby. Its gentle rocking themes effect a skilful marriage between the rondo of the finale and the opening bar of the first movement. (A clarinet and then a horn make the point clear to those who haven't spotted the relationship.) As the music slows to a majestic tempo a magnificent chorale rises through the orchestra only to be swept away in the whirlwind final page.

There had been many cello concertos before this but none had explored so wide a range of emotion nor been so richly endowed with melodies. As long as there are cellists to play it, it will remain a firm favourite and justifiably so.

ELGAR
1857–1934

One evening, back in the closing year of the nineteenth century, a still relatively unknown English composer was recovering from a long and trying day's teaching by improvising gently on the piano. It wasn't his instrument really; he was a violinist. But one can't believe that his playing would have been unmusical, even if he hadn't got a facile technique. Anyway, the theme that came into his mind and out through his fingers was a slow one, tinged with melancholy. Her attention caught by a tune she'd never heard before, his wife asked him what it was. 'Oh, nothing', replied Elgar 'but I might be able to do something with it.' And then, for no particular reason except a flight of fancy, he started to amuse himself by imagining how some of his musical friends might have treated the theme. For instance, there was a man called Nevinson, a cellist, with whom Elgar used to play trios for pleasure. That very evening Elgar imagined how an amateur cellist would approach the theme, and there and then he improvised on the piano to show his wife.

Her reaction was to suggest to Elgar that he'd hit upon a brand new idea for a work, and straight away they made a game of it, he playing the theme in various ways and she guessing who he was imitating. And so this English classic was born, the whole work being written within a fortnight. The Enigma Variations were to prove a most significant breakthrough for Elgar. The first performance, in June 1899 under Richter, was hailed as a triumph, and the work was soon in the repertory of European orchestras. Here's Elgar in a letter to his close friend A.J. Jaeger who worked at Novello's the publisher:

> Since I've been back I have sketched a set of Variations on an original theme: the Variations have amused me because I've labelled 'em with the nickname of my particular friends — you are Nimrod. That is to say I've written the Variations each one to represent the mood of the 'party'. I've liked to imagine the 'party' writing the var. him (or her) self and have written what I think *they* would have written — if they were asses enough to compose. It's

a quaint idea and the result is amusing to those behind the scenes and won't effect the hearers who 'nose nuffin'. What think you?[1]

But though the Variations had scored a great success at their first performance, Richter and others, including Jaeger, had expressed misgivings about the ending. Elgar's reaction to the criticism is fascinating in its mixture of schoolboy slang and serious musical talk. Again he's writing to Jaeger:

As to that finale, it's most good of you to be interested and I like to have your opinion. I have my doubts as to some of the rest 'cos it's generally *suggested* to them. Now look here, the movement was designed to be concise. Here's the difficulty of lengthening it. I could go on with those themes for half a day but the key G is exhausted. The principal motive (Enigma) comes in grandioso on page 35 in the tonic and it *wouldn't do* to bring it in again. Had I intended to make an extended movement this would have been in some related key, reserving the tonic for the final smash. In deference to you I made a sketch yesterday but the thing sounds Schubertian in its sticking to one key. I should really like to know how you heard that Richter was disappointed. He criticised some of it but not the end. The actual final flourish was spoilt in performance . . . You see there's far too much of this sort of thing said. Somebody wants to find fault and in course of conversation says 'the end did not please so and so, I find it very poor, *don't you?*' The other chap hadn't thought of it at all but says 'Yes, it's very abrupt' and so it goes on. This sort of thing is of no value to me. What *you* say is your own opinion and would be given on anybody's work. All the other fellows would never have made a remark if the work had been written by any great man. If I find, after New Brighton that the end does not satisfy me, I may recast the whole of the last movement but it's not possible to lengthen it with any satisfaction, I fear. If I can find time to make a readable copy of my 'end' I'll send it to you and then you'll see how good E. Elgar is at heart.[2]

In fact the revised ending proved to be a significant improvement and Elgar admitted that Jaeger's judgement had been right. (The mention of 'page 35' in the letter above suggests that Jaeger had been given a piano reduction since in the full orchestral score the 'grandioso' passage would have been at least a hundred pages later.)

Although Elgar had written a considerable quantity of music in the years prior to 1899 he had remained a 'local' composer whose works were not widely known. He earned a none too handsome living doing a variety of musical jobs, mostly with amateur musicians; he was for a time organist at St George's Church, Worcester; he conducted various local choral societies and orchestras; he played the violin in the augmented orchestra that was assembled for the Three Choirs Festival and once, in 1884, played under Dvořák's baton. His marriage in 1889 was an important step for him for his

[1]Basil Maine, *Elgar: His Life and Works*, p. 86 (Bell, 1933).
[2]Op. cit.

wife had some means of her own and gave him some freedom to escape the worst of the musical drudgery which had been his lot. With her encouragement they moved to London, hoping for greater things; but the unknown from a rural cathedral city found little response in the capital and in just over a year they returned to the country they knew so well and settled in Malvern. It was a difficult time for them both. Elgar, the son of a piano-tuner and shopkeeper, had married the daughter of a Major-General, Sir Henry Roberts, KCB. They made an oddly assorted couple within the rigid structure of Victorian society; furthermore Elgar was a Catholic in a staunchly Protestant community. However, success began to come his way in the mid-1890s, mostly with choral works such as 'King Olaf' or 'Caractacus', compositions which reached London or Leeds but which still had no international standing. The 'Enigma' Variations were to change all that. It seemed as though he had suddenly found new confidence in his ability, and the enthusiastic endorsement of Hans Richter, the great conductor, gave him the feeling that he was now fully equipped to tackle the major musical forms. Self-taught as he was, he had forged a style that was uniquely his own, indebted to no 'school'; to achieve this from so unpropitious a background confirmed that here at last, for the first time since Purcell's day, was an English composer to whom the word genius could honestly be applied.

Variations on an Original Theme for Orchestra Op. 36

Enigma

Dedicated to my friends pictured within.

Malvern 1899

The word 'Enigma' was added to the manuscript score in pencil, apparently as an afterthought. In the programme note which he wrote for the first performance Elgar set a riddle which has caused much food for thought for those with a taste for codes and ciphers.

> The Enigma I will not explain — its 'dark saying' must be left unguessed, and I warn you that the apparent connection between the Variations and the Theme is often of the slightest texture; further, through and over the whole set another and larger theme 'goes', but is not played. . . . So the principal Theme never appears, even as in some late dramas — e.g. Maeterlinck's *L'Intruse* and *Les Sept Princesses* — the chief character is never on the stage.

It is the mention of 'another and larger theme' that has tantalised musical scholars ever since, for it is a musical impossibility that any specific tune could fit against the Theme *and* against all the variations. A number of solutions have been proposed[3] ranging from 'Auld Lang Syne' to abstract conceptions such as 'Friendship'. Elgar was fond of anagrams, acrostics and word puzzles. The name of his house, 'Craeg Lea', is an anagram of his own name and his wife's initials, C.A.E.[4] An early composition dedicated to some friends called Gedge used their name as a basis for the musical material — 'Allegretto on G.E.D.G.E.'. I am therefore inclined to favour an ingenious solution proposed by Vernon Jones in an article for the Royal Academy of Music magazine, the summer issue of 1970. He shows how the theme, if transposed into A minor, becomes a musical translation of the name of Elgar's daughter Carice, which itself is a contraction of his wife's names Caroline Alice. Since the final variation is headed EDU, a pet name for Elgar that his wife had invented, it seems quite likely that the 'larger theme' that 'goes' with all the variations is family love. The snag to almost every solution is the authentic story of Elgar improvising the theme at the piano; it is inconceivable that he would by chance have hit upon a melody that would fit in perfect counterpoint against another tune as different in character as 'Auld Lang Syne', even though, by somewhat Procrustean methods 'Auld Lang Syne' can be

---

[3]See *An Elgar Companion* ed. Christopher Redwood (Sequoia, 1982).
[4]Or possibly Carice, Alice, Edward, incorporating his daughter, wife and himself.

adjusted to fit against the 'Enigma'. But many musicians have played the musical spelling game that makes tunes from letters — for instance Schumann's ABEGG Variations, Ravel's '*Menuet sur le nom d'Haydn*' and '*Berceuse sur le nom de Gabriel Fauré*', not to mention a number of compositions based on B.A.C.H. Knowing this, and taking into consideration Elgar's love of word-puzzles, is it not quite possible that Elgar jotted down the musical equivalent of his daughter's name, perhaps to delight her on some future occasion, and then began to improvise around those notes? '*I might be able to do something with it*': 'might be able' to write a piece depicting his daughter, or perhaps amuse her by describing friends she would also know? When Elgar first played the completed work to his wife he exclaimed 'Japes!' as he began, which, together with 'High Jinks', was a favourite expression. Yet on another occasion he wrote that the opening bars of the theme depicted 'the loneliness of the artist'. As Elgar's stature as a composer grew he became increasingly irritated by any discussion of the 'Enigma' and it may well be that what started as an intimate family game proved to be unsuited to more public exposure. Since the riddle has no definitive solution it is as well that we should not dwell on it too long; the music stands on its own merits as the sole English orchestral masterpiece to emerge from the nineteenth century.

A glance at the theme (see below) shows that it falls into three sections, six bars in G minor, four bars in G major, then a reprise of the first six bars plus a final bar which momentarily touches G major again. Thus the tonality of theme is itself 'enigmatic'.

(Notice the numerous directions to the players that are characteristic of Elgar: '*ten.*' is an abbreviation of '*tenuto*', 'held' or 'lingered on': '*Mesto*' means 'sadly'.)

An unusual feature of the theme is the absence of first beats in the two G minor sections, an absence which makes their provision in the central part all the more effective. What is not shown in the example is the glorious counter-tune which surges up in the middle register in bars 13–16. The last note is sustained by the violins who then provide an expressive two-bar link that feels its way back to G minor and Variation I. Very properly, since it was at her behest that the work came to be written, it represents Elgar's wife, Caroline Alice. The silent first beats of the theme are now filled in, giving it an air of greater confidence while the delicately syncopated arpeggios in unison violins and cellos suggest her moving quietly about the house anxious not to disturb the composer. Oboe and bassoon have a quite prominent little figure with a triplet rhythm; destined to reappear in the finale, it was apparently a fragment that Elgar used to whistle to show his whereabouts. The variation grows to a sudden impassioned climax in the middle, revealing the depth of feeling this very devoted woman aroused in him.

Variation II is notoriously tricky to play and supposedly represents a pianist friend called H.D. Steuart-Powell who was in the habit of 'limbering up' at the keyboard by dashing off a few technical exercises. The music is a mischievous caricature since Steuart-Powell would select rather facile passages, whereas these patterns are extremely awkward. The theme doesn't appear until the eighteenth bar when it makes a somewhat grumpy entrance in the bass, as though Elgar was saying 'Why can't we get on with it?'

Variation III portrays Richard Baxter Townshend, an author of boys' books who delighted in amateur theatricals. The oboe has a cheeky if slightly breathless version of the theme, now all in G major; it describes Townshend playing the role of an old man and adopting a senile falsetto voice to do so. This would cause much mirth since his normal voice was very deep, as a bassoon shows towards the end of the variation.

Variation IV uses the full orchestra for the first time. The theme is hammered out — no time for rests! — while the G major section becomes a whirlwind. It seems that W. Meath Baker was a rather choleric country squire who tended to treat his house-guests as though he was a commanding officer. Here he gives the orders for the day and sweeps out of the room, leaving his friends at the breakfast-table laughing affectionately at the display. (A jocular little section for woodwind.) His reappearance at the end is good-natured bluster.

Variation V begins with a grave new melody on the violins beneath which the lower strings and bassoons play the first part of the theme, now in C minor. Richard Arnold, son of the poet Matthew Arnold, was serious in bearing but witty in speech; both aspects are vividly conveyed, the gravity by the strings, the wit by the woodwind. The music moves smoothly without a break into the next variation, Ysobel. The archaic spelling is a scant disguise for Isabel Fitton, an amateur viola player who had been a pupil of Elgar's. As an affectionate tribute to her there is a prominent part for solo viola. The theme, reduced to fragments, is given to the bassoons but our attention is inevitably drawn towards the gracious viola tune and the smiles of approval that the clarinets seem to give as the 'pupil' explores unaccustomed heights.

Variation VII is technically one of the most demanding for the orchestra. The first four bars allude to the rhythm of the theme but in a very abrupt and alarming manner; the rising phrases that follow are derived from the central portion of the theme and, when given to the trombones, sound positively menacing. The explosive timpani rhythms give the impression that Troyte Griffith was extremely ill-tempered. In fact he was one of Elgar's closest friends, although he had a habit of blurting out unexpected remarks. The portrait is therefore unexpected, but its air of ferocity should not be taken seriously. Elgar himself offered this explanation:

> The uncouth rhythm of the drums and the lower strings was really suggested by (his) maladroit essays to play the pianoforte; later the strong rhythm suggests the attempts of the instructor (Elgar) to make something like order out of chaos, and the final despairing 'slam' records that the effort proved to be vain.

It would seem that Elgar was not the most patient of teachers . . .

Variation VIII is one of the most enchanting episodes, putting the framework of the theme into the major and changing the rhythm into a flowing 6/8. The piquant little trills on the oboe followed by delicate staccato figures on the flutes describe Winifred Norbury's characteristic laughter, light-hearted but refined. The variation ends with a phrase that is warmly affectionate. Its final note is held for a long pause, the tonic of G major poised to be transformed into the third note of the key of E flat.

So begins Variation IX, 'Nimrod', its name being a typical Elgarian pun. Nimrod was 'the great hunter' of mythology, and 'hunter' in German is 'Jaeger'. A.J. Jaeger worked at Novello's, the music publishers, and was more than a dear friend to Elgar; he was also someone on whom he could rely for totally honest criticism as well as unflinching support. He idolised Beethoven and would often discuss Beethoven's music with Elgar as they walked together on the Malvern hills. It was for this reason that 'his' variation begins with a subtle allusion to the slow movement of the 'Pathetique' sonata:

Beethoven (transposed)

Elgar

This noble theme is orchestrated in such a way that the sound accumulates; the first eight bars are for strings only. Woodwind and horns are then added to enrich the texture, while a soaring counterpoint in cellos and violas recalls the passionate phrase that appeared towards the end of the original theme. A soft timpani stroke signals an ingenious new treatment of bars 7–10 of the theme in which it is inverted by violas and cellos. Then, after a sustained crescendo the 'Nimrod' theme is heard for the third time, now with full orchestra. The penultimate phrase is repeated three times with ever-increasing intensity. The last three bars demand a quite extraordinary diminution of tone from the fullest *fortissimo* to an almost inaudible *pianissimo*.

Elgar described this famous variation as 'a jolly fine tune. It's just like you,' he wrote to Jaeger, 'you solemn wholesome hearty old dear.' The heartiness is not evident but the solemnity is such that the piece has acquired an almost religious significance.

There follows an Intermezzo which cannot really be regarded as a variation although the first entry of a solo viola may be an allusion to the rising phrase in bar 7 of the theme. The name at the top of the page is Dorabella, a reference to one of the characters in Mozart's '*Cosi fan tutte*', which perhaps Miss Dora Penny may have appreciated. If she was anything like as charming as the music she must have enchanted everyone who met her. Elgar said that the music suggested 'a dance of fairy-like lightness' and the delicate trills on the violins and the fluttering phrases in the wind do give an impression of gossamer wings hovering in the twilight. The soft sustained lines on solo viola or flutes are a master-stroke of scoring. A contrasting episode beginning with a swift upward scale from the violas takes us by surprise and for a moment or two the music shows greater animation. Notice particularly the contributions from the woodwind; every note counts and the whole Intermezzo is a supreme example of the fastidiousness of Elgar's scoring.

Variation XI is a curiosity. Supposedly a portrait of Dr. George Sinclair, the organist of Hereford Cathedral, it is more concerned with his bulldog Dan of whom Elgar was immensely fond. He even used to write fragments of music in the Sinclairs' Visitors' Book to illustrate Dan's mood of the day. On one occasion Elgar and Sinclair were walking by the river Wye when Dan slithered down the bank and fell in; he paddled frantically back towards dry land, scrambled out, shook himself and gave a triumphant bark. 'Set *that* to music' said Sinclair. 'I did' said Elgar after the variation had been written. Bar 1 shows Dan falling in, bars 2–3 show him paddling back to safety, the swift chromatic run in bar 4 is the dog shaking himself; clarinets, bassoons, horns and lower strings provide the bark in bar 5 and we even hear the chink of a triangle to capture the sound of Dan's name-plate medallion on his collar. The whole incident takes less than ten seconds but it provides Elgar with material for a brilliant variation. The dog's paddling becomes synonymous with Dr. Sinclair's nimble pedalling, the full brass grab hold of the theme and make it sound like a cathedral organ playing a fanfare; a musical joke becomes a virtuoso showpiece that is entirely relevant to the theme. Particularly ingenious is the compression of the theme in bars 2–3.

Variation XII depicts a cellist friend, Basil Nevinson, who used to play trios with Elgar and Steuart-Powell (see Variation II). Not surprisingly it opens with a cello solo. The other cellos soon join in to share the broad singing melody whose relationship to the theme is easy to comprehend.

Variation XIII is headed with three asterisks and the word 'Romanza'. The only reference to the theme is a gently rocking phrase on a pair of violas. Elgar's own note reads: 'The asterisks take the place of the name of a lady who was at the time . . . on a sea voyage. The drums suggest the distant throb of the engines of a liner, over which the clarinet quotes a phrase from Mendelssohn's "Calm sea and prosperous voyage".' There is a small mystery here. In later years Elgar himself pencilled in the name of Lady Mary Lygon, later to become Lady Trefusis. It seems though that Lady Lygon was not at sea in the first months of 1899 when Elgar was orchestrating the work since she and Winifred Norbury both went to his home to have tea on 21 February. If anything it was Elgar's memory that was at sea since it has recently been suggested that the asterisked lady was Helen Jessie Weaver to whom Elgar had been engaged some sixteen years earlier. Owing to religious differences the engagement came to nothing but Elgar was deeply affected by their enforced separation. Helen Weaver subsequently went to New Zealand, and it was no doubt because he was thinking of her at the opposite end of the world that he quoted the Mendelssohn phrase in this way.

The second appearance of the Mendelssohn quotation, on trombones and low trumpets, is truly impressive, perfect music for a film shot of a great ocean liner ploughing tirelessly across an infinite sea.

The finale, Variation XIV, is headed E.D.U. which, as we have seen, was his wife's pet-name for Elgar. (The full stops are certainly there to mislead the over-curious.) It starts as if it might well be a 'Pomp and Circumstance' march, though none of them had yet been written. The music symbolises the enormous gain in self-confidence which came with the writing of this work. The first references to the theme come in the brass after two powerful chords for full orchestra. Some way in, the brisk tempo eases back as cellos refer to the rising central phrase of the original theme; set against it is a new melody which Vernon Jones shrewdly points out spells E D U according to the musical 'alphabet' playfully used by many composers.

This theme spreads through the orchestra as the central section of the original theme becomes more openly displayed. Suddenly the full brass produce the theme transposed into the major, a moment of triumph celebrated with a magnificent descending scale in counterpoint. The music increases in tempo then breaks off for a momentary pause. Softly the march begins again, building more rapidly than before. Abruptly it halts in mid-flight and the music seems to freeze on a low E flat. Loud and clear we hear the triplet figure from Variation I, the private signal that Elgar used to whistle to his wife. We hear a distant echo and then, ever faithful, she appears — an exact quotation from her 'portrait' in the first variation. It is an oasis of calm in the excitement of the finale. Soon the music gathers impetus as though Elgar himself were striding with quickening steps towards the goal of recognition too long withheld. The theme reappears majestically, the orchestra now reinforced with the organ. The final climax is immense with the trombones proclaiming the first five notes of the theme in a hugely drawn out version. Small wonder that the work has retained its popularity ever since its first triumphant performance.

Introduction and Allegro for Strings (Quartet and Orchestra) Op. 47

The majestic opening bars of this splendid work do little to suggest that it was inspired in the first place by the sound of a few Welsh voices singing in the distance. Elgar was taking a holiday at the time and, so far as is known, had no particular project in mind; but the distant music touched a response which lay dormant in his mind. Some time later he was sitting one evening on his beloved Malvern hills and again he heard Welsh voices from far off. The sound was too remote to be able to identify the tune with any accuracy but one interval, a falling minor third, seemed to predominate. Fascinated by the elusiveness of the sounds and perhaps feeling that the dual experience was a prompting that he should not disregard, he took out the notebook he habitually carried round with him and jotted down a tune with a distinctly Welsh inflection (see top of page 223).

At that moment he probably had no particular idea as to its possible use but as he mulled it over it must have seemed especially suited to string tone. That decision made, he set to work on a most original plan, paying homage to the baroque concerto grosso by contrasting a solo string quartet with a larger

body of strings while at the same time writing what could be described as a gloriously free extension of the traditional concept of Prelude and Fugue. A postcard to his friend Jaeger, dated January 1905, reads: 'I'm doing that string thing in time for the Sym. Orch. concert. Intro. and Allegro — *no working-out part but a devil of a fugue instead, G major and the 2nd. divvel in G minor.*'

'That string thing' was finished on 13 February and performed at the Queen's Hall the following month, proof if needed of Elgar's ever-growing confidence. It is an extraordinary work, reconciling a variety of ideas that hardly seem to belong to the same world. The tempo fluctuates wildly, as it often does in Elgar's music, while ranging in emotion from majesty to tenderness, from frankly sentimental to fiercely intellectual and all within a span less than that of a symphonic first movement.

The first four bars, (I) are as grand a proclamation of the key of G minor as has ever been devised. Having made the point in so powerfully rhetorical a way, the main body of strings yields gracefully to the solo quartet who offer a brief contrasting phrase, (II) in which the rhythm ♫♫ should be especially noted for future reference. The 'orchestral' violins take the hint but the listener should pay greater heed to the lower strings whose rather sombre curve (III) is due to appear in a very unexpected role later in the work.

For four bars quartet and orchestra contemplate Theme I in a somewhat sweetened version and then, impatiently, the quartet moves on into II which, this time, is picked up with rather more emphasis by the orchestral violins, the sombre counterpoint of III now more intense in feeling. With a sudden and magical change of mood the solo viola from the quartet allows us to hear the 'Welsh' theme which was the genesis of the whole work. It is duly taken over by the main body of strings building to a climax of great warmth before dying away mysteriously as though receding into the night. A powerful crescendo on a single chord brings back Theme I, slightly modified, and terminated by three massive chords; as the last of these dies down we hear the quartet quietly meditating on the 'Welsh' tune. So far then these have been four distinct ideas, only one of which has been allowed to develop at any length; it is truly an Introduction in which the characters make their identities clear, each so different from the other.

But now there is a distinct change as the orchestral strings begin to develop II at greater length. Occasional interjections by the quartet attempt to sentimentalise it, but the 'orchestra' always moves the tempo forward again. Notice too how Theme III emerges from the depths, appearing in the violin parts for the first time. A sudden crescendo out of nothing halts the music in mid-flight. A new subject appears, (IV), instantly recognisable by its non-stop chatter of semiquavers. Treated at first as a dialogue between the quartet and the main body of strings, it builds to an exciting climax that spills over into a torrent of descending scales. Without any prior warning Theme I appears triumphantly in unashamed D major. An impassioned new theme grows out of it with an exhilarating striding bass. Brilliant scale-passages show off the violinists' technical skills; they lead to an agitated figure that opens out in contrary motion. It is a moment worth remembering for it is due to be repeated at a later point with a different sequel. Here it leads to a rather more lyrical version of Theme I which gradually subsides as the quartet again offers a tender reminder of the 'Welsh' tune. The music appears to come to a complete halt.

If we are to take the words on Elgar's postcard to Jaeger at their face-value it would seem that he had second thoughts here for the 'devil of a fugue' makes its unexpected entry in G minor, not G major as he suggests. Nor does there appear to be a second fugue; presumably he decided that one was sufficient. Whatever the truth of the matter the fugue is remarkable enough in itself. Beginning on the second violins it has a curiously hopping gait with sudden little upward spurts of notes that suggest a cloak swirling around a slightly grotesque figure. The entries would have been approved by Bach himself although the gradual infiltration of smooth legato lines deprives the theme of some of its spikiness. It is the entry of the quartet that brings the greatest surprise for instead of joining in the fugal dance they bring back Theme III which, amazingly, provides a perfect counterpoint to the continuing fugue despite its very different mood. The compositional problems that Elgar sets himself in the development of the fugue are very challenging, the more so for one who had never been through any conventional course at a conservatoire or university. After some striking examples of contrapuntal ingenuity the music gradually loses its forward thrust and the fugue subject makes an exit via the basement. Like a whisper, fragments of the 'chattering' theme return. With a sense of release a recapitulation of sorts begins, picking up the music at a point which was originally ten pages in. Familiar landmarks pass by, easily recognised since each element has so clearly defined a character. At the 'contrary motion' climax already mentioned Elgar plays his ace. Instead of the reversion to Theme I which we had previously, he offers a grandiose version of the 'Welsh' theme, no longer tender and distant but blazing with fervour. It is one of the richest examples of string orchestral writing in the entire repertoire and must lift our hearts however often we hear it. Some soaring fanfare-like figures bring the work to a conclusion that combines brilliance with nobility. 'I have finished the string thing and it's all right; of course, it will take you some time to get used to it, but it will sound really wholesome and bring out much tone from the strings.' So wrote Elgar after he had completed the score; those of us who have 'got used to it' find it a good deal more than 'wholesome'. 'Totally inspired' would be a better description of a work that can be classified as one of the greatest ever written for string orchestra.

Symphony No. 1 in A flat
Op. 55

To Hans Richter, Mus. Doc.
True Artist and true Friend.

These words appear on the title page of Elgar's First Symphony and Richter repaid the compliment handsomely when, at the rehearsal for the first London performance in December 1908, he began by saying to the orchestra, 'Gentlemen, let us now rehearse the greatest symphony of modern times, written by the greatest modern composer — and not only in this century.' Elgar had cherished the idea of writing a symphony for ten years; he had even contemplated following the precedent of Beethoven's 'Eroica' by relating the work to a contemporary hero, General Gordon. 'The Gordon thing possesses me but I can't write it down yet,' he wrote to Jaeger at one time. Perhaps it is as well that the plan was dropped; somehow the title 'Gordon Symphony' sounds amateurish. In the event the First Symphony turned out to be purely musical in concept with no suggestion of a programme. It is a long work taking some fifty minutes to play, but Elgar handles this largest of pure musical forms with great assurance. Prior to its composition he had suffered a long period of depression; he felt, with some justification, that the musical establishment in England had not yet given him due recognition. For example in 1908 Stanford had written a book of essays largely concerned with English music without so much as a mention of Elgar's name. Admittedly he had been given the professorship of music at Birmingham University but his duties there were not sufficiently practical to hold his interest; lectures on music were no substitute for conducting performances of his own works. Perhaps in an effort to rejuvenate his tiring muse he turned to some music he had written as a child of fourteen. Reworking the material with the skill of a mature master the fifty-year old composer produced two charming suites called *The Wand of Youth*. The relatively simple task gave him some relaxation so that at last he felt ready for the daunting task of writing a symphony. Considering its length it is remarkable that the work was written in two months, June/July 1908. The orchestral score was completed in the Autumn, the first performance given in Manchester in December. Within a year the symphony had been played over a hundred times, a response which must have delighted the composer even though he was so exhausted mentally that for several months he could not bear to hear a note of music. For relief he turned to chemistry, which fascinated him, or the occasional game of golf which he thought 'a grand game because you can think of nothing else when playing'.

The orchestra can certainly think of nothing else when playing this symphony since it is a work demanding virtuosity from every player. The opening pages give little hint of the perils ahead; two preliminary bars for timpani and low strings are like an initial clearing of the throat before making a speech. Elgar then gives us a magnificent tune with a hymn-like character.[5] At the first statement its tone is subdued, the texture virtually confined to two parts — the tune and a solemn marching accompaniment. The second 'verse' is scored for full orchestra and is richly harmonised until the closing bars which die away to a quiet sustained A flat in the bass. A tune as complete as this is not really good symphonic material since it is already fully grown; it leaves no room for development. (Schubert had a similar problem at the start of his great C major symphony.) It is not really surprising then that mood and tempo change abruptly as the 'true' first movement begins. The surprise lies in the key, D minor, a violent contradiction of the unadulterated A flat major that has preceded it.

The new theme (I) surges restlessly against a curiously angular bass, quickly reaching a climax before breaking into an urgent sequence in the strings goaded by off-beat chords for wind and brass. (I) returns in cellos and clarinets, now in G minor; it again climbs to a peak from which the descent is made to seem more precipitous by a change of the rhythmic pulse from 2/2 to 6/4. (This means that each 'beat' is subdivided into three instead of two, thus giving the impression of an increase in speed.) Gradually the agitation lessens, making way for a more relaxed theme (II) in the first violins. It is a precursor of the second subject, anticipating its shape but not its full span. That materialises a moment or two later, easily identified by the octave rise to a high A and the more leisurely descent. The music becomes increasingly lyrical, drifting through several keys while isolated dabs of sound from the flutes give a suggestion of scattered raindrops. Just as we think that peace is restored, an element of unease creeps in; the brass re-enter the fray (note the

---

[5]See Ex. 2 for a later version in C major.

high trumpet part) provoking an extremely vigorous response from the violins, leaping upwards in a sequence of mounting fifths. Rapid-fire chromatic scales in trumpets and trombone are the signal for a descending cascade in the strings out of which emerges a fragment of I. It is no more than a reminder and much more dramatic use is made of a phrase which originally appeared as a subsidiary to theme II. Here are its two versions, the first so discreet, the second so forceful:

Ex. 1

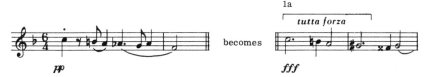

The tempo eases back and as if from a great distance we hear the very opening theme on muted horns; it seems to grow quite logically from the second part of the example above as a comparison of the first four notes will show.

Ex. 2

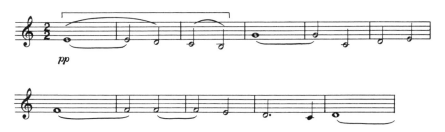

This reminder of things past signals the beginning of the Development which takes up more than a third of the movement. It starts with a 'wailing' motif on strings that has not appeared before, but a reversion to the 6/4 pulse causes some anxiety. The woodwind parts become notably more active, soon infecting the strings with their swiftly running figuration. Fragments of II appear in wind, horns and strings in turn, but they are shortly displaced by a strange new pattern whose awkward gangling shape proves to be surprisingly fruitful.

Ex. 3

It is the intrusion of such seemingly irrelevant passages that have laid this symphony open to criticism. It has been described as 'shapeless', 'sprawling', 'an improvisation rather than a symphony'. On being asked to account for its diffuseness Elgar exclaimed, 'All this is beside the point because I *feel* and don't invent. I can't even invent an explanation.'

To catalogue every happening in this extensive Development would be wearisome; the sounds alone should be thrilling enough. All the same we should not fail to recognise the dramatic re-entry of the second subject, its initial rising octave stretched to a tenth, its character transformed as the timpani thunder beneath it. There is also a remarkable expansion of Ex. 3 that goes from *pp* to *fff* in three bars. At a later point the music loses all momentum, coming to a virtual halt; quietly the 'wailing' motif reappears, ethereally scored. It is a useful landmark warning us that the recapitulation is about to begin. Although Elgar accepts the convention willingly enough, he finds plenty new to say; after the unmistakable re-entry of the rhythm shown on page 223 on horns and trumpets we should stand by for the extensive coda. We can hardly miss the imposing gateway that leads to it — three downward steps on bass trombone and tuba followed by a dramatic rising arpeggio in the violins.

The opening theme of the movement makes a ghostly appearance played by the back desks only of the strings while the 'wailing' motif provides a tender counterpoint. As the texture thickens again the opening phrase becomes more prominent until it appears radiant in the strings and wind. The gangling figure Ex. 3 crops up briefly but fails to establish any authority. Inevitably we sense that the movement is nearing its close as the tempo grows more and more relaxed. The end, when it comes, is almost inaudible, just two clarinets and a hushed pizzicato note from cellos and basses.

The second movement is a brilliant scherzo in which Elgar's earlier skills as a violinist stood him in good stead since the violin parts are superbly written to show the instruments' agility to the greatest advantage. After four introductory bars the first violins begin a sort of *moto perpetuo* figure which, though extremely quiet, fairly crackles with energy. The woodwind interpolate a less excitable phrase as the violins seem to pause momentarily as if to take breath. Soon the strings set up a more aggressive pattern which is skilfully divided between them. The wind, abetted by muted trumpets, respond to the challenge. Then violas and clarinets introduce a firmer footed idea beginning with the same note repeated three times. There is a vaguely martial feel to this, a brisk march for light cavalry rather than plodding infantry. The sound increases layer by layer until the high trumpets provide a fitting climax. The aggressive string pattern begins again, this time with horns giving a hard edge to the overall shape. The advent of the full orchestra plus a clash of cymbals heralds a new theme descending by thirds from a top A; it is a striking anticipation of an important theme in the violin concerto which

Elgar was to write two years later.[6] Strongly rhythmical chords from the full orchestra bring us back to the opening *moto perpetuo*, now played by unison strings, a passage that must have brought a smile to Elgar's face as he put it on paper. 'High Jinks' indeed for the cellos particularly!

After this exhibition of virtuosity the music appears to slow down by the simple process of doubling the value of notes. Flutes change the mood completely with a cheeky but casual little tune which is the equivalent of the Trio in a classical Scherzo. Clarinets (in thirds) offer a companion theme which has a touch of Dvořák about it. The violins find it irresistible; so do we all when it turns out to make a perfect counterpoint to the bustling *moto perpetuo*, now in violas and cellos only while the flutes whistle away cheerfully far above. For some time Elgar rings the changes on by now familiar themes, alternating the march with bustling semiquavers or even combining the two. The cheeky theme appears in full military uniform only to be displaced by a fairy troop. At last fatigue seems to set in as the semiquavers of the *moto perpetuo* are turned into triplets and then into crotchets. (Flutes and oboes in unison far below a sustained violin chord.) Gradually the music disintegrates until nothing is left but a quietly sustained F sharp in violins and violas.

Without a break Elgar leads us into the ensuing Adagio, a slow movement of which Richter said, 'ah, this is a *real* Adagio — such an Adagio as Beethoven would 'ave writ'.[7] And here we must pause for a moment to appreciate the amazing ingenuity Elgar shows. First let us take a look at the *moto perpetuo* from the scherzo, remembering that it should be played as fast as possible.

Ex. 4

Ex. 4a on page 230 shows the beginning of the Adagio; close comparison reveals that the actual notes are identical even though the outline is heavily disguised by the change in note-values. Elgar himself makes the point clear a few bars later when half of the second violins and violas are given Ex. 4 to play in equal semiquavers, although of course at the much slower tempo. Meanwhile the first violin part has developed into an impassioned melody of Mahlerian intensity. One of the most interesting things about this sublime

[6]See Ex. Ia on page (232).
[7]See W.H. Reed, *Elgar* (J.M. Dent, 1939).

Ex. 4a

movement is the contrast between long sustained melodic lines and tiny wisps of phrases. The influence of bird-song is apparent and despite the difference of idiom it seems to have much in common with Dvořák in its evocation of nature's beauty. Two solemn chords on trombones with a mutter from the timpani announce a soaring melody which has descending scales as a counterpoint. Notice also the extravagantly ornamented dialogue between clarinet and solo violin. Further reference is made to the opening theme before a coda of exquisite tenderness introduces yet another theme in this richly endowed movement. In the very closing bars there is a stroke of genius in the orchestration when muted trombones, timpani and harp are mingled together in the softest possible blend. The little triplet figure with which they interrupt the strings' elegy looks like a fatal miscalculation, but Elgar's touch is absolutely sure and the effect works to perfection.

A sudden blast of sound would have been too cruel a way of breaking the spell of this remarkable movement. Elgar tactfully begins his finale with a slow introduction whose opening bar should be barely audible. Bass clarinet and cellos seem to lift a curtain revealing a darkened stage. (Their notes incorporate the first bar of Ex. 3). Bassoons and pizzicato cellos present a ghost of a theme, all bones and no flesh. Faintly we hear a memory of the opening theme of the symphony, so faint indeed that it seems in danger of being blown away by a sudden flurry of notes from flute, harp and bassoon. Trombones take up the spectral march; the strings give a more forceful reminder of Ex. 3; there is another abortive attempt to introduce the opening theme. The music seems to be in a limbo, uncertain of its direction. After a moment's silence the solution is found; a rushing scale pitches us into the finale proper with a theme whose obsessional insistence on one rhythm (♩. ♪) is a stern corrective to the deliberately amorphous introduction. (The constant repetition of one rhythm is so characteristic of Elgar that it seems presumptuous to call it a weakness; we shall find it again in the finale of the Second Symphony and in the first movement of the Cello Concerto. Whereas repeated rhythms are acceptable as an accompaniment — as in Holst's 'Mars' — they become dangerous when they occur in the actual theme.) The dotted–crotchet–quaver pattern continues unbroken for twenty bars, forty times in all, so that when the music does break out one has a sense of escape to freedom. After some further developments the 'spectral march' from the introduction appears, crisply confident and building swiftly to a climax. The obsessional rhythm returns for another eighteen bars before the horns start a game of 'Hunt-the-march' that spreads through the brass in thrilling style. After some time the excitement dies down and once more the back desks of the strings give us a distant reminder of the opening theme, slightly altered. It has a wonderfully soothing effect on the 'march' which is promptly converted into a lyrical melody by the violins. Violas and cellos follow in imitation while the harps provide a rippling accompaniment. This new treatment is developed at some length leading to a fine climax.

The obsessional rhythm returns but with added interest in the shape of a sustained line in the horns. More excitement is whipped up with the march theme, urged on by fanfares from horns and trombones. As a final apotheosis the opening theme returns in glory, the surrounding arpeggios seeming like banners dipping in salute. It is a fitting climax to a work of the grandest stature, the first great symphony ever to have been written by an Englishman.

Concerto for Violin and Orchestra
Op. 61
(1910)
'AQUÍ ESTÁ ENCERRADA EL ALMA DE . . . . .'

This brief Spanish quotation, 'Here is enshrined the soul of . . . .', is inscribed on the dedicatory page of the concerto. It is a second Enigma that has caused much speculation. The five dots would seem to have some significance and it is unfortunate that the two most likely candidates to occupy the space both have names with five letters in: Alice and Helen. At one time Elgar wrote to a friend of whom he was particularly fond, Alice Stuart-Wortley, and told her that she was the one whose soul was enshrined in this intensely romantic work. But towards the end of his life, after his wife had died, Elgar confided to his close friend Ivor Atkins that the concerto had been inspired by Helen

Weaver, the girl to whom he had been briefly engaged in his mid-twenties.[8] White lies are a convenient way of concealing painful truths; men in their fifties are only too likely to have nostalgic memories of early romances. It seems quite probable to me that with his wife still alive — and his devotion to her is not in doubt — Elgar might well have used a harmless affection for Alice as a cover to hide a more profound feeling he had experienced nearly thirty years earlier. The cadenza in the third movement, a unique feature of the concerto, is a profoundly expressive contemplation of past events in a musical sense, a survey of the principal themes steeped in nostalgia. Helen Weaver was an accomplished violinist and I do not find it the least improbable that Elgar's cadenza was a musical symbol of 'If only . . .' There are many crossroads in all our lives and when it comes to affairs of the heart which of us does not at some time contemplate what might have happened if we had chosen an alternative?

Following the great precedents established by Beethoven and Brahms, Elgar begins his concerto with a substantial orchestral exposition, a classical convention which had fallen out of fashion by 1910. Even by Elgar's generous standards the first movement is unusually rich in material and there are no less than six clearly identifiable themes in the exposition. The 'first subject' group contains four, the 'second subject' a mere two; however, the continuity of the music is such that there is no impression of bittiness while subtle relationships between some of the themes help to preserve unity.

   The opening phrase has an easily recognisable contour but it is worth noting that nowhere in the entire work does the solo violinist play these actual notes.

The two-bar phrase is immediately repeated in a slightly modified version, more powerfully orchestrated. Its first subsidiary (Ia) follows at once, its descending pattern mirrored by a comparable ascending shape in the bass.

8See Enigma Variations, Variation XIII.

Again there is a slightly modified repetition before the announcement of (Ib) whose initial rising semitone (F♯–G) shows at least that it is a member of the same family.

Since this phrase is only a single bar it merits a four-fold repetition to balance the preceding patterns, but whether by modulation or by ornamentation each repetition introduces some variation. The entrance of the fourth theme (Ic) brings a change of mood. Although the melodic line continues to be lyrical there is a slightly sinister counterpoint on horns while a timpani roll adds a further touch of menace.

This is the first of these four themes to be developed at some length, sixteen bars in all. A slight *allargando* (broadening) makes room for the true Second Subject (II).

This too is considerably extended, the initial rising phrase being common to every variant; then, as though saying 'I've indulged myself long enough', Elgar quickens the pace and introduces the sixth theme (IIa), its rhythm strongly marked.

Another roll on the timpani accompanies the return of Ic, its two elements changing places so that the 'sinister' horn counterpoint now appears on top on violins and oboes. Waspish trills and swift ascending scales heighten the tension, summoning the trombones to make an impressive appearance. Theme I reappears in a more agitated mood and builds to a climax notable for some sensational writing for the horns. Ia makes its strongest effect yet, the rising bass reinforced by a tuba. Suddenly calm, the violins repeat Theme I, awaiting a reply. It comes from the soloist who, in a notably original entry, finishes off the orchestral phrase, bringing it to rest on a darkly coloured chord of B minor.

Although Elgar had been a professional violinist at the start of his career, it is likely that in his fifties his playing skills had considerably deteriorated. He therefore turned for practical help to W.H. Reed, a fine player who was for many years leader of the London Symphony Orchestra. In a very fascinating essay about the early birth-pangs of this work Reed describes the genuine delight that the novel entry of the soloist gave to the composer.[9]

Elgar was always very lavish with his printed instructions to performers and there is hardly a bar in this work that does not have a *crescendo* or *diminuendo*, a *tenuto* on one vital note, a change of tempo or any one of the wide range of dynamics between *ppp* and *fff*. There are six indications of tempo changes in the first nine bars of the solo part, showing that while Elgar wanted the soloist to adopt an improvisatory style of playing, the improvisation should be strictly according to Elgar rather than a matter of personal caprice.

Having rounded off the orchestral tutti in so satisfying a manner the soloist begins a quiet rumination beneath which the violas offer a tender reminder of the opening theme — a touchingly beautiful 'Lest we forget'. Soon the soloist arouses himself from this trance-like state and launches into a powerful statement of Ia, joining it seamlessly to Ic. This is developed quite extensively by soloist and orchestra with increasingly elaborate ornamentation in the solo part. Displaced from its original position, Ib now comes to the fore, exciting a somewhat breathless and agitated response from the soloist, not to mention a figure that is borrowed from the 'Introduction and Allegro'. The solo part grows increasingly athletic with wide sweeping scales covering two octaves or more. At last a fleeting reference to IIa brings a release and with touching simplicity the solo violin presents us with the second subject, shorn even of the dotted rhythm. The melody, seeming like a folk-song in its total lack of pretentiousness, is extended in a passage of notable beauty which, rather surprisingly, brings the Exposition to an end.

A sighing recollection of Theme I from the violins signals the start of the Development which soon involves a new theme. Accompanied by restless syncopations on horns and a quiet rumble from the timpani, it strides purposefully through wide-spaced intervals. The orchestral violins will have none of it and offer instead a neatly contracted version of Theme I.

---

[9]Reprinted in *An Elgar Companion*, pp. 251–7 (Sequoia, 1982).

This proves to be very productive and leads to the first open display of virtuosity from the soloist, rapid and aggressive chords that were revised several times before appearing in their final spectacular form. Having arrived at last on an altitudinous top C sharp, the soloist has a dazzling chromatic descent beneath which oboes and clarinets make four frustrated attempts to reintroduce Ic. It is the cue for an extensive orchestral tutti which effectively reduces the soloist to silence for a while. This centrepiece treats the material more dramatically than has been the case so far. First there is a full orchestral version of Ic; next a complete transformation of the tender second subject. Having put it into the minor with majestic new harmonies, Elgar extends it upwards on unison horns and clarinets while the violins have a turbulent passage in triplets which even continues as fragments of Theme I pass by in the woodwind. The music broadens as the first phrase of II is built into a four-fold sequence which spills over into more brilliant triplets in unison strings, harried by off-beat chords in brass and wind. The effect is almost overwhelming and one wonders how the voice of a single violin will make itself heard against such a volume of sound. Needless to say Elgar has things under control and the reappearance of Theme I in the violins has the necessary calming influence. The soloist takes over the pattern of the first three notes of I turning it into a descending sequence. A beautifully free improvisatory passage now begins while the orchestra offer expressive reminders of II. The soloist finishes his extempore style by returning to Ic in a substantially slower tempo. As the speed quickens again clarinet and violin engage in a dialogue while a restless figure like a sudden gust of wind surges through the strings. We are now in a recapitulation of sorts in which we find many recognisable features — a reworking of Ib and, in due course, a more passionate version of II. Passionate though it may be, it ends with a phrase of touching simplicity.

A soft timpani roll and the sudden menace of trombones brings an agitated reaction from the soloist with Ic and soon we sense that the pace is increasing as Elgar sees the final cadence ahead. The writing for the soloist grows ever more brilliant until we reach a suggestion of a cadenza. It is an indulgence Elgar denies himself, saving it for the last movement. A quick sprint for home brings the movement to an end.

The slow movement begins with an unaffected tune of great simplicity, its smooth flow interrupted in the second and fourth bars by curiously static chords from the woodwind. After a mere eight bars the solo violin enters not with the melody but with an independent inner part; it is a surprise as ingenious as the initial entry in the first movement. As the phrase shifts into the minor the soloist joins the orchestral violins briefly, only to leave them in a wonderfully ethereal ascent to the topmost register of the instrument. A new theme appears in the strings, mystical and reverent. This too comes to a halt on a sustained chord of E major. (Note how subtly Elgar darkens the harmony by dividing his cellos and adding a discreet roll on the timpani.) Over this chord the soloist offers a phrase of profound beauty that rises and falls again like a sigh. The strings disregard it, repeating their previous phrase a little tentatively. The soloist is not to be denied, however, and extends the sighing phrase into a melody of great warmth accompanied at one point by trombones, a blend of sheer genius on Elgar's part. This arouses a passionate outburst from the orchestra, positively Wagnerian in intensity, to which the soloist adds a searing comment.

A brief reminder of the opening theme serves to cool the passions. A capricious element now enters into the solo violin part as the music eddies to and fro. The orchestra is anxious to stress the importance of their secondary theme (to which the soloist adds a deeply expressive extension), but soon the capricious figures begin their tantalising dance again. A restoration of order comes from the horns and once more the secondary theme reasserts itself, freely decorated by the soloist. There is a particularly poignant episode in B flat minor in which a solo horn reiterates a mournful falling sixth, but in time the opening theme returns.

Although the movement appears to be loosely constructed, one may regard this as a recapitulation. From here to the end the music is unashamedly lyrical. The capricious element is banished; every phrase is profoundly expressive. Indeed it is hard to think of a single slow movement which can rival it in its exploitation of the violin as a 'singing' instrument.

From a purely formal point of view the finale is the most original of the three movements. Basically it is in a loosely constructed sonata–form but room is made for a substantial quotation from the slow movement before the remarkable cadenza which surveys material from the whole concerto.

We hardly have time to hear a soft rustle on the strings before the soloist starts a swiftly spiralling climb up the arpeggio of B minor. (After the unorthodox B flat major of the slow movement it is important to restore the 'proper' tonality.) From the outset it is clear that this movement is aiming to exploit technical virtuosity to a greater degree than its predecessors. The first significant theme does not appear until the twenty-eighth bar when the orchestra, determined 'to get a phrase in edgeways' against the soloist's perpetual chatter, interrupt the flow with this very positive statement (I).

Instantly it is taken over by the soloist who then reverts to the bustling semiquavers to provide a nimble variation. The orchestra restates the theme even more firmly but the soloist playfully rejects it, preferring to play 'catch-me-if-you-can' with clarinet or flute. Tiring of the game, he allows the orchestra to introduce a fine new theme which was briefly suggested earlier but disregarded.

This is treated majestically with some counterpoint from the brass but the soloist remains unimpressed by its seriousness, responding with sparkling scales and a positively flirtatious little phrase in elegant double-stopping. Having toyed with us in this enchanting and very feminine manner Elgar now introduces the second subject, a tune easily identified by the three repetitions of its first note. The orchestra gives a rather melancholy tinge to this tune but the soloist refuses to be downcast and embarks on some delightful variations. For a moment the 'flirtatious' phrase aspires to the grandeur of Brahms, only to become even more enchantingly capricious.

The initial spiralling arpeggios return, indicating the start of the development. The material follows very similar lines to the exposition, one significant difference being a powerful version of I played by the violin alone in three-note chords (triple-stopping). As before the orchestra has a brief but impressive tutti based on II; as before the second subject is introduced by the soloist, though this time the orchestra is allowed to relish it to the full.

The next significant landmark is signalled by a sequence of trills in the violin part culminating on a high sustained F sharp. Richly harmonised, the orchestra brings back the second main subject of the slow movement, inspiring the soloist to rhapsody. Just as the emotion seems about to become overwhelming there is a sudden scurry in the strings as though Elgar was sweeping away all thoughts of romance. The soloist produces a bold version of I above the rushing strings followed by a sequence of trills which brings back a brief reference to II. This is soon extended by the orchestra and unexpectedly scaled down until it is reduced to little more than a sigh. We are at the threshold of the cadenza which, far from being a firework display, is profoundly expressive. It begins with a touch of sheer magic, a ghostly reminder of Theme I from the first movement, just six notes. The soloist has a different recollection and with infinite tenderness suggests Ic (see page 233), extending it lovingly. Suddenly we hear a completely new sound, never used by any composer before; it is a harmony sustained by a soft thrumming as violins and violas play their instruments guitar-style. Against this mysterious background the violin wafts arpeggios upwards, lingering time and again on the falling third E–C♮. Once this wonderful meditation on Ic is ended it is the turn of the second subject from the opening movement. The mere reminiscence is enough to start an ornate extemporisation which alternates swift flights of notes with impassioned double-stopping. Virtually the whole time there is some orchestral support, usually a murmur but occasionally moved to share moments of exceptional intensity. Only towards the end of this unique section is the violinist left to muse alone. A soft trill beckons the strings back with a whispered reminder of the slow movement's secondary theme which seems to merge naturally into the comparable theme from the first movement. Then, with greatly intensified emotion, the orchestra again recalls Theme I from the first movement to which the soloist this time gives the logical response.

The rustle from the strings and the spiralling arpeggios bring us out of the dream and the final coda begins. Here too Elgar has a surprise for us for the tender second theme from the slow movement, so emotionally treated in the cadenza, is transformed into a broad singing melody that strides out energetically. The orchestra also gives us a stirring version of the rather neglected second subject of the finale — the theme beginning with the same note thrice repeated. A sequence of rough-hewn chords on the orchestra marked *strepitoso* (noisily) is cut short by a dramatic roll of drums such as might herald the last and most daring act of a circus acrobat. The soloist obliges with the triple-stopping version of I (see page 236), drawing each chord out to the full. Horns and cellos proclaim a simplified but triumphant version of the very first theme, now translated into the major, as the soloist provides some glorious fanfares to bring the work to a heroic conclusion.

Symphony No. 2 in E Flat
Op. 63

In addition to the conventional title the full score carries the following inscription:

> *Dedicated to the memory of His late Majesty King Edward VII*

At the foot of the page there is a further sentence:

> *This Symphony, designed early in 1910 to be a loyal tribute, bears its present dedication with the gracious approval of His Majesty the King.*
> *March 16th 1911*

On the inside of the fly-leaf there is a brief quotation from Shelley:

Rarely, rarely comest thou, Spirit of Delight!

The death of King Edward VII while Elgar was actually working on the symphony caused the dedication to be modified in this way. The first performance was given on 24 May 1911 and earned the seal of Royal Approval by the award of the coveted Order of Merit the following month. Curiously enough the première was received with less enthusiasm than Elgar had expected and afterwards he remarked to the leader of the orchestra 'What's the matter with them, Billy? They sit there like a lot of stuffed pigs.' It seems that the 'Spirit of Delight' was absent on that occasion, though the relevance of the quotation is characteristically enigmatic; does it greet the arrival of the Spirit or bemoan its absence?

At the end of the score we find the words 'Venice — Tintagel, 1910–11', but it is now known that sketches for the symphony date back to 1903. In December of that year one of Elgar's dearest friends, A.E. Rodewald, died in Liverpool. Hearing of his sudden illness Elgar at once journeyed north but arrived too late. He was distraught by the tragic news and wandered aimlessly through the streets unable to believe that the man who only two months previously had been his genial host in Bettws-y-Coed would never again help him with proofs, never offer valued criticism nor encourage him in his recurrent periods of depression. Unable to face the jouney home, he ended up in a room at the North-Western Hotel where he unashamedly wept. It was almost certainly this personal loss, so deeply felt, that resulted in the 'funeral march' in the Second Symphony, since the score was completed *before* the death of Edward VII.[10] If we relate the Shelley quotation to Elgar's nostalgic recollection of his friendship with Rodewald it makes a great deal more sense than if we try to associate it with the inevitably remote figure of a monarch.

The first movement, *Allegro vivace e nobilmente*, begins with an immensely energetic theme whose frequent syncopations give it an impression of tumbling forward impetuously. Like the overture 'In the South', which he had written some six years previously, it shows the influence of Richard Strauss in the sheer exuberance of the writing — the pagan whoops on the horns for instance which are a striking feature within seconds of the start. It is hard to pick out the most significant themes from the welter of sound with which the symphony begins but it is worth noting Elgar's love of contrary motion; if the violin phrases rise, the bass will tend to fall and vice versa. After more than forty bars of intensely animated music the pace slackens a little as a curiously angular pattern of triplets passes down from violins to violas. A new theme appears which one is tempted to hail as the second subject;

[10]W.H. Reed maintained that the slow movement was written subsequently but early sketches disprove this; it could well be that Elgar rescored the movement in a grander way after the King's death.

however it is extremely unstable harmonically with two shifts of tonality in each bar. (G major to E flat, A flat to the dominant of D minor, G minor to the dominant of E flat — and all in the space of four bars!) It is this wayward refusal to settle down that makes me prefer to call it a bridge passage (a swaying rope bridge . . .) since it seems to be the origin of a much calmer theme for the cellos, the first extended lyrical tune of the symphony. Beginning with a sustained B flat in the high tenor register, it climbes by stages to a top F, although Elgar curbs delusions of operatic grandeur by the restraints of *dolce*, *delicato* and frequent warnings to make instinctive *crescendi* small. The restless uneasy figures of the 'bridge' disturb this brief period of calm and soon the full orchestra is involved in strongly accented chords marked *Impetuoso* followed by a giddily see-sawing pattern that is whipped on by brilliant triplets in the trumpet parts. The tempo quickens again only to ease back slightly as we reach a huge climax with more conventional battle-calls from the trumpets cutting through the general hubbub.

Some respite is offered with the emergence of some soft harp chords though there is still some uneasiness in the strings. Then, as the agitation dies, quiet string chords drift downwards in a strange ghostly interlude. There are still murmurs of unrest but the effect is nocturnal, veiled in mist through which the occasional swift chromatic run suggests a bird winging its way back to its nest high above. A barely audible rumble from timpani and bass drum adds a touch of menace. Only the cellos seem confident as they spin a golden thread of tone, yet even their theme seems to lack a conventional sense of key. It is not surprising that the first audience was puzzled for this was a very different Elgar from the one who had bewitched them with the violin concerto. That had tunes in abundance, but could this cello theme, surrounded by strangely groping harmonies, be called a *tune*? (Tune or not, it is as well that we should stow it in our memories since it is destined to appear nearly a hundred pages later in the middle of the scherzo.) The drum-beat slows as the ghostly interlude continues until it dies away to nothing but sombre clarinets and bassoons. The strings remove their mutes and a revival begins with a repeated phrase in the lower reaches; it spreads to the wind then to the horns. Within eight bars animated figures from the earlier section of the symphony sweep through the orchestra. The tempo quickens as the music grows more violent; imposing unisons from horns and trombone summon an awe-inspiring climax of extraordinary intensity that leaves us literally gasping. Although we are unlikely to realise it at the time, it is the start of the recapitulation, and after a moment's silence we are pitched into the second full bar of the initial theme, the preceding cataclysm having been a hugely magnified version of the first bar. (Even the prolonged B flats on horns and trombone are a giant extension of the very first notes of the symphony.)

It would be unlike Elgar to give us a literal recapitulation and there are many additional touches even though the basic framework is clearly recognisable. The most noticeable difference is the omission of the 'nocturnal' section. As it is, bell-like harmonics on the harp give us due warning that the coda is imminent. It introduces a sustained tune on the violins that we have not heard before. Its emphasis on flattened sevenths (D flats in an E flat major context) gives it a sense of yearning and for a moment or two we wonder if Elgar will follow in Brahms's footsteps by giving us a twilight ending. But no; the restless rhythms begin to surge again and the final bars flare up like a consuming fire.

The Larghetto which follows is for the most part a very controlled expression of grief. A few introductory bars from the strings set the mood and then flutes, bass clarinet, trumpet and trombone present the main theme with the greatest simplicity. Against this sustained threnody quiet but weighty chords on the second and fourth beats suggest the solemn tread of a funeral procession. (It is by such means that Elgar may have given a public face to private grief diminished by the passing of the years.) Soon the violins take over the melodic interest, bringing their more openly expressive tones to a more elaborate theme. After ten bars the initial theme returns now on horns and trombones alone; but it seems that we catch only a glimpse of the *cortège* at this moment for after one phrase the interest shifts to the woodwind with a gently rocking motif that is like a sad lullaby. ('Come lovely and soothing death . . .')

For the first time the strings are left completely on their own with a new theme beginning with a rising fifth that soon reaches out to become an octave. At first in three parts only and sounding like choral writing rather than orchestral, it soon grows more impassioned, building to a strong *forte* phrase which is echoed almost inaudibly — such an effect as may come naturally in a great cathedral. Suddenly the music seems to be racked by paroxysms of anguish as scales, trills and arpeggios sweep through the string parts while the darker woodwind have a theme that is heavy with grief. Unison horns extend this further until the music spills over in a passionate outburst out of which emerges one of Elgar's noblest tunes. The key, F major, brings release from the wrought-up tension of the preceding pages; it is a passage that rivals 'Nimrod' in its solemn beauty, but unlike 'Nimrod' it finds no reconciliation in the end. Softly oboes and then clarinets bring back the 'sad lullaby' which, by a brief extension, leads into a reprise of the first main theme. Despite the essential simplicity of the tune the texture here is very complex. In the bass we find a constantly reiterated figure in this rhythm ♪ ♫ ♩. Meanwhile divided violins, violas and cellos have dense clusters of harmony, four notes to a beat, over solemn chords for brass and harps reinforced by drums — all off the beat. But the truly inventive ingredient, the touch of genius, is a forlornly wandering oboe part, almost like a sad version of 'Jesu Joy', flowing with complete freedom through the deliberately measured rhythms that surround it.[11] Out of this grave processional comes a

[11] The thought comes that this might by a symbol of Elgar's aimless wandering on that private via dolorosa in 1903.

passionate theme from the violins; we have heard it once before as early as the nineteenth bar, but not with such emotional intensity. The horns seem to give a solemn rebuke to this almost operatic display of grief and the strings, repentant, return to the quiet three-part 'choral' theme. From this point on there is the sort of reprise that is needed in a symphonic movement on this scale. After the anguish comes the noble tune that I compared to 'Nimrod', now in its 'proper' key of E flat. This is no funeral march but a triumphant cry of 'Death where is thy sting, Grave, thy victory?' Even so the movement ends not in glory but in sorrow as the awareness of bereavement strikes a cold chill into the heart.

The third movement is labelled Rondo on the score instead of the more traditional Scherzo. Its components are extremely simple to grasp; the first could be described as a flick of a theme:[12]

Ex. 1

while the second once again employs Elgar's favourite rhythm:

Ex. 2

The first section, which is repeated, is concerned entirely with Ex. 1 and its derivatives. Despite the initial suggestion of Puckish humour there is a frenetic haste about some passages that gives the music a nail-biting intensity and although the raucous appearance of Ex. 2 may seem to suggest the entry of Bottom and his fellow-rustics into a fairy glade, the music is too harshly driven for comedy. Even when this second theme is treated more delicately the constantly shifting tonalities are unsettling, so much so that when the first theme returns on flutes and oboes it is cruelly distorted. After some scampering chromatic runs in the woodwind the violins produce a new theme against

[12]Elgar said that he had heard the phrase from a group of itinerant musicians in the Piazza San Marco in Venice.

a barrage of three-note patterns derived from the very first bar. These and subsequent derivations are very obvious even to the untrained ear since the initial 'flick' is instantly recognisable.

After one particularly energetic passage of hustle and bustle the wood-wind propose a change; it is an innocent enough little theme:

Ex. 3

It is not developed in any significant manner but it keeps nudging its way into the score as though determined to stake a place. The strings disregard it entirely as they start on a new episode that has the naiveté of a nursery song. Still the wind persist in their interpolations of Ex. 3 until at last the violins are forced to acknowledge it — once!

In due course, after some stalling in the strings, the rondo theme returns. As it does so, the second violins add a new counterpoint that seems of little importance:

Ex. 4

Gradually it displaces the darting flicks of the rondo, lengthening the span of the phrases. The timpani begin a softly insistent beat, the only warning that we are about to be thrust into a nightmare. Against an extraordinary throbbing pulse Ex. 4 is transformed into the long cello tune from the 'nocturnal' section of the first movement (see page 240). There too it was accompanied by the rumble of drums, but now the beat is relentless. Elgar is said to have had in mind the lines from Tennyson's 'Maud':

> The hoofs of the horses beat,
> Beat into my scalp and my brain.

This theme from the first movement is transferred from the violins to trombones in a passage of astonishing drama. The 'hoof-beats' pound out on the heavy percussion while fragments of the rondo theme seem to hurl themselves against this unwelcome invader. One can see why Elgar avoided the word Scherzo, for this is clearly no jest. As the shattering tumult dies down we even hear faint allusions to the drifting string harmonies from the 'nocturne'. At last the music comes to a complete halt on a sustained dissonance from horns and bassoons. Almost tentatively Ex. 2 reappears, as though emerging from hiding. Soon it gains confidence and initiates the semblance of a reprise. What differences there are are self-evident but inevitably the rondo theme regains its eminence towards the end. When Elgar described this work as being 'on a totally different psychological plane from that of the first symphony' he must surely have been thinking of this movement in particular; the central section is the most disturbing passage that he ever wrote. In a letter he wrote to Alice Stuart-Wortley he said, 'I've just put the last notes to the third movement and very wild and headstrong it is . . .'

These are not words one would be likely to apply to the finale which begins with a theme that glides along '*con dignita*', scored darkly for bass clarinet, bassoons, horns and cellos. (The horn-section had some justification for their complaint that it was extremely difficult to play, though the modern instruments of today's orchestras ease the problem somewhat.) Once more Elgar lays himself open to the criticism of sticking closely to one rhythm; it may be that since the symphony was completed in Tintagel the music was inspired by the tireless sweep of the waves. The secondary theme that follows has a more energetic spring to it, leaping through a fifth, a sixth and then an octave before falling back again. It has the most unusual instruction '*ff ma dolce*' (very loud but sweetly). By this time Elgar had written his three oratorios as well as such early choral works as 'King Olaf' and 'Caractacus'. I only mention this because his treatment of this new theme tends to follow the precepts of traditional choral practice with a first entry on tenors, then altos, sopranos and so on. In other words although it is certainly not a fugue, it follows a fugal concept. It builds to a fine climax emphasised by a splendid ascent in the trombones and a brilliant martial figure in trumpets and horns. A gradual broadening leads to the true second subject, a fine expansive tune which fully deserves Elgar's often used instruction '*Nobilmente*'. It runs its full course without interruption until, having come to a peaceful cadence, the cellos give us a brief reminder of the opening theme.

It is a cue for the development to begin. With a complete change of texture Elgar begins an agile treatment of the leaping secondary theme with athletic counter-subjects that remove all suggestions of choral music. The music makes increasing demands on the virtuosity of the players, the string parts being especially brilliant. At the climax the trombones (abetted by timpani) present an abrupt staccato version of the opening theme that quite changes its character, an act of aggression which the strings soon do their best to mollify. Just to show it can be done Elgar then combines the smoothly rolling first theme with its leaping subsidiary, although as a symbol of reconciliation both are now hushed.

A new theme now appears (III) starting high on the violins and falling by intervals of a fifth and a fourth through just over two octaves. It proves to be an effective new counterpoint to the first theme and the two are worked together for some time. (Do not miss a demanding pizzicato passage for the cellos which must lead to sore fingers at any lengthy rehearsal.)

The recapitulation in this relatively conventional movement is easily recognised although the participation of III gives it the appearance of novelty. Anyone who has absorbed the material of the exposition should have no difficulty in appreciating the reappearance of now familiar themes. As one would expect, the '*Nobilmente*' subject is re-stated majestically, after which an even bigger climax suggests that the symphony is heading for a triumphant conclusion. Surprisingly the flames flicker and die. A quiet drum-roll and the re-emergence of the first theme signal the beginning of an unexpectedly tranquil coda to which the harps lend a golden sheen. The tempo slows as though indeed all passion is spent. Elgar was steeped in Shakespeare, and the Duke's lines — 'That strain again! It had a dying fall' — would suit these closing pages admirably. Only one concession is made to convention, a fortissimo chord for full orchestra that seems to court applause. But then 'too vulgar' thinks Elgar and marks a long diminuendo until only strings and a few woodwind are left fading to silence.

Concerto for Violoncello and Orchestra
Op. 85

Despite its impressive opening phrase I doubt if in the whole repertoire of concertos there is one so reticent, so essentially introverted as this. It was written in the aftermath of four devastating years of war during which Elgar had of necessity composed various patriotic works such as *The Spirit of England* and a set of songs to Kipling's words called *The Fringes of the Fleet*. These were performed with scenery and action at the London Coliseum until Kipling for some obscure reason withdrew permission for his poems to be used. The composer, now in his sixties, was growing weary and retreated to a cottage called Brinkwells in a beautiful part of Sussex. As though reflecting his wish to escape from public life, from rousing patriotic concerts and from the constant reminders of the huge death toll across the water, he began to write chamber music — a violin sonata, a string quartet and a piano quintet. These works represent a huge reaction from the orchestral splendours of the symphonies; they are intimate and restrained, the private thoughts of a man in his sixties who sensed perhaps that his creative fire was on the wane.

These same qualities prevail in the cello concerto which he actually began in the last month of the war. The first performance was given a year later on 27 October, 1919. The audience was in the mood for something more spectacular and only those who knew Elgar well fully appreciated the work's unique character. Even Donald Tovey, normally the most perceptive of writers, stresses its humour rather than its pathos, drawing the dangerous analogy of 'slipping on a banana-skin' as he describes a passage in the last movement.

The work begins with an arresting declamatory passage for solo cello which the woodwind make an abortive attempt to copy, quickly suppressed by a 'Hush' from the strings. The initial recitative continues with an express-ive ascent whose final note dissolves almost imperceptibly into a gently meandering theme for the violas, completely unaccompanied. Here surely is a symbol of Elgar wandering alone through the Sussex woodland thinking of the numerous friends who had met a painful and frightening death in the endless massacres that had turned France into a human slaughterhouse. Most unusually for Elgar the music is almost devoid of expression marks as though true feeling must be kept behind a mask. (The time for weeping comes at the end of the work.) The soloist takes over the orchestral phrase as discreetly and unostentatiously as a couple, long-married, might link hands wordlessly as they stroll along a favourite path. Richer harmonic support from the orches-tra brings greater intensity of tone from the soloist who, with a magnificent ascending scale summons a brief majestic tutti. It lasts for a mere six bars, too massive for a theme of such intimacy. The soloist resumes as before and then, with the utmost simplicity, brings the phrase to rest with two pizzicato notes and a final sustained low E.

Clarinets and bassoons now introduce a pastoral phrase that is not so much a dance as a recollection of one. It is a memory the soloist seems to share, a memory tinged with sorrow for days that can never be recaptured. The orchestral participation is tactful and sympathetic but if we listen to the cellos and basses we can hear the suggestion of a salon orchestra in this strangely haunted ballroom, full of memories though the furnishings are bare. The cello part grows more passionate but elicits no response. The vision fades and the wandering theme resumes its leisurely pace. The ascending scale — the one concession to virtuosity in the whole movement — again rouses the orchestra to a show of strength but it is even shorter-lived and almost before we are aware of it the movement has died away to a single held note in the bass.

Three plucked chords from the cello remind us of the opening recitative; they are cut off by a dramatic orchestral gesture. A strange miniature cadenza follows, as though the soloist is searching for a suitable theme for a scherzo. A restless little fragment is tried and then rejected with two pizzicato chords —

tried again, and again rejected. Yet again we find this curious indecision; then, as though in exasperation at this mental block the pizzicato chords are wrenched aggressively into a brisk ascent culminating in an extraordinary cry of anguish (now 'bowed') as though the very idea of writing a happy-happy scherzo is more than can be endured. Two more tentative attempts are made before the movement at last gets under way.

It proves to be a strange sort of scherzo, a will-o'-the-wisp movement that flits and darts like a dragon-fly. The orchestral part is minimal, only occasionally chasing after the soloist in imitation of some especially notable flight. Only one phrase seems to have real flesh on it, a characteristically Elgarian theme that is at once endorsed with healthy enthusiasm by the orchestra. (It is their first *forte* in the movement!) Within seconds the cello returns to its *moto perpetuo* style of playing. Indeed there are only two elements in this movement, the dragon-fly motif and the brief Elgarian phrase; even that is never allowed to develop at any length and the movement ends its hovering flight by coming to land most elegantly.

The slow movement is only four pages long compared to the fourteen of the violin concertos. It is scored for two clarinets, two bassoons, two horns and strings. It has scarcely a *forte* in the orchestral part and little visible contrast. Yet so deeply felt is the emotion that time seems of little consequence; perhaps only the Cavatina from Beethoven's Op. 130 Quartet says so much in so concentrated a form. Eight introductory bars set the mood; then, with the last beat of the eighth bar the main theme begins. Apart from a single bar's rest the cello line remains unbroken for the rest of the movement. One falling phrase needs to be stored in the memory so that we may better appreciate its return towards the end of the concerto. Otherwise all we have to do is to surrender to this sublime meditation.

The orchestra begin the finale purposefully with a brisk march rhythm but the soloist declines to share their mood and turns their crisp little theme into a declamation. A brief cadenza ensues, culminating in a brilliant rush into the extreme upper register. Having thus established total dominance, the soloist sets the march going at a slightly steadier pace. The strong accents on the second beat of every alternate bar give the music a splendid forward thrust and the wind and brass welcome the chance to show a bit of muscle after their long silence. For a moment or two we are in a mood of Pomp and Circumstance but the cellist, as if saying 'we've done with marching now' takes a capricious turn and introduces a more lyrical theme with a delightfully skittish tail. Elgar develops this in a series of sequential repetitions which, in due course, are treated as material for variations in a continuous pattern of semiquavers. The orchestral accompaniment is kept very light so that every note of the solo part can be heard. At last the soloist tires and has a charming 'sit-down-and-rest' phrase on descending minims. 'You take over' he seems to say, and the wind do so with the little march theme. Gaining confidence, it begins to spread through the orchestra until a rocking arpeggio figure from the soloist magically transforms the march into a light-footed dance. It is the happiest moment of the whole concerto, a symbolic emergence from the rigours of war.

There is a tiny gap after three stamping chords and then the cello resumes the first theme in a recapitulation of sorts. Again the orchestra is given the chance to show its full strength — rare in this work, and again the cellist resorts to caprice to change the mood. But a sustained timpani roll, the first in the movement, casts a sudden shadow and all the spring suddenly goes out of the music. Five repeated C sharps plucked on the double basses sound like a funeral drum. Strings and soloists together share a phrase of heart-breaking poignancy as though Elgar was questioning the propriety of writing cheerful music when so many millions had died in the mud and filth of Flanders. The ensuing lament is one of the most profoundly expressive passages in the cello repertoire, the more so when a quotation from the slow movement makes its unforgettable appearance. The cynical might argue that Elgar overplays his hand here by too many repetitions of the wailing chromatic phrases, but the cynical have not experienced the grief that Elgar was expressing for all those whose loved ones had been killed. The last note of this heart-felt lamentation dies away to silence; then, solemn and majestic, the very opening phrase of the concerto reappears. Two explosive chords like gunshots over a grave interrupt its progress, but it continues on its way, even though it is not too fanciful to suggest that the phrase seems to shed tears as it descends to a dramatic low E. As though from a great distance the crisp little march tune begins again, though the soloist is too wrapped in grief to be able to respond to the change of mood. But the rhythm grows more insistent until, almost unwillingly, the cello is forced to join in. It is a coda that seems almost indecently short after so profoundly moving an episode but 'life must go on' it seems to say, even if only to deny Death the added satisfaction of dragging the living into the pit of despair.

CÉSAR FRANCK
1822–90

Franck's talent for music manifested itself at an early age although the family had been noted for producing painters of quality for a number of generations. His father earned his living as a banker but was a keen amateur musician. Every encouragement was given to the young César to develop his innate abilities and he made his first concert tour in his native Belgium when he was still only eleven years old. At fifteen he was admitted to the Paris Conservatoire where after less than a year's study he played the Hummel Piano Concerto in A minor so expertly that he seemed certain to gain the first prize. However there was also a compulsory sight-reading test. Hoping to impress the examiners Franck read the piece flawlessly while simultaneously transposing it down a third. The jury were astonished except for Cherubini who, jaundiced pedant that he was, claimed that the rules had been broken and that Franck should therefore be failed. Only the vehement protests of the other professors persuaded Cherubini (who had the final say as Director) to agree to make a special award, a *Grand Prix d'Honneur*.

Franck was to become the greatest organist in France but despite his prodigious gifts he was not appreciated by the powerful musical Establishment and for a long time his sole income came from the church and from teaching private pupils. Times were difficult in Paris with the political disturbances of the second revolution and, later, the Franco-Prussian war. Franck would habitually rise at five-thirty in the morning to give himself time to compose before setting out to give the daily round of lessons. Not until he was well into his forties did acknowledgement of his qualities as a composer begin to come. At the age of fifty he was offered the post of organ professor at the Conservatoire where he soon became adored by his pupils and disliked by the staff; his method of teaching was too liberal and too unorthodox to be acceptable to narrow academic minds. His modesty was such that he was incapable of promoting his works yet he continued to compose on an ambitious scale. Only the enthusiasm of his devoted pupils enabled many of his compositions to be performed at all, and when a grudging government finally awarded him the order of Chevalier of the Legion of Honour it was for his abilities as an organist, not as a composer.

In 1887 his pupils organised an entire concert of his works but insufficient rehearsal and Franck's inexperience as a conductor prevented it from being a success. He was not to receive a real public ovation until 1889 when his String Quartet was performed at a concert of the *Société Nationale de Musique* which, incidentally, Franck himself had founded some years previously. The persistent calls for the composer at last persuaded him to take a bow. The next day the sixty-eight year old Franck said to his pupils, 'You see, they are beginning to understand me.' Recognition had indeed come, though cruelly late for the following year he died after months of illness. Although posterity has denied him the status of true greatness, a certain number of his works have retained their place in the repertoire. Of these the violin sonata, the piano quintet and the Symphonic Variations show him at his best, while his bequest to organists is considerable. Liszt declared that Franck could have had no equal as an improviser since Bach himself and it is our loss that recording had not been perfected in his time so that his inspired improvisations could have been preserved for later generations to marvel at.

Symphonic Variations for Piano and Orchestra

The Variations, which are played without a break, are based on three themes, two of which are heard in the initial dialogue between the orchestra and soloist. The conception of the opening is remarkably similar to the slow movement of Beethoven's Fourth Piano Concerto, a resemblance of which Franck must surely have been aware; since Beethoven's mould is soon broken, the point is not worth labouring. It is enough to say that the opposition between aggressive strings and conciliatory piano simplifies the listener's task since the two themes are so different in character that they cannot be confused. Here then are themes I and II.

Notice that the strings have a *diminuendo* in their first phrase, a concession that Beethoven certainly does not allow in his G major concerto.

The dialogue is repeated at a higher pitch after which the orchestra, subdued but obdurate, continue to develop their theme, the offbeat chords above emphasising the gradual increase in tension. Meanwhile the piano intervenes with romantically expressive phrases designed to avert any more open conflict. The orchestra remains unmoved by the piano's protestations and in time the dotted rhythm of Theme I becomes powerful enough to persuade the pianist to accept it as well; however the alternate phrases still express argument rather than agreement. The sudden flare-up soon subsides and after a rippling arpeggio from the piano we meet Theme III. Its first presentation is not all that encouraging; woodwind and pizzicato strings present it rather drily over a quiet drum-roll.

A brief linking passage from the piano brings us to Variation I. It is for piano alone and is an extension of Theme II, more lyrical, more impassioned and accompanied by a figure in the left hand that is a Franck hallmark.

At their next entry the cellos and basses continue to grumble away about Theme I. The piano's renewed attempts to calm their irritation come to nothing and the orchestral part builds to a considerable climax. The dispute between soloist and orchestra is renewed but it is a contest which the piano easily wins. A brief orchestral link offers several hints that it's time to give more serious consideration to Theme III. So begins Variation II, in a far more expressive version than the one shown in the above example. It is a theme with many silences in it, silences which are soon to be filled in the delightful second part of the variation. For the first time pianist and orchestra are reconciled and in an enchanting dialogue they share the theme turn and turn about.

Another variation follows at once with violas and cellos turning Theme III into a fully sustained melody while the pianist is given a delicate accompaniment of 'raindrop' chords. No sooner is this section ended than another variation begins. It involves quite wide skips in the piano part which centre round reiterated C sharps — the dominant of F sharp minor. With the increased participation of the orchestra this becomes much more resolute, leading into a powerful new variation in which the melodic shape of III is combined with the rhythmic drive of I. Were it not in 3/4 time one would think of it as a march; certainly it is 'heroic' in concept, developing into quite a menacing storm. However this is not a work in which the pianist readily accepts the role of hero-figure and an extension of this variation soon follows with the strings quietly continuing the 'march' version of I-plus-III while the pianist has a sort of 'skater's waltz', with dancing triplets and bell-like upper notes. Gradually the music slows down for the two central variations which structurally serve the purpose of a slow movement.

At a much slower tempo the pianist begins a softly rippling figure in F sharp major. Tempting though it is to give all our attention to this dreamy nocturnal music, the heart of the matter lies in the cellos who are given a beautiful variant of III, dark in tone and deeply expressive. The second half of the variation is shared by the woodwind and occasional pizzicato chords from the strings though the piano figuration remains constant throughout.

A return to F sharp minor reduces the pianist to a purely accompanying role whose harp-like figures give the cellists sympathetic support in the next variation. Here the material is taken from II, now extended and converted into a profound sigh. Muted strings provide a hazy background which modulates through several keys before finally coming to rest on a wide-spaced chord of C sharp major. A subtly disguised chromatic scale enables the pianist to escape from the hypnotic arpeggio figures which have persisted throughout the variation. A trill rouses the woodwind from their slumber with dancing crotchets that are derived from III, while the lower strings offer a far more cheerful version of II, its angular intervals smoothed out, all sadness banished.

Infected by the new mood, the pianist joins the woodwind with a happy clatter of chords before embarking on a free episode in which the left hand figuration from Variation I plays a vigorous part. Three bars of piano solo prepare the way for the next variation, a carefree treatment of I whose nimble athleticism is a sheer delight. The orchestra takes over for a few bars in much rougher fashion, but the pianist woos them with a new tune in which the two hands move in parallel chords. Down in the orchestral bass there is a cleverly sketched version of III. A brief orchestral tutti produces yet another treatment of II, sinister and exciting. It breaks off abruptly having built to a dramatic peak.

As if in gentle rebuke, the pianist now has an extended episode of a lyrical character loosely derived from I. Although it isn't at all dramatic it has an intriguing rhythm in which the right hand is playing in 6/4 while the left hand is in 4/4. It gives a slight unease to an otherwise conciliatory passage.

The entry of a flute with the cheerful dancing version of II is enough to produce a change to a more frivolous mood. The rhythmic ambiguity of the piano part is resolved into a nimble waltz which fairly flies over the keys. In due course there is an easily recognised reprise of two of the more joyous variations and the work ends with Theme II transformed into a peal of bells. Apart from its purely musical qualities this work shows Franck at his best since although the craftsmanship is brilliant, three concise themes being all that he requires, there is throughout a feeling of spontaneity so that one imagines that each variation was improvised on the spot rather than being the product of purely intellectual decision.

GRIEG
1843–1907

Grieg inherited his musical talent from his mother who, although not a fully professional musician, was sufficiently gifted to play in concerts in Bergen. She began to give piano lessons to young Edvard when he was still only six; his natural tendency was to improvise in a rather formless way, searching for beautiful and exotic chords. He once wrote that his happiness at discovering a dominant ninth (CEGB♭D) knew no bounds. Hearing him dreaming away at the piano his mother would come in and reprimand him, redirecting his thoughts towards more systematic study of the pieces he was supposed to be learning. Since Grieg at the time nursed a childish ambition to be a pastor who could harangue congregations from the pulpit he saw no reason why he should play the piano other than for pleasure. A significant turning-point came when Norway's most famous violinist, the delightfully named Ole Bull, became acquainted with the Grieg family. He it was who took an interest in the fifteen-year old's attempts at composition and urged his parents to send him to Leipzig for proper musical tuition.

It was not an experience which Grieg particularly enjoyed although he did strike up a friendship with a fellow-student from England called Arthur Sullivan. He soon realised that his mother's dilatory approach had caused him to fall far behind the standard required; much though he hated the drudgery of technical exercises and theoretical study he began to work feverishly to make up lost ground. The result was a complete breakdown and a severe attack of pleurisy which left him with one lung permanently impaired.

During the summer of 1864 Grieg spent some time at Ole Bull's country home on the island of Ostery. Although he had an international reputation as a concert violinist, Ole Bull was a true Norwegian at heart and had a profound conviction that the folk-music of Norway should be the proper source of inspiration for any Norwegian composer. This was a welcome philosophy to young Grieg who had been stifled by the conservatism of Leipzig where Chopin and even Schumann were regarded as dangerously 'modern'. To hear the violinist whom he idolised playing folk-songs and dances with such fervent enthusiasm fired Grieg with a determination to find a new path, untainted by the German school. From then on, he decided to concentrate on establishing a specifically Norwegian style of composition. Another young musician called Rikard Nordraak encouraged him still further, and Grieg began to mount his own concerts in various cities, and even founded a Norwegian Academy of Music when he was still only twenty-four. I't was married the same year. The following summer, soon after the birth of a baby daughter, Grieg composed the piano concerto. (1868).

A grant from the Norwegian Government enabled Grieg to visit Rome where he met Liszt, at that time the most renowned musician in Europe. It was on a second visit to the Liszt household that the famous episode concerning the piano concerto occurred. Grieg described it vividly in a letter home.

> I had fortunately just received the manuscript of my pianoforte concerto from Leipzig, and took it with me. Beside myself there were present Winding, Sgambati, and a German Lisztite, whose name I do not know, but who goes so far in the aping of his idol that he even wears the gown of an abbé; add to these some young ladies of the kind that would like to eat Liszt, skin, hair, and all, their adulation is simply comical. . . . Winding and I were very anxious to see if he would really play my concerto at sight. I, for my part, considered it impossible; not so Liszt. 'Will you play?' he asked, and I made haste to reply: 'No, I cannot' (you know I have never practised it.) Then Liszt took the manuscript, went to the piano, and said to the assembled guests, with his characteristic smile, 'Very well, then, I will show you that I also cannot.' With that he began. I admit that he took the first part of the concerto too fast, and the beginning consequently sounded helter-skelter; but later on, when I had a chance to indicate the tempo, he played as only he can play. It is significant that he played the cadenza, the most difficult part, best of all. His demeanour is worth any price to see. Not content with playing, he at the same time converses and makes comments, addressing a bright remark now to one, now to another of the assembled guests, nodding significantly to the right or left, particularly when something pleases him. In the adagio, and still more in the finale, he reached a climax both as to his playing and the praise he had to bestow.
>
> A really divine episode I must not forget. Toward the end of the finale the second theme is, as you may remember, repeated in a mighty fortissimo. In the very last measures, when in the first triplets the first tone is changed in the orchestra from G sharp to G, while the piano part, in a mighty scale passage, rushes wildly through the whole reach of the keyboard, he suddenly stopped, rose up to his full height, left the piano, and with big theatric strides and arms uplifted walked across the large cloister hall, at the same time literally roaring the theme. When he got to the G in question he stretched out his arms imperiously and exclaimed: 'G, G, not G sharp! Splendid! Splendid!'

In the event it was a pianist called Edmund Neupert who gave the first performance of the concerto, although it was perhaps ironic in view of Grieg's nationalist feelings that it was given in Danish Copenhagen. Grieg himself soon acquired a very considerable reputation as a pianist and as a conductor and was much admired in England, France and Germany as well as in his homeland. On one of his trips to London a newspaper diarist noted that audiences for his concerts had started to queue at eleven in the morning. If his standing is not so high today as it was in his lifetime it is because his genius failed to develop in the larger musical forms of concerto, symphony or opera; nevertheless the piano concerto has greater claims to originality than it is usually allowed, as a closer look should reveal.

Piano Concerto in A Minor
Op. 16

Since this concerto has suffered from becoming too well-known, it is worth while to place it in its proper context. It was written just over twenty years after the Schumann concerto and fourteen years before the Tchaikovsky. Looked at in this light one can begin to appreciate its genuine originality. Grieg was only twenty-five when he wrote it, and although he had written a symphony while still a student — recently unearthed and recorded — it is extremely unlikely that he had ever heard any of his music played by an orchestra. The fact that he revised the orchestration a number of times in later years gives proof of his insecurity.

After a preliminary drum-roll the piano has a brief cadenza, a fine rhetorical flourish that establishes the tonality of A minor very positively. The woodwind then announce the first subject material which comes as two contrasting ideas, the first crisp and detached, the second smooth and sustained; the strings shadow both of these tunes, only coming to the fore during the repetition of the second stanza. This whole exposition (only twelve bars in all) is then repeated by the piano with relatively little assistance from the orchestra. Suddenly there is a complete change of mood as the pianist launches into a capricious passage that suggests an elfin dance and it is here that Grieg shows an individual idiom that he certainly did not learn in Leipzig. (Without documentary evidence one cannot be certain but it seems very probable that it was passages such as this and the dance-finale that prompted Ibsen to invite Grieg's collaboration in the dramatised version of 'Peer Gynt'.)

A descending scale in chromatic thirds leads to a duet between oboe and piano which, having reached a momentary climax, dissolves into the lyrical second subject. This is given to the cellos[1] with a soft accompaniment from trombones and horns; each short phrase is approved by the woodwind in a charming way. The pianist takes over the melody with slightly Chopinesque decorations, extending it substantially in a rising sequence which increases in passion and intensity until it explodes into an exciting display of octaves in the right hand which, after a rather trite cadenza, leads into an orchestral tutti in C major. This is derived from the very first notes of the piano part though their effect is naturally very different. The cellos and basses have an important response which is an ingenious development of the first subject that takes just its first five notes as a starting point. A big *crescendo* leads to a trumpet fanfare which is very similar to a famous passage in Tchaikovsky's Fourth Symphony, an allegation easily made but which one hastily withdraws on learn-

[1] Liszt advised Grieg to put it on the trumpet!

ing that the Grieg was written nine years earlier. Even so, such passages offended Debussy in his capacity as music critic. He said that he could not understand 'why it should be broken up by martial trumpet-blasts, usually announcing the beginning of nothing more than a languishing little tune'. Grieg would no doubt have replied that the 'trumpet-blasts' give the movement a heroic stature that it would otherwise lack for it is undoubtedly true that in general the movement is more of a lightweight than its dramatic initial gesture would suggest.

Three quiet pizzicato chords lead us into the development which begins with a lyrical treatment of the first part of Theme I from flute and horn in turn. A melancholy version of the second limb of the theme follows, an exchange which is repeated in a different key. Suddenly the brass arouse us with a powerfully different approach to the same theme which elicits a tremendous arpeggio from the pianist covering almost the whole range of the keyboard. It is now the turn of the second part of the theme to be developed in a series of rising sequences. Trombones and wind interrupt with an angry statement of the first bar of the main theme against hammering triplets from trumpets, horns and timpani. Twice the pianist responds to the challenge with double octaves that are derived from the opening cadenza, but the crisis is soon resolved and in a moment we are at the start of the recapitulation, easily recognisable when the soloist takes up the opening theme exactly as before. The development section is therefore quite unusually short, a mere twenty-eight bars, or, if we include the orchestral tutti as well, at most forty-four.

A strict recapitulation follows, only differing by the necessary modulations that bring the second subject into the 'proper' key of A major. A five-bar outburst from the full orchestra heralds the arrival of the cadenza, musically the finest part of the movement. It begins in a freely improvisatory style much indebted to Liszt both in style and harmony; there is then a splendid development of the first theme with wide-spaced arpeggios in the left hand. It reaches a climax with a descending cascade of double octaves followed by a massive treatment of the same theme, its progress interrupted by thunderous rumbles in the bass. A greatly augmented version of the second part of the theme then appears, surrounded by a positive torrent of notes. Gradually the storm subsides and a series of trills finally fades into near silence as the orchestra enter with a most expressive version of the second part of the theme. A short coda rounds off the movement beginning with a seemingly new tune on oboe and bassoon in unison. It is enough to suggest an inversion of the initial cadenza to the pianist who, having made the point quite wittily, brings the movement to a resounding conclusion with a majestic restatement of the opening bars, giving them a finality that would have been quite out of place at the start of the work.

The slow movement is notable for the beauty of the orchestral theme with which it begins. The first phrase, four bars in length, is in D flat major. By a simple process Grieg then repeats it, starting on the second degree of the scale; this effectively transposes it into E flat minor, giving it a markedly more poignant quality. A series of shorter phrases follows, their chromatic harmonies very similar to César Franck in style. Yet all the large-scale works of Franck, the symphony, the quartet, the violin sonata and so on come from a later period and apart from Wagner Grieg should be given credit for being one of the very first composers to use harmony of quite such chromatic richness. Certainly he must have had a considerable influence on Delius.

The entry of the solo piano brings an elaborately decorated alternation of tonic and dominant, naive in harmony but sophisticated in ornamentation. Strong bell-like accents are the most original feature. The whole nine-bar sequence is duly repeated at a higher pitch before flute and clarinet start to remind us of the opening theme. This time the piano adds swathes of colour to the orchestral texture and a substantial *crescendo* leads to a majestic statement of the original theme by the pianist with a skilfully contrived cello part following in its wake a bar later. The second portion of the theme is continued in the orchestra with nicely harmonised comments from the soloist. A brief coda with bird-song trills from the piano brings this essentially lyrical movement to an end.

Without any interruption Grieg begins his finale with a staccato rhythm on clarinets and bassoons that recalls a similar moment in Beethoven's Fourth Concerto, albeit with a very different outcome. An arpeggio shoots rocket-like across the keyboard and sizzles down to earth in a brilliant descent. A strongly rhythmic accompaniment begins in the left hand telling a Norwegian audience that Grieg is going to incorporate a favourite national dance, the *halling*, into the concerto. The pianist develops the theme at some length before the orchestra is permitted to express its rather noisy appreciation.

A new episode in the solo part seems to suggest the entry of a particularly nimble dancer. It is a passage that demands considerable dexterity from the pianist who must feel a certain relief when it gives way to a more sustained tune in crotchets. One of the characteristics of the more energetic type of folk-dance is for individual dancers to take turns in showing off fancy steps of their own devising, the men in particular trying to excel each other in athleticism. This movement suggests such a dance quite vividly since the episodes, short in themselves, follow one another in rapid succession. Next to appear is a very virile theme with a military rhythm; it is announced by three C major chords but quickly subsides as the orchestra takes over the thematic interest. The rhythmic pattern here (three repeated crotchets followed by four semiquavers) is taken directly from the first piano solo though the effect is rather different. Accompanied by fluent arpeggios from the pianist the orchestra builds up a stirring sequence which culminates in a powerful tutti. It is interrupted abruptly by the pianist who is allowed a brief cadenza before restarting the *halling* even more energetically than before. At last the dance ends in a general collapse.

An almost imperceptible shift to F major enables Grieg to change the mood entirely as a solo flute introduces a pastoral melody whose tranquil beauty suggests a lakeside scene at dawn. The shimmering string accompaniment is played *sul ponticello* (the bow very close to the 'bridge') an effect which conveys not just brightness but the icy clarity of sunlight reflected off a glacier. The soloist duly takes up the same theme in an expressive improvisation. A solo cello sustains the bass notes, an ingenious device to aid the relatively weak effect of the sustaining pedal on the pianos of the 1860s.[2] This central section occupies quite a substantial portion of the movement and the theme is destined to reappear in much more heroic guise at the end of the movement.

First, though, we must have a return to the dance. More tactfully than we might expect the woodwind quietly awaken us from our reverie with the tap-tap rhythm. The piano responds and a classic recapitulation follows for some eighty-two bars. At this point the *halling* is transformed into something far more serious with sweeping scales in the orchestra and Lisztian rhetoric from the pianist. An exciting orchestral crescendo leads to a bravura display of double octaves which one can imagine Liszt sight-reading with particular relish. There is a brief silence and then, with a change from 2/4 to 3/4, the final section begins. The tempo is quicker — *quasi presto* — and the dance is changed to another national favourite, the *springdans*. There are definite reminiscences of Schumann here in the sudden shifts of accentuation and in the rapid modulations. As the pianist executes a swift downward scale covering the whole span of the keyboard, trumpets give a ceremonial welcome to the splendid coda, a triumphal version of the central tune, now transformed from the dawn-song of a lark to a patriotic hymn. It was in this section that Liszt hailed the G natural with such enthusiasm; those of us who regard the concerto as altogether too predictable would do well to remember how original it seemed to Grieg's contemporaries, even to one so daringly innovative as Liszt himself.

---

[2]It was reliably reported that Schumann would improvise for an hour at a time without ever changing the pedal.

HAYDN
1732–1809

Although the names of Haydn and Mozart are often loosely coupled together
they could scarcely have led more different lives. Mozart through force of
circumstance was a prodigious traveller from early childhood onwards;
Haydn was most fortunate in his patrons and hardly travelled at all until the
latter part of his life when he enjoyed two hugely successful trips to London.
Mozart died in his mid-thirties, poverty-stricken; Haydn lived to be seventy-
seven and was well provided for for almost the whole of his adult life. Mozart
was a public performer accustomed to the acclaim of audiences in the concert-
hall or the opera-house even though applause did not necessarily bring
adequate financial reward; Haydn mostly performed to small select groups
invited to a princely palace and was quite overwhelmed by the experience of
public concerts in London. But perhaps the most significant difference came
about through Haydn's long attachment as resident musician at the court of
the Esterházy family, for there he had a permanent orchestra at his disposal
with which he could experiment as he liked in matters of orchestration.

Although Haydn had a sound musical education at a choir school he had
none of Mozart's prodigious gifts as a child. Indeed his first adult years were
something of a struggle during which he scraped a precarious living teaching
and playing in small orchestras at aristocratic parties. Not until he was
twenty-six did he find regular employment with a Viennese nobleman,
Count Morzin. He had already developed great fluency as a composer and
had a number of works to his credit including sonatas, concertos, quartets,
church music and even his first essay at opera. The appointment to Count
Morzin's household would not have come unless Haydn had already given
proof of his abilities; but within two years the Count had to cut down his
establishment for financial reasons and Haydn found himself jobless. It was to
prove a most fortunate dismissal for the following year he was engaged by
one of the wealthiest Princes in Europe, Paul Anton Esterházy. He remained
in the service of the family for nearly thirty years during which time he was
required not only to compose but to act as musical director in the Prince's

private chapels and opera theatre. Winters were spent at Eisenstadt, some thirty miles from Vienna, summers at Esterháza in Hungary where Paul Anton's successor, Prince Nicolaus, built a magnificent palace that was rivalled only by Versailles. It was in such protected surroundings that Haydn was able to work without either financial worries or the distractions of a public life. Even so, his works gained recognition in other countries and in 1784 a set of six symphonies was commissioned by a young French aristocrat for performance by the finest Parisian orchestra, *Le Concert de la Loge olympique.* By then Haydn had become one of the most celebrated composers in Europe and his music was frequently performed in Germany and France, though it should be remembered that such performances gathered no royalties. The Paris commission brought an offer of twenty-five *Louis-d'or* for each symphony, a sum which seemed 'un prix colossal' to Haydn who up to then had received no specific payment for the numerous symphonies he had written as a matter of course for his royal patron. However, the most significant commission was to come after the death of Prince Nicolaus in 1790. The new Prince, another Anton, cared little for music and disbanded his orchestra; to Haydn he gave not only his freedom but a generous pension. The gratified composer left Esterháza for Vienna with the prospect of a new, more independent life-style opening before him. News of his availability brought a number of invitations of which the most important was the most informal. One morning, without even a preliminary request for an audience, a German violinist who had established himself as a successful impresario in London arrived at Haydn's apartments. 'I am Salomon of London,' he said; 'I have come to fetch you to England'. With this historic summons came a contract for £1,200 for six symphonies, an opera and twenty lesser compositions. By the standards of the day it was an enormous sum and Haydn willingly accepted.

He bade a tearful farewell to Mozart, with whom he had struck up a warm and admiring friendship. Mozart had of course spent nearly a year in London as a child and asked Haydn how he would manage when he spoke not a word of English. 'My language is understood all over the world' replied the older man. It was a remark justified by events for he was to score a huge success with London audiences. He and Salomon arrived there on 2 January, 1791. Six days later Haydn was writing to a woman friend in Vienna:

> My recent arrival in London caused a great sensation and I was giving newspaper interviews for three days running. Everyone wants to know me. I've dined out six times already, and if I wanted, I could be entertained every day. But I must consider my health first, and also my work. Everything is terribly expensive here. I wish I could fly for a time to Vienna to have more quiet in which to work, for the noise from the streets outside is intolerable.

The first concert of the series Salomon had planned was given early in March; it caused a sensation, earning ecstatic reviews in the newspapers.

Haydn thrived on the unaccustomed adulation he received on every side and was easily persuaded to stay for a second season. In July, 1791, he was given an honorary Doctorate at Oxford; meanwhile he had cultivated wealthy friends with country estates where he could escape from the 'intolerable noise' of the streets and compose in peace. The demand for his music was such that his pen was kept busy providing new works. An added zest to his visit came when he fell in love with a widow, Rebecca Schroeter, whom he would happily have married had he not left a Frau Haydn in Vienna. (His marriage was one of the less successful aspects of his life.) At the end of his two-year stay he had earned as much as would have taken him twelve years in the service of the Esterházys. After returning to Vienna in 1792 he paid a second and equally successful visit to England in 1794. The following year found him back in Austria once again attached to the Esterházy household. (He was persuaded to do so by a second Prince Nicolaus.) His duties were not arduous and he turned his attention increasingly to religious music, producing some magnificent settings of the Mass as well as *The Creation* and *The Seasons*. His last works were for string quartet, although in the final six years of his life his faculties diminished and further composition was beyond him. All the same, to have continued composing with ever increasing brilliance until he was nearly seventy was remarkable enough and it is clear that the English visits gave him a stimulus that inspired him to heights that he might not otherwise have attained.

Sinfonia Concertante in B flat
for oboe, bassoon, violin and cello
(1792)

As a musical form the *Sinfonia Concertante* was a direct descendant of the *Concerto Grosso* of the Baroque period, a work in which a small group of players was given a more virtuoso role than that of the supporting orchestra. Audiences enjoyed the display of any especial talents in the orchestra and such works were very popular. Noting the enormous success of Salomon's Haydn concerts, a rival organisation, 'The Professional Concerts', offered a contract to one of Haydn's pupils, Ignaz Pleyel,[1] then resident in Strasbourg. London audiences were perpetually hungry for novelty and it was hoped that the arrival of a newcomer on the scene would do something to displace Haydn in their affection. Haydn swiftly defused any potential sparks by publicly embracing Pleyel and applauding his compositions warmly; but, since Pleyel had scored his greatest successes with his *Sinfonie Concertanti*, Salomon no doubt suggested to Haydn that he would best dispose of the opposition by writing a comparable work. The autograph manuscript shows that it was composed in considerable haste although in no way to its detriment.

The blend of instruments is unusual. The most obvious choice would be to place a string quartet or wind quartet in opposition to the orchestra but Haydn of all people had a dislike of the obvious. (The symphonies are full of experimental ideas as, for instance, the point in the finale of No. 60 where the violins have to re-tune their lowest string before proceeding.) The instruments he chose as soloists offer several options, whether as a pair of woodwind and a pair of strings, as an oboe and a cello matched against a violin and a bassoon, or simply as a quartet with two unmatched treble and bass pairs.

The opening exposition is forty-eight bars long but the solo quartet are by no means idle. Salomon, as leader, would have played the main orchestral part as well as his solo contributions, but there are moments when all four soloists are given passages that stand out from the main tutti. The work is not a concerto but a symphony with concerto elements and Haydn is careful to establish this convention quite early.

The first bars are unusually lyrical; he usually has a preference for something more positive but here we find a phrase which might suitably introduce an operatic aria. However it is instantly followed by a passage for full orchestra (including all four soloists) to which horns, trumpets and

---

[1] In all probability Pleyel was responsible for the theme on which Brahms based the so-called Brahms-'Haydn' Variations.

timpani give a splendid bounce. A busy tutti comes to a close on the dominant (F major) in bar 18. The implied modulation is contradicted at once by a gentle phrase which coincidentally would make a perfect response to the very opening theme. It is treated as an elegant conversation-piece by the solo quartet with the added participation of the first violins. Sixteen bars later the full orchestra rejoins the fray with a back reference to the 'bouncy' theme into which the quartet interjects a cheeky comment. A very positive cadence in B flat signals the end of the orchestral exposition.

The soloists now begin an elaborate discussion of the opening material with the violin and cello parts in particular showing a greater element of virtuosity. An expressive little phrase in F minor provides a momentarily touching contrast, but it should be taken no more seriously than a heroine's 'attack of the vapours' and Haydn wittily switches back to bustling frivolity. (The violinist's ascent to a high B flat tells us what an exceptional violinist Salomon must have been.) A cadenza-like passage in which all four soloists show their dexterity in playing scales ends with the conventional trill that warns the orchestra to stand by for action. A substantial 'symphonic' tutti follows, ending, or so it seems, with the same cadence in the dominant. Typically, Haydn foils expectation with a sudden shift into the totally unheralded key of D flat major. A wonderful development of the opening theme now materialises in which Haydn draws upon his substantial operatic experience. Apart from the advantage of sheer range that instruments have over voices, it is laid out exactly as an operatic quartet might be. It is the first moment to touch our hearts rather than merely to entertain us. And then, just as we are thinking 'how beautiful', the bassoon reverts to comedy with a grotesque skipping phrase which dispels all pathos. A progression of trills from the two wind players leads us towards an emphatic cadence in quite the 'wrong' key — the dominant of G minor, whose F sharps totally contradict the proper tonality of B flat to which we should have been heading by rights. The Gordian knot is severed by the violinist who with a brief (unwritten) cadenza steers us back into home waters.

It is a strange way to approach a recapitulation but that is what we now find, bars 163–80 being exactly comparable to the first eighteen bars. At such moments we should be on our guard since Haydn regards predictability as synonymous with laziness. He by-passes fifty-one bars and picks up the thread at the point where previously he had given us a moment or two of pathos in F minor. It is now in B flat minor but the substance is the same; indeed it continues on orthodox lines towards the traditional pause that precedes the cadenza in a solo concerto. Such cadenzas were normally improvised by the performer in Haydn's day but that would clearly be impractical with four soloists. The easy solution would have been to omit the cadenza entirely, nor would he have been censured for so doing. Instead he gives us a brilliantly contrived cadenza for all four players, thirty-four bars of music that marries expressive beauty to virtuosity while humour dances attendance on them both.[2] Even the final trill has an element of surprise, for the bassoon cannot resist the temptation to throw in an extra arpeggio just as we think that the resolution is upon us. The closing tutti is brief and to the point, reasserting the tonality of B flat from which the solo quartet has strayed delightfully during the cadenza.

The slow movement is in Haydn's most elegant style, the essentially simple theme being lavishly decorated. Perhaps even more than the first movement it shows us what outstanding players Haydn had at his disposal. One should remember that oboes and bassoons in his day were far less perfect mechanically than modern instruments yet in the first eight bars we find that a top B flat is expected from the bassoon and a top D (twice) from the oboe-player. Such notes are extreme for the instruments and even today's players would regard them as a challenge. The cello part ascends to the high E an octave and a bit above 'middle' C while also containing some very rapid accompanying figures which demand great fluency.

The movement begins with a four-bar phrase which is treated as a duet, first for violin and bassoon and then for oboe and cello. Violin and cello are then paired together and after a short transitional passage mainly for violin they present us with a second subject in the dominant, the violin now accompanying the cello. This tune has a subsidiary extension whose brief phrases evoke elaborate comments from violin or bassoon. The appearance of the opening theme on the full orchestra for the first time serves as a central landmark after which the preceding material is presented anew with the individual roles exhanged. Towards the end of the movement we are kept in suspense for a long silence before a tiny coda in which the horns have a dangerously high entry. (Haydn's horn writing is often extremely demanding; even in a symphony as early as No. 5, written in the late 1750s, he produced a horn-part which is one of the most challenging in the whole symphonic repertoire — and this for valve-less 'natural' horns which were notoriously tricky to play.)

The finale begins with a spirited tune that shows the composer in his most rustic mood; starting with everyone in unison, it ends in rumty-tumty fashion with a deliberately silly cadence. With mock solemnity the violin declaims a vocal-type recitative that sounds like a stern admonishment to abandon such frivolity. After a slightly stunned silence, the orchestra begins again as before only to be checked in mid-flight by further admonitions from the solo violin. In case anyone should be so obtuse as to take this seriously, Haydn then gives the violin a delightfully mischievous phrase that almost seems to be giggling as it goes on its way. This new tune, a derivative of the opening theme, is

[2]Had Mozart perhaps shown him the miraculous cadenza for soprano and wind instruments in the '*Et incarnatus est*' from his C minor Mass? It might have served as a model.

taken up with enthusiasm by the full orchestra. From this point on Haydn exploits the contrast between the solo quartet and the full orchestra to great comic effect. Soon the violinist embarks on a tricky solo that is the musical equivalent of a tongue-twister, a solo which the bassoonist courageously tries to match. Each member of the quartet is given a chance to display his technical dexterity, the most fearsome challenge being given to the cellist. The tutti which follows this is built around a descending chain of notes around whose measured steps fragments of the opening theme dart and play. A brief excursion into minor keys leads into a huffing and puffing tutti which clearly fails to blow the soloist's house down since the cello sets them dancing again at once. The music continues happily until suddenly halted at a portentous pause. Again the violinist assumes the mantle of an oratorio singer and again the attempt to be serious dissolves in laughter. Soon the quartet begins an absurd slow-motion trill, all four of them in unison; the rest of the players cannot refrain from joining in. It is a signal for a last display of high-spirited virtuosity from the quartet, violin and cello in turn climbing to such dizzy heights that Haydn gives them silent beats to enable them to find the right place on the finger-board. The final tutti is notable for some two-octave skips in the violin parts that even *look* comically awkward to play as well as sounding hilarious. The whole movement is a remarkable display of musical wit; it is immense fun to play as well as to listen to.

> A new concertante from HAYDN combined with all the excellencies of music; it was profound, airy, affecting, and original, and the performance was in unison with the merit of the composition. SALOMON particularly exerted himself on this occasion, in doing justice to the music of his friend HAYDN. (*Morning Herald*, 12 March 1792)

> A new Concertante, for a Violin, Violoncello, Oboe, and Bassoon was performed for the first time with admirable effect. The solo parts were finally contrasted with the 'full tide of harmony' of the other instruments, and they were very ably sustained by the respective performers. (*Morning Chronicle*, 12 March 1792)

Symphony No. 94 in G
(The 'Surprise')

Simple as a nursery-rhyme, the slow movement of this symphony has rebounded against its creator by becoming too well-known. Thousands of children must have had it thrust upon them as a first introduction to so-called 'classical' music, probably coupled with the apocryphal legend that the loud bang that interrupts its tiptoe progress was put in by Haydn to wake up any old ladies in the audience who might have dropped off to sleep. He himself denied this, saying that he merely wanted to surprise his audience with something new. The surprise bang is a very small part of a large symphony, though a part that has caught the popular fancy ever since. Needless to say it isn't a surprise any more and I can't help wishing that Haydn had left a note in the score giving the conductor leave to insert something different at each performance. A ting on a triangle would make a nice change and would cause people to sit up more effectively now that they know what to expect. The trouble about such a noticeable feature is that it attracts a disproportionate amount of comment. Like a pretty daughter in a family of plain boys the slow movement has hogged all the attention; for all too many of us the rest of the symphony is relatively unknown.

Haydn wrote this work in rural Hertfordshire where, on his first triumphant visit to England, he stayed for a couple of months with the family of a banker. 'I work hard', he wrote to a friend in Austria, 'and when in the early mornings I walk in the woods alone, with my English grammar in my hand, I think of my Creator, my family, and all the friends I have left behind.' This letter itself contains a surprise, for just as you think he's going to say how homesick and miserable he is, he says: 'How sweet this bit of liberty really is! I had a kind Prince, but sometimes I was forced to be dependant on base souls. I often sighed for release, and now I have it in some measure.'

Although he was caught up in a whirl of social life, Haydn could not forget his obligations as a composer, and every now and then he would withdraw from the scene for a few weeks to dash off another symphony. Numbers 93 and 94 were written in the early spring of 1792 and were received with the habitual ovation which Haydn was to know everywhere he went in England. The London Symphonies give us an interesting insight into the standards of orchestral playing at the time; Haydn makes considerable demands on the players. He was an eminently practical musician, and would never have doubled up flutes, oboes and bassoons on the very first page if he hadn't been confident they would play well in tune.

The slow introduction we find here was his normal way of beginning a symphony, a hangover from the earlier suite from which the form had developed. The first phrase from the woodwind is like a caress to which the strings give a nodding approval. A second and sweeter caress follows which also brings a smile from the strings. The interest now passes to the cellos who begin a somewhat tortuous ascent, opening doors to several different tonalities on the way but never staying for long enough to settle until they regain the dominant of G. An isolated phrase from the first violins leaves us in mid-air waiting for the expected resolution into G major. It is at such moments that Haydn proves himself a true master of surprises far more subtle than the crash in the slow movement. The first subject of the ensuing

Vivace assai ('rather lively') appears with great delicacy in the 'wrong' key of A minor before having second thoughts and reverting to the proper tonality of G. The safe arrival at this desirable goal is greeted with enthusiasm by the full orchestra whose bouncing 6/8 rhythm and lusty brass give a hunting flavour to the music. After seventeen exuberant bars the violins are suddenly left on their own save for some fragile support from the other strings. They seem unnerved by the situation and play the same bar three times before breaking off, as if hoping someone will come to their aid. The lack of offers causes them to go back to square one and start again with exactly the same routine as before. Once more the return to G major is hailed as a cause for rejoicing, but this time the tutti effects a proper modulation to the dominant, D major.

According to convention the repeated As we find at this point should lead into the second subject which without a shadow of doubt should be in D major. Haydn scorns convention and produces three 'surprises' in the space of two bars. First of these is the non-appearance of the second subject, second the substitution of D *minor* for D major, third a rapid shift to the alien key of F major — and all with the first subject cheekily usurping the rightful position of the second. Not surprisingly this causes some consternation and for a while there is an impression of chaos in the orchestra as the violins rush around in D minor or the lower strings and woodwind try to force their way back to a respectable dominant (A) from which there is a chance that sanity — in the shape of D major — will return. It does, although the displaced accents seem to indicate a rather bumpy landing. The violins take up their position on the dominant (A), seemingly ready to make amends for their earlier indiscretion; surely this time the second subject will appear . . . But no. Like a kitten trying to catch its own tail, they twirl round and round with a phrase whose deliberate banality is underlined by the 'vamped' accompaniment which continues patiently underneath. (It is an early example of the old music-hall accompanist's 'till ready' fill-in). At last, twenty-six bars late, the second subject does appear, all neat and tidy and anchored firmly to a sustained D in the bass. It skips happily along with the insouciance of a child until a bit of an argument breaks out in the woodwind. All is well, though, as the full orchestra heads for a glorious cadence in D major that will bring the exposition to a proper and satisfying conclusion. But does it? Only by showing what convention would dictate can I reveal how unconventional Haydn is. This is what we might rightfully expect, the first three bars being Haydn's.

All very fine but all very obvious. This is what he actually does — and how well deserved the nickname 'Surprise' seems when we encounter such diversions:

Admittedly landing up on these repeated B naturals does facilitate the conventional repeat of the exposition since that is the note the *Vivace* started on; but the total avoidance of a proper cadence at this point leaves the violins in mid-air. Where should they go from here?

Haydn's solution brings another extraordinary surprise, a smooth modulation into C major, a key which nobody would ever predict in such a context. As though to confirm that he really means it, he spells out the scale of C in a unison phrase for wind and strings; but then doubts creep in and in a marvellously imaginative passage the strings drift in and out of F minor before settling back into C. A sudden blast from brass and wind produces a dramatic shift to D minor and for some thirty bars there is a veritable storm in which modulations from key to key are too frequent to be listed. Heavy accents mark the majority of the main beats and the mischievous geniality of the previous music seems to be forgotten.

The sudden emergence of quiet repeated Bs on the violins gives us some reassurance that a way back may be found. They sound like raindrops and when the first subject makes its welcome return the addition of a flute an octave above is like a pale ray of sunlight. It is the beginning of a recapitulation in which, though the material is familiar, there are still surprises for the attentive listener. For instance Haydn's little joke of leaving the violins on their own and then breaking off in bewilderment is omitted completely. There is also a delightful new event when four detached chords seem to be bringing the movement to a conclusion. Low horns give vent to a tuba–like note that sends the violins loping upwards to start yet another game with the first subject, a game that the woodwind then enjoy on their own. The second subject duly makes a graceful last appearance before a rousing tutti puts an end to a remarkable movement.

The famous slow movement is a set of variations on a C major theme. It is ironic that the sudden *ff* chord from which the symphony gets its name was an afterthought of which there is no sign in the original autograph. Haydn was particularly concerned that the second-beat crotchets in bars 2, 4 and 6 should be fully sustained in a basically staccato context; he therefore marked *ten.* for *tenuto* (held) on each one. The theme itself is simple enough to need no description except to underline that it only contains one modulation — and that to the adjacent dominant (G).

Variation I gives the theme unaltered to the second violins, adding a neat and elegant decoration in the first violins which are joined by a flute in the second phrase.

Variation II brings a fundamental change of character, a shift to C minor and a much stronger version of the theme. The initial severity is quickly mollified by an apparent switch to A flat major in the strings, a deception which is soon explained as it turns out to be an intermediate step on the way to E flat major. This fails to bring the peace one might expect and the second half of the variation is extremely dramatic. References to the theme are confined to its first five notes while agitated figures in the violins soon spread to all the strings as brass and timpani add their considerable force to the score. A sweeping upward scale in full strings and woodwind suddenly leaves the first violins out on their own. As if not quite certain how to extricate themselves from the situation, they have a rather tentative little phrase which at least enables them to reach Variation III.

This features a delightfully stuttering oboe who gains confidence when he is joined by a flute. Together they provide an enchanting descant to the theme.

Variation IV covers the theme with glory, trumpets, horns and timpani bestowing full military honours on it while the violins stand in for the cavalry. With the audience reeling from the sudden assault, Haydn plays one of his most characteristic jokes — a change of mood so sudden that one suspects the players may have turned two pages by mistake. Out of the hurly-burly emerge the strings *pianissimo e dolce* with a smoothly gliding version of the theme that changes its character completely. As though resentful of this seductively feminine intrusion, the gentlemen of the military summon their forces to bring the variation to a rousing conclusion — or such is their intention. Heading for a final cadence they are brought to a sharp halt by a diversionary chord that holds us all in suspense. Tentatively the strings suggest a way out and then relax onto a series of cushion-like harmonies of a positively voluptuous kind while oboe and bassoon say a fond farewell to the theme. The movement ends like the Cheshire cat, so that all that is left is the smile on Haydn's face.

The term *Menuet* which Haydn applies to the third movement is a meaningless gesture towards convention since the indication of the tempo, *Allegro molto*, clearly precludes any possibility of courtly dancing. In fact he is preparing the way for the Beethoven-type Scherzo not only in the speed of the music but also in its humour. The first eight bars are rustic in the extreme with their rum-ti-ti accompaniment and very basic harmonies. Beware, though, for another surprise is imminent; instead of matching eight bars with another phrase of comparable length Haydn extends the second stanza to ten bars. The repetition of these first eighteen bars gives us an opportunity to enjoy its lack of symmetry. As if to compensate for those extra two bars he then gives us a three-bar phrase followed by a six-bar one, a defiance of the laws of proportion which causes quite an upset. Accompanied by strident chords on the woodwind, the violins hop through a swift sequence of keys, G minor, E flat major, C minor, and back to the dominant of G, all in the space of eight bars. The music breaks off, uncertain of where to go. Flutes and oboes have a flick of a phrase that seems to ask 'Up here?' Bassoons and a solo cello reply 'Or down here?' Neither is right, as the orchestra confirms by returning full of confidence to the opening theme, confidence that is misplaced since in the eighth bar the music grinds to a halt. Somewhat chastened, violins and wind make a couple of abortive attempts to get started again. Help is forthcoming from flute, cellos and basses and the main part of the 'menuet' is concluded with the aid of the brass and timpani.

The central Trio features bassoon and violins in unison, an unusual match to say the least, so much so that in the second part the bassoon seems to miss his cue and the violins have to circle round D several times waiting for him to catch up. The normal repetitions of the 'menuet' are duly observed in a movement that is too easily taken for granted.

'The Finale is one of the most sophisticated examples of a sonata rondo that Haydn (or anyone else) ever composed.' I quote the opinion of H.C. Robbins Landon, the great expert on Haydn's music, who goes on to describe it as 'a phenomenal movement'. The term 'sonata rondo' should perhaps be explained. Rondo form involves a recurring theme with intervening episodes, usually described in the textbooks as ABACADA. (B, C and D will most probably be in related but contrasting keys while A always represents a return 'home' to the original or 'tonic' key.) A 'sonata rondo' combines elements of sonata and rondo forms; it should have three sections, (corresponding to the exposition, development and recapitulation of a sonata-form movement) as well as two episodes of which the first will probably reappear in the dominant key while the second consists of a further development. We should realise that such forms are not rigid and may be manipulated in a number of ways by composers of genius.

The tempo of the finale is very brisk, *Allegro molto*, and the first theme slips by so quickly that it is just as well that Haydn instantly repeats it with the addition of a flute to give extra brightness to the subdued violins. The tune has an extensive second limb with a nice 'double take' in the middle. In the thirty-eighth bar we find the first tutti, notable for the fiery runs in the violin parts (here in unison for maximum brilliance). At one point there is an oblique reference to the first subject, now in the dominant (D), but for the most part the intention is to leave us breathless. A sudden break and a silent bar seem to confirm that the violins have indeed run out of steam. A quiet pizzicato bass and a dancing rhythm in the second violins announce the arrival of the second subject, graciousness personified. As with the first subject we are given two opportunities to hear it before another exhibition of virtuosity by the violins brings the exposition to a brilliant close.

The emphatic D major chords which end the exposition are quietly contradicted by the three C naturals which follow. In a trice we are whipped back to the first subject, a move calculated to fool the more knowledgeable listener into thinking that Haydn has observed the convention of repeating the exposition. We are soon shown that the assumption is wrong when he takes a drastic short cut. The original first subject material occupied thirty-seven bars before the first tumultuous tutti. At this later point we are given a mere eight bars to assimilate what has happened before the tumult begins again. After twenty-nine extremely energetic bars the music breaks off, makes several comic false starts, and then gets back on the rails again with a return to the main theme. After another eight-bar spell the entry of brass, timpani and full woodwind signals a shift to G minor, an event which leads to an almost frenzied series of modulations into a number of totally alien keys. After a searing climax everybody drops out except for the first violins who, finding themselves thus exposed, scuttle around for a little before finding safety in a reprise of the initial rondo theme, here given new colour by the participation of flute and bassoon two octaves apart. Once again Haydn takes an ingenious short cut by omitting twenty bars from his original plan, but the second subject duly makes its gracious entrance, complete with the preliminary silent bar. However, its proper termination is rudely interrupted by trumpets, horns and timpani.

A new treatment of the rondo theme now appears, woodwind thirds over a soft timpani roll with strumming pizzicato violins adding a comic effect. Suddenly the timpani roll grows louder, bringing a startled reaction from the full orchestra who plunge into E flat major without a hint of warning. After a noisy few bars the first violins extricate themselves neatly from an awkward situation and lead a joyous return to G major. This solution is received with jubilation by all and sundry, especially the timpanist who looses off a cannonade in celebration. And so this remarkably inventive movement finishes; 'Laus Deo' says Haydn at the end of the score, 'Praise to God' being a more pious expression of gratitude for reaching the end than 'Thank God'.

The effect on the audience of the day was stupendous and Haydn related how the cry of 'Encore' came from every throat. How disappointed he would have been to feel that the symphony would become so famous for the wrong reason — a practical joke in one bar of the slow movement, and an afterthought at that.

Symphony No. 98 in B Flat Major

There are many unusual features about this symphony, the first of which is the key of the Introduction — B flat minor. For technical reasons to do with intonation it is probably the least used key in music and without extensive research I can think of only one symphony in the entire repertoire that is actually *in* B flat minor and that is Walton's First. Since tonality was so important an aspect of all musical forms in the eighteenth century, Haydn must have realised that to begin a work in this manner would be appreciated as unusual to say the least. Furthermore the Introduction is exceptionally powerful and severe in character with all the strings declaiming the main theme in unison, each minim being marked with a heavy accent.

Notice the abrupt cut-off in the fourth bar and the dramatic pause that follows. The phrase is then repeated in a modified form, *piano*. After a second pause we find another modification of the opening phrase, this time with the original fierce dynamics intensified by an angry trill. Two brief chordal passages in dotted rhythm bring this impressive introduction to a close. It seems to be designed to prepare us for matters of grave import; how typical of Haydn it is when we discover that it is an elaborate hoax, for the *Allegro* that follows is delightfully entertaining. Despite its totally different mood Haydn evolves it from the introduction with great skill, as a comparison with the previous example will show at a glance.

The change to B flat major contributes greatly to the transformation, but so do the slurs in the third bar, so different from the stern crotchets in the Introduction.

Towards the end of his life Haydn had become increasingly concerned with unifying his larger orchestral works. Slow introductions were a relic from the days of the French 'Ouverture', the opening movement of the orchestral suites from which the symphony as a major form was partly derived. (The Italian overture or '*sinfonia*' was normally in three sections, fast-slow-fast.) Although Haydn had a great fondness for slow introductions, he felt instinctively that there was a danger that they might seem irrelevant to what followed; thus it was that in Symphonies 90, 97, 98 and 103 we see a positive effort to establish a recognisable thematic link between the introduction and the main part of the movement.

The first movement of this symphony is conceived in the broadest terms that Haydn could envisage. Once the link shown above has been securely established (with a captivating variant the second time round), the full tutti is used for the first time in a robust confirmation of B flat major. After some considerable activity the music settles onto a sustained C enabling him to modulate convincingly to the anticipated dominant key of F. We are justified in expecting the second subject to appear at this point, but Haydn surprises us by returning once again to his opening theme, extending it in a number of ingenious ways. Not for the first time in his music we hear echoes of Mozartean opera, as for example in the pleading voices of the strings and the peremptory interruptions from wind and brass. A tinge of F minor casts a momentary shadow which is brusquely dispersed by some energetic passages for strings and wind.

The second subject is one of the strangest aspects of the symphony since it sounds more like a transition than a theme. Accompanied by throbbing strings, it consists essentially of four semibreves on a solo oboe (C, C♯, D, B♮). The rest of the orchestra show little sympathy for it and the exposition ends with brilliant triplets cascading through the violin parts. The dominant key, F major, is firmly underlined by the closing chords. It is a point worth making since the first bar of the ensuing development brings a shock.

Contradicting the preceding tonality completely, Haydn re-introduces the first subject in what seems like D major; that it turns out to be the dominant of G minor in no way lessens the surprise. Then, as if feeling that this is no way to carry on, he cranks the music up a semitone and tries the theme out in E flat major in much more positive tones. This is the signal for a quite remarkable demonstration of contrapuntal skill in which the first three notes of the theme are made into the basis of a free fugue whose running counter-subject gradually dominates the scene in a bustling quaver run that keeps the violins fully occupied for thirty-two bars, 256 quavers non-stop! A more sustained section follows as a much-needed contrast, descending expressively at last to the recapitulation. Although this follows a fairly predictable course, the second subject is allowed a little more scope than before while the coda introduces a new treatment of the opening theme with the off-beats pounded out with some gusto.

The second movement, a deeply felt *Adagio*, has in its opening bars a suggestion of 'God Save the King' which may indeed be a subtle compliment to Haydn's hosts. Yet the emotional content corresponds poorly with any such gesture and it seems more likely that the movement is a private lament for Mozart's death, an event which had seemed a grievous loss to Haydn. (The idea was put forward by Donald Tovey.) Certainly there are a number of passages which have a truly Mozartean flavour once the violins introduce the second main subject. The softly repeated woodwind chords which seem to give a blessing to each violin phrase are a device Mozart frequently used in operatic arias, as are the little hesitations which give such poignancy to the melody.

The central part of the movement brings a storm of anguish with the serene opening phrase cruelly distorted in the bass — surely an unlikely treatment to be meted out to the National Anthem? The storm ceases as abruptly as it had begun and the opening phrases return with the addition of an expressive new counterpoint from a solo cello. The initial serenity is hard to regain after the emotional upheaval in the centre of the movement and even when the two oboes sing the opening theme in a mellifluous duet the string parts show a continuing unease. The final harmonisation of the opening phrase is tinged with extraordinary pathos and the movement ends with two *pianissimo* chords. This in itself was extremely unusual for Haydn who, having grown accustomed to the English habit of applauding every movement, would normally end even the most touching *Adagio* with a loud chord regardless of context.

The *Menuet* has a certain roughness about it that is different from mere rustic cheerfulness. First beats are accented with an upward scoop that has a whip-lash effect while the extensive use of brass and timpani removes the music from the ballroom. In other words it is a truly symphonic movement whose impact the occasional gentler phrases do little to soften. The central Trio is more forgiving, with its naive melody scored as a duet for violins and bassoon, yet even this innocent little tune is roughly handled in a weighty unison for full wind and strings. One cannot help feeling that Haydn was beginning to resent the convention that demanded a 'menuet' now that he had attained his freedom from aristocratic patronage.

Although the last movement is marked as a *Presto* 6/8, its unusual stresses can most easily be described as one-two-THREE-four, one-two-THREE-four, the 'THREES' standing out not as accents but as the only sustained notes in this nimble-footed theme. Nimble it may be in the hands of the violins or a solo oboe, but the full orchestra attack it with the exuberance of a party of drunken males at a hunting lodge. Three separate chords on the dominant (F) arrest the dance in mid-flight. There is a momentary silence and then the violins make three tentative attempts to get things started again. It is such a witty idea that it is almost as though Haydn is winking at the audience. 'This is fun' he seems to say, and then lets the flute and violin proceed, light as a ballerina. Her toes are swiftly trodden on by the raucous throng who, judging by the oboes and bassoons, appear to have a collective bout of hiccups.

A second subject appears, trying to inject a vestige of calm; but it is soon whisked away in a rising swirl of triplets. The passage that follows has the sort of enchanting silliness we more readily associate with Rossini. It simply consists of fragments of scales over a galloping accompaniment, now here, now there, like the insistent calls for Figaro in 'The Barber of Seville'. A sudden outburst of 'Tally-ho's' from the full orchestra must have delighted the hunting fraternity in the London audience while the coy response from the violins no doubt gave equal pleasure to their wives. The exposition ends riotously with dominant harmonies slapped on top of a tonic bass — and 'the Devil take your rule-book'.

A silent bar with a pause over it allows any shocked academicians time to recover their equilibrium, only to be bowled over again by Haydn's next move. Having ended the exposition in F major he now begins a delicate oom-pah accompaniment in the strings in the foreign key of A flat major, while Mr Salomon toys playfully with the Rossini-esque theme on his own. He too gives the audience a wink with three confidential asides. They are greeted with a roar of appreciation from unison strings and wind, whereupon the flute joins Salomon in the game. 'Enough fooling' says Haydn, and launches a massive tutti that could be mistaken for Beethoven at his angriest. The music literally grinds to a halt, uneasily swaying between D and C sharp before settling on D for a long pause. 'What shall we do next?' is the question that hangs in the air. Well, in moments of such grave crisis what can a fellow do but go oom-pah oom-pah in another key (E flat) and whistle a careless tune — which is just what the solo violin seems to do. It doesn't seem quite right, though, so it is followed by a slightly embarrassed silence. He tries again but still seems to be getting nowhere. There follows a delightfully witty link which haltingly finds the way back to the original tune, still treated as a violin solo.

This restoration to normality is greeted with loud acclaim by the full orchestra, hiccups and all. Something like an orderly recapitulation follows, but just as we think the movement is about to end, Haydn breaks off in mid-phrase. Picking their way with the care one expects from the barely sober, the violins embark cautiously on the theme, '*Più moderato*'. It is one of Haydn's best jokes for he uses a slower tempo to make the music seem faster.[3] The steadier beat enables the players to pack more notes into the bar, and after a mere seven bars of groping from the violins, the whole orchestra sweeps into a torrent of semiquavers that must have overwhelmed the audience. Yet even now this astonishing composer has not finished with us. Twice more the music breaks off abruptly. Then, as the violins again play the tune at the slower tempo, a glittering figure appears on the piano, played by Dr Haydn

---

[3]Beethoven uses a similar technique to much more serious purpose in the finale of his Op. 110 piano sonata.

himself to the huge delight of those present. Its merry tinkling has a musical-box effect and must have seemed as novel as the famous celesta solo in Tchaikovsky's 'Dance of the Sugar-plum Fairy'. Although Haydn directed his symphonies from the keyboard, it was unheard of for the instrument to be featured in this decorative capacity. The symphony ends with eleven more exuberant bars from the full orchestra, a fitting close to a masterpiece in which humour, intellect and sensibility have combined to give us a musical feast.

Symphony No. 101 in D Major (The 'Clock')

As with the 'Surprise' symphony, the public reputation of this work tends to rest unfairly on the slow movement. (So far as I know nobody has yet tried to call Beethoven's Eighth Symphony the 'Metronome' even though to do so would at least have more substantiation than to call the Fifth Piano Concerto the 'Emperor'.) In Haydn's case the many nicknames attached to his symphonies came about purely because of the sheer number that he wrote. When a composer produces 104 works of the same genre it does create problems of identity and it is only fair to say that such soubriquets as 'Clock', 'Surprise', 'Drum-roll' or 'London' do have some value in helping instant recall. The objection that Haydn himself would surely have raised is that the nickname often draws attention to a relatively unimportant feature.

The introductory *Adagio* is in D minor and would seem to be in a totally different mood from the extremely lively movement that follows. In fact the seeds of both first and second subjects of the main movement are planted here, though the relationships are perhaps easier to comprehend through the eye than the ear. Here is the opening of the *Adagio* and its derivative.

And now bars 5–8 of the second violin part followed by its transformation some 73 bars later:

Thus although it may be said that 'coming events cast their shadow before' the solemnity of the Introduction in no way prepares us for the frivolity that lies ahead. What we should be aware of is the subtle way in which the 'shadows' lengthen, for Haydn begins with a four-bar phrase, follows up with one of eight bars and ends with eleven bars. This lack of symmetry is a notable characteristic of Haydn's style and when the *Presto* begins we should realise that it is far more sophisticated than its dancing rhythm suggests. Two phrases of five bars are followed by one of three, one of eight and one of four — scarcely a predictable pattern. What *is* predictable is that the delicacy of the initial presentation will be offset by a display of full orchestral strength. This comes to a halt on the dominant chord of A, leading the gullible listener to suppose that the second subject is about to appear. Foiling expectation in his usual mischievous way, Haydn proceeds to give us quite an extensive development of the first subject, twisting it this way and that until it comes to an abrupt stop.

Scored with extreme delicacy, the second subject makes its appearance. Frail though it may seem, it is destined to dominate the central section of the movement, something it can do without offence since it represents no real change of character. (This shows no lack of invention on Haydn's part but rather an increasing preoccupation with unity within a movement.) The tail-end of the second subject shows a curious cessation of activity as though the music suddenly loses its way before joyfully resuming its skittish dance. The exposition ends on a much more positive note with a bold descending figure quite different from anything else in the movement. Having reached base by climbing heavy-footed down to a low A, it discharges a couple of rockets into the air which explode into five cadential chords. The sparks sizzle down in two swift but quiet descending scales; to go back to the obligatory repeat all Haydn has to do is to reverse the direction of the scale. (Omission of the repeat means the loss of this delightful pun.)

The development begins with an urgent though whispered discussion of the second subject initiated by the second violins but soon spreading like gossip through all the strings. It is with some shock that we suddenly find ourselves plunged into the very 'wrong' key of C major. As if the world has indeed gone crazy, the first subject promptly appears upside-down. Somehow a way out of this impasse must be found and Haydn begins a tiered sequence of modulations using a pattern derived from the second subject. Higher and higher he climbs until an exciting climax is reached, swaying perilously between F sharp major and B minor. The strings extricate themselves with a bustling unison passage which seems to have found G major after a fashion, but a sudden blast from brass and timpani blows them off course again. Eight terse chords from the full orchestra tell us that B minor it has to be. As though they can scarcely believe it, the strings spell out the notes of a B minor chord in slow motion. It is a moment of extraordinary magic. Violins and flute again begin to discuss the second subject in hushed tones but soon there is a rapid crescendo towards an immense dominant seventh chord through which hurtles a descending scale. There is a silence, enabling us to absorb the fact that this chord is indeed the gateway back to the tonic key of D major. We stand by for the recapitulation.

It is all very well to identify where we are in the overall plan of the movement but Haydn is in far too inventive a mood to be content with a slavish repetition of past events. After seventeen bars — or roughly seventeen seconds! — he changes course with a sudden lurch into D minor which causes considerable agitation. The passage to the second subject is now very much stormier than it was in the first place but it is also very much shorter — fifteen bars from the diversion just described instead of the original forty. Needless to say the orchestration is changed, cellos now taking the place of violins. Haydn seems intoxicated with his material, constantly finding new tricks to play with it. There is one particularly subtle passage near the end where the violins mutter away on their lowest string in a state of indecision before being prodded on their way by four chords on horns and bassoons. As for the ending, it could scarcely be more brilliant, deserving the storms of applause which so delighted the composer but which we are now too good-mannered to bestow.

The second movement has the slow tick-tock accompaniment from which the symphony derives its name. Above it the first violins begin an elegant and courtly dance-tune, extremely aristocratic in its manner after the sparkling ebullience of the first movement. Yet even here Haydn plays a little joke on us for the beautifully poised four-bar phrase is matched by an equally beautifully poised four- . . . sorry, *five*-bar phrase. As the music continues into the next stanza the dynamics are surely humorous in intent, the dainty dotted rhythm of the first two beats followed by a clumsy *forte* on the next two, as though an accomplished girl dancer finds herself lumbered with a fat and arthritic partner. A long sustained note on a solo oboe introduces a new touch of colour as the violins provide an extension of the rhythm of the first bar of the tune, building it up in sequences until, after taking a slight stumble, it returns to the first phrase once more. (Note the addition of a flute and the extra pizzicato chords in the viola part, previously silent.)

After the affected manner of this somewhat foppish theme the last thing we would expect is a stern-faced excursion into G minor, but that is what happens. Complete with horns, trumpets and drums, the orchestra embarks on a dramatic and fully symphonic episode whose only connection with the previous music is the rhythmic pattern ♪♪♪♪ which now, instead of mincing along, acquires a severity more suited to a passage from an oratorio. Indeed, as the music progresses to the intensely dramatic centre it seems like a setting of the *Dies Irae*. There is no logical or programmatic explanation for this truly extraordinary passage, but it gives a potent demonstration of what I call the two-way process of composition. Haydn makes an intellectual decision to go into G minor; once there, the very sound of the music generates an emotional reaction deep in his inner self that demands release in this extravagant display of power.

The return to the 'Clock' theme seems positively irreverent after this storm, the more so with the enchantingly eccentric orchestration Haydn now provides. The tick-tock figure is given to flute and bassoon more than two octaves apart while the effect of a musical toy is enhanced by the combination of flute, oboe, bassoon and first violins. One of the delights of the palace at Eszterháza was a puppet-theatre and this section of the movement might aptly be described as a Puppet Serenade. It comes to a stop exactly as marionettes do; there is a silence. The second violins begin the tick-tock figure on G and B flat. Not another excursion into G minor surely? No; it is even more of a surprise, a shift to E flat major. The violins make a brave attempt to reintroduce the opening theme in this new key but it only leads to trouble. There is a minor crisis which is resolved to everyone's evident relief by a return to G major, the 'proper' key for the theme, now in a much more robust mood. Just as the music seems to be fining down to its original daintiness there is a violent intrusion of heavy brass and pounding timpani that must have had the ladies clutching their escorts in terror. 'Didn't really mean it' says Haydn, and allows the movement to trickle away into silence.

Before we move on to the Menuetto is is worth pointing out that the form of the slow movement is wholly original; it is part Rondo, part Theme and Variations. But the stormy central section gives it a symphonic weight that neither term adequately conveys. Donald Tovey, that eminent musical scholar, describes it as having 'an audacity and genius without parallel in earlier or later music'. Some clock!

The Menuetto scarcely deserves its Italian diminutive since it is the longest of all in the Salomon symphonies. The theme, rather square and solid at first hearing, is artfully constructed. The first beat of bar 1 is a D, bar 2 an E, bar 3 an F sharp, bar 4 a G, bar 5 an A, bar 6 a B — at which point he seems to say 'that's high enough for the moment' and gently slides back to E. The phrase begins anew as if it is going to be a straight repetition; instead it climbs by a quicker and more direct route to a high E, taking an extended and tortuous path down again to the dominant (A). Some rough syncopations confirm this to be a genuine modulation rather than a brief call on a neighbour. This first section of 28 bars is duly repeated according to the convention of the time.

The following passage shows some intriguing contrasts between quiet chromatic phrases in the strings accompanied by soft drum taps and a pastoral response from oboes and horns. This is extended in a richer texture before arriving back to Theme I in a lengthened version.[4]

There follows a Trio of rustic charm in which the strings set up an

[4]The two sections of the Menuetto are respectively 28 and 51 bars in length.

unchanging 'drone' accompaniment above which a solo flute acts the part of a shepherd-boy's pipe. (The resemblance between this and the corresponding part of Beethoven's First Symphony is so striking that it lays the latter open to a charge of petty theft.) The first time the flute tune occurs the accompanying harmonies refuse to budge even when propriety demands that they should; furthermore the 'rustic charm' is rudely dispelled by a rowdy interruption from the full orchestra. The second time round the strings pay more attention to the flute and make the required adjustment to the harmony, except for the cellos and basses, who are too idle to change. In the second portion of the Trio there is a would-be elegant duet for flute and bassoon in which one feels that the peasants are mimicking the affectations of the gentry. Soon the violins have a deliciously comic 'cadenza' in which they get hypnotised by one circling phrase, ultimately repeated seven times. The rest of the orchestra come to the rescue with the greatest confidence only to fizzle out in a bewildered way leaving an embarrassed silence. The rustic 'drone' begins again in a rather tentative manner, the sense of insecurity justified when the horns plonk down a bottom D a bar too early. The whole Trio is a 'village band' joke comparable to the one in Beethoven's 'Pastoral' Symphony written fourteen years later.

The finale, *Vivace* starts with deceptive innocence. For once the tune is a symmetrical one of two four-bar phrases of which we need to remember two fragments marked below.

This artless tune is duly repeated, after which there is a twelve-bar sequel which plays at modulating into new tonalities without really getting anywhere; Theme I then returns to reassure us that nothing alarming has occurred. At such moments we should be on our guard, for with a thump on the timpani and a blare from the brass Haydn straightens our backs up with whipcrack phrases on the violins. Unison strings then begin a crisp development of B, doubling its speed as the trumpets sound a call to arms. A brisk skirmish follows out of which a single oboe emerges unscathed, cheerfully piping its repeated Es. The strings offer a second subject of sorts, so akin to the opening theme that it could be taken for a variation. Some confusion is generated when the first violins lose their place and play across the beat for six bars. It is just after this that we are given the first inkling of the tremendous events that lie ahead. Against a brilliant running counterpoint in violins and flutes the lower strings (reinforced by the brass) turn A from Theme I into massive footsteps which then become a jogtrot of tremendous energy.

After a pause for breath a new episode begins, altogether calmer in mood and based on the twelve-bar sequel already mentioned; here again it seems anxious to modulate but horns and violas supply a firm anchor. Slyly, so that we hardly realise it's happening, the violins introduce a devious version of Theme I, a piece of frivolity which is forcibly corrected by the full orchestra — the first time the theme itself has been played at all loudly. A swifter variation soon follows but this is no time to sit back with a confident feeling that we've heard all this before. For the next fifty bars we are battered by a fierce storm in D minor, as great a shock as the one in the centre of the slow movement. It ends as abruptly as it began.

Haydn now begins a double fugue[5] where the dextrous mastery of contrapuntal skills rivals even that of Mozart. (The young Mendelssohn may well have studied this closely before writing the brilliant fugue in the last movement of his Octet.) The whole fugal episode is played as quietly as possible until a brief crescendo summons the full orchestra, *fortissimo*. The ensuing tutti seems to be heading towards the final cadence but Haydn cannot resist a last leg-pull. Tenderly he says farewell to his theme with a new harmonisation that gives it a suggestion of a tear. Twice he detaches the fragment B from the theme. Will the music end on tiptoe? 'No!' says Haydn, and doubling the speed of B turns it into a dazzling sequence of ascending quavers that lead us towards the triumphant close.

Symphony No. 103 in E Flat (The 'Drum Roll') 1795

The more we know the Haydn symphonies, the more amazed we should be by his unflagging inventiveness. The very first bar of this work — a simple drum roll — was totally original and, so far as I know, has not been duplicated in later times. It is followed by a quiet sustained phrase for bassoons, cellos and basses that within the idiom of the eighteenth century has a mystery comparable to the start of Schubert's 'Unfinished'.

---

[5]Two subjects sounding at once but both being treated fugally.

Soft wind harmonies provide a modulation to the dominant with the last two notes of the above; a phrase of similar length takes us back to the tonic. Violins take over from the lower strings, the theme in the 'firsts' being followed by tentative steps from the 'seconds'. Gradually the texture thickens slightly, ending with a unison descent through the arpeggio of C minor to a low G, nudged disturbingly by the adjacent A flat. There is a pause.

Seemingly indifferent to this mysteriously veiled opening, the strings begin a perky little dance, *Allegro con spirito*. Its two brief phrases are repeated an octave lower before the full orchestra offers a joyous comment which continues in a carefree mood for some time. The oboes' contribution is worth noting as they pick out a phrase on their own, provoking a wriggle of delight from the strings. A loud drum-roll and a sustained brass chord serve as a useful landmark to help us identify a significant moment we could easily miss. Without drawing attention to it in any way, Haydn gives this phrase to his violins:

A comparison with the opening theme (see above) shows how close the relationship is, yet Haydn, having made the point to his own satisfaction, passes on happily to the second subject. The tune is folk-like in character and has the most unsophisticated of accompaniments. The end of the exposition has an unmistakable air of finality.

The development begins with a tightly woven web of counterpoint based on fragments of the '*con spirito*' theme. This continues with growing energy until it is brought to a sudden halt on the dominant of C minor (G). Cellos and violas begin an obvious reference to the opening *Adagio*, turning it into an ambling accompaniment against which the violins offer the sort of fragmentary phrases that Beethoven was to use so effectively. Again there is a halt and a brief pause. An enterprising new development of the first few notes of the '*Allegro*' leads us to a reprise of the second subject, now in D flat major and instantly recognisable with its pizzicato bass. Its peasant origins are soon obscured in some symphonic hullabaloo that need not be taken seriously since Haydn arrests it in mid-flight. There is another pause, a feature of this movement, followed by a perfectly proper recapitulation. As we have grown to expect, the road to the second subject is considerably shortened. However, just as things seem to be going along according to plan there is an extraordinary upheaval, a musical earthquake of shattering force that ceases as unexpectedly as it had appeared. With a master-stroke of ingenuity Haydn brings back the opening *Adagio*, the initial drum-roll now seeming much more sinister in such a context. In the ensuing coda he returns to the *Allegro con spirito*, openly revealing its relationship to the introduction. There have been shocks enough and sixteen brisk bars end the movement.

While we often describe Haydn's themes as being *like* folksongs it is not often that we can know precisely whether he was drawing on childhood memories, quoting songs that were still current in Austria or Hungary during his adult years, or simply inventing them *à la mode*. In the case of this slow movement (and in the finale) it is possible to be more specific and researchers have established that the two themes on which Haydn wrote an elaborate double-variation movement both came from the district of Oedenburg, the nearest town to Eszterháza. Rather than quoting the folk-tunes exactly, Haydn used them as a starting-point, continuing on more interesting lines after the first few bars. Since one theme is in C minor and the other in C major they are easily distinguishable even though the actual melodies are rather alike in shape; indeed at a first hearing one might mistakenly presume that the second tune is a legitimate, if rather free, variation on the first.

The form of the movement is simple enough:

Theme I   (C minor) in two sections, both repeated.
Theme II   (C major) in two sections, both repeated.
Theme I   Variation 1, no repeats.
Theme II   Variation 1, violin solo with repeats.
Theme I   Variation 2, first section only repeated.
Theme II   Variation 2, no repeats.
Coda.

There are several points worthy of comment. Notice the gruff sound of the double basses, tuned down to an exceptional low C to give a suitably rustic trudge to the accompaniment. Theme I is initially for strings only; Theme II highlights oboes, bassoons and horns to give it a quite different tonal colour as well as a different tonality. Theme I, Variation 1 sees little change in the string parts but new interest is added by solo wind instruments. Theme II, Variation 1 has a highly decorative violin solo, a further opportunity for Salomon to show his skill though Robbins Landon suggests that in this case Haydn was writing for his friend Viotti.

Theme I, Variation 2 is altogether different, with brass and timpani conscripting the humble peasant tune into the army. The second portion involves some very brilliant passages for the violins. In contrast Theme II, Variation 2 is rather frivolous, with perky oboes and an ornithological flute. Towards the end of the variation note the strangely growling bass. The music then breaks off on an ascending phrase and there is a little pause before the delightful coda in which we find ingenious imitative counterpoint in the strings, a humorous dissection of the subject and a salvo of artillery near the end.

The Menuetto is notable for the sharp rhythmic kick that occurs in alternate bars. This is a real country dance and one can easily imagine the stamp of heavy boots and the slap of horny hands on *lederhosen*; in fact the tune itself is almost certainly meant to be a yodelling song. The second section begins rather timidly as though the aristocracy are slightly alarmed by this rowdy display; but with the return of the initial rhythm Haydn plays a nice joke on us since the dancers are no longer together, the lower strings lagging a bar behind. This produces a flustered reaction from the violins who take some time to get back in line and re-start.

The central Trio begins with a gracefully curving figure which is passed from hand to hand, possibly representing the flags or coloured ribbons that are often used in folk-dances. A curious little passage based on repeated quavers conjures up a picture of girls running tiptoe to their appointed places for the next part of the dance, but the main feature here is the transparent delicacy of the texture in comparison to the boisterous rusticity of the Menuetto.

The final movement is remarkable for its concentration on one theme virtually throughout. Only in the first movement of Beethoven's Fifth Symphony do we find a comparable limitation of themes, although to very different purpose. Curiously enough both composers use themes that exploit repeated notes:

Haydn begins the movement with a quiet passage for two horns suggesting the lure of the chase to his English audience. It could have been a mere prefix but turns out to have an additional function as accompaniment to the theme above. This too is based on a Croatian folksong, suggesting that despite his huge popularity in England Haydn's thoughts were beginning to turn homewards.

The omnipresence of the theme makes it extremely difficult to pick out any notable landmarks, but one point that even the tone-deaf would notice is the first tremendous climax in which full brass and timpani join forces with the rest of the orchestra. Out of this considerable eruption emerges a quiet tapping figure on violins and violas, preparation we feel sure for a second subject. But no; refusing to make way for any such intruder, the cellos come in with Theme I yet again, eliciting a confirmatory response from the flute. The tapping accompaniment continues as the cellos and basses set out on a mysterious journey that ultimately produces a mirthful reaction from the full orchestra. Theme I now seems momentarily to lose its way as the strings grope around by semitones; however, they are soon put right by their colleagues and after a typical Haydn pause the development section begins. (One might mistake it for the recapitulation but the movement is conceived on a very large scale and though the material may seem not overimpressive, Haydn is astonishingly inventive in his treatment of it.) The actual arrival of the recapitulation is very clearly signposted with the entire orchestra (save for the timpani) stamping out four repeated Gs.

The final coda makes the most of the opening horn call, now doubled by trumpets and wind as the timpani whip up the excitement by playing at ever increasing speed. To have based 386 bars of music on one short theme may seem to be carrying economy to a ludicrous level, but the movement is a splendid justification of Haydn's self-imposed restriction, and we are swept along on the flood-tide of his inspiration.

ACKNOWLEDGMENTS

In the course of preparing a book of this nature it is obviously wise to check facts as thoroughly as possible. Opinions remain my own and I hope that I have made clear the difference between speculation and verifiable fact. Needless to say the New Grove has been a valuable source in general terms, as have the admirable *Pelican* books on symphonies and concertos, both edited by Ralph Hill; but the short bibliography below lists some other *aides-mémoires* that I have consulted.

BACH   Malcolm Boyd. (Master Musicians, J.M. Dent, 1983.) Schweitzer. (A & C Black)

BEETHOVEN *Essays in Musical Analysis:* D.F Tovey. (O.U.P., 1935.) *The Nine Symphonies of Beethoven*: A. Hopkins. (Heinemann, 1981.)

BERG   *The Second Viennese School*: Rognoni. (John Calder, 1977.)

BRAHMS   *His life and work*: Geiringer. (Allen and Unwin, 1948.)

BRITTEN   Michael Kennedy. (Master Musicians. J.M. Dent, 1981.)

CHOPIN   A Biography; Adam Zamoyski. (Collins, 1979.)

DEBUSSY   Edward Lockspeiser. (Master Musicians. J.M. Dent, 1936.)

DVOŘÁK   Alec Robertson. (Master Musicians. J.M. Dent, 1945.)

ELGAR   *An Elgar Companion* ed. Redwood. (Sequoia, 1982.) *Life and Works: Basil Maine* (Bell, 1933.)

FRANCK   *Five Great French Composers*: Donald Brook (Rockliff, 1946.)

HAYDN   H.C. Robbins Landon. (Thames and Hudson, 1976–81.)

I would also like to express my gratitude to Beatrix Taylor for her great help in producing an exemplary typescript, and to Tabitha Collingbourne for her preparation of the music examples.